# *Solaris Management Console Tools*

Janice Winsor

*Sun Microsystems Press*
*A Prentice Hall Title*

10 9 8 7 6 5 4 3 2 1

ISBN 0-13-061762-8

*Production Supervisor:* Wil Mara
*Acquisitions Editor:* Greg Doench
*Associate Acquisitions Editor:* Eileen Clark
*Editorial Assistant:* Brandt Kenna
*Marketing Manager:* Debby van Dijk
*Buyer:* Alexis R. Heydt
*Cover Designer:* Anthony Gemmellaro

Sun Microsystems Press:
*Publisher:* Michael Llwyd Alread
*Marketing Assistant:* Bequi Gomez

**Sun Microsystems Press**
**A Prentice Hall Title**

# PREFACE

This book is for system administrators who are familiar with basic system administration and with the tasks described in the *Solaris System Administrator's Guide*, Third Edition, published by Sun Microsystems Press, a Prentice Hall title.

## A Quick Tour of the Contents

This book is divided into six parts, one appendix, and a glossary.

Chapter 1, "SMC Introduction," introduces the Solaris Management Console packages, toolboxes, commands, components, and software developer's kit.

Part One, "SMC Overview," provides an overview of SMC in three chapters.

Chapter 2, "SMC Console," describes the elements of the graphical user interface, the SMC Console preferences, logging into a server, and opening a toolbox.

Chapter 3, "SMC Server," describes how to start and stop the SMC server.

Chapter 4, "SMC Toolbox Editor," describes how to start the SMC toolbox editor and how to use it to customize the SMC Console tools and create custom toolboxes.

Part Two, "System Status" contains two chapters describing the Processes and Log Viewer tools that are part of the System Status category.

Chapter 5, "Processes," describes how to use the Processes tool to search for a process, sort process information, suspend and resume a process, and delete a process.

Chapter 6, "Log Viewer," describes how to start the log viewer, view the details of a log entry, change log file settings, back up log files, open backed-up log files, and delete log files.

Part Three, "System Configuration," contains six chapters describing the tools that are part of the System Configuration category.

Chapter 7, "User Accounts," describes how to get started with user tools, set user policies, add single and multiple user accounts with either a wizard or with templates, assign rights to a user, copy a user account to a group or mailing list, edit user properties, and delete user accounts.

Chapter 8, "User Templates," describes how to create a new template, clone an existing template, change template properties, and set user policies.

Chapter 9, "Rights," describes how to add new rights, view and edit properties of existing rights, and delete rights.

Chapter 10, "Administrative Roles," describes how to create a role, assign an administrative role, assign rights to a role, edit the properties of a role, and edit a role.

Chapter 11, "Groups," provides information about groups and describes how to add new groups, how to paste user accounts into a group, how to modify groups, and how to delete a group.

Chapter 12, "Mailing Lists," provides information about mailing lists, e-mail recipient formats, and special mailing lists. It describes how to add a new mailing list and view or modify the contents of a mailing list.

Part Four, "Services," contains one chapter that describes the Scheduled Jobs tool.

Chapter 13, "Scheduled Jobs," describes how to start the Scheduled Jobs tool, add a scheduled job, set scheduled job policies, view and edit properties of a scheduled job, and delete a scheduled job.

Part Five, "Storage," contains two chapters that describe the Disks and Mounts and Shares tools.

Chapter 14, "Disks," provides information about disk formats and disk partitions and describes how to start the Disks tool, view disk partitions, view properties of disks, create Solaris disk partitions, copy disk layout, create `fdisk` partitions on an IA computer, and change active `fdisk` partitions on an IA computer.

Chapter 15, "Mounts and Shares," describes how to start the Mounts and Shares tool, how to make file systems available, display a list of mounted file systems, display or modify the properties of mounted file systems, add a new NFS mount, and unmount a mounted file system. It also describes how to share files from a server, display a list of shared directories, add a shared directory, display or modify the properties of shared directories, and unshare a directory

Part Six, "Devices and Hardware," contains one chapter that describes the Serial Ports tool.

Chapter 16, "Serial Ports," describes how to start the Serial Ports tool, view serial port properties, and set up modems and character terminals.

Appendix A, "SMC Commands," describes the commands available to supplement the SMC graphical user interface tools.

# Conventions Used in This Book

## Commands

In the steps and the examples, the commands to be entered are in bold type. For example: "Type **su** and press Return." When following steps, press Return only when instructed to do so, even if the text in the step breaks at the end of a line.

## Variables

Variables are in an italic typeface. When following steps, replace the variable with the appropriate information. For example, to print a file, the step instructs you to "type **lp** *filename* and press Return." To substitute the file named quest for the *filename* variable, type **lp quest** and press Return.

## Mouse-Button Terminology

This book describes mouse buttons by function. The default mouse-button mapping is shown below.

- SELECT is Left.
- ADJUST is Middle.
- MENU is Right.

Use the SELECT mouse button to select unselected objects and to activate controls. Use the ADJUST mouse button to adjust a selected group of objects, either adding to the group or deselecting part of the group. Use the MENU mouse button to display and choose from menus.

## Platform Terminology

In this document, the term IA (Intel Architecture) is used instead of x86 to refer to the Intel 32-bit processor architecture, which includes the Pentium, Pentium Pro, Pentium II, Pentium II Xeon, Celeron, Pentium III Xeon processors, and comparable microprocessor chips made by AMD and Cyrix.

## Storage-Medium Terminology

In this book, we distinguish between three different types of media storage terminology in the following way.

- *Disc* is used for an optical disc, CD-ROM, or DVD disc.
- *Disk* is used for a hard-disk storage device.
- *Diskette* is used for a floppy diskette storage device. (Note: Sometimes, screen messages and mount points use the term *floppy*.)

# ACKNOWLEDGMENTS

Many people contributed to the design, writing, and production of this book. The author would particularly like to acknowledge the following people for their contributions.

Michael Alread, Marketing Manager, Sun Microsystems Press, for his help in promoting this book.

Sally Beach, Larissa Brown, Tom Hardesty, Maria Santiago, and Beauty Shields of Sun Microsystems, Inc., for enabling me to participate in the Solaris 8 Beta programs and for answering numerous questions.

Rachel Borden, Publisher, Sun Microsystems Press, for her unfailing enthusiasm, support, and friendship.

Greg Doench, Executive Editor, Prentice Hall, for his continuing support, encouragement, and friendship.

Sandra Carrigan, Sun Microsystems, Inc., Sun – PC Networking, for answering questions about the SMC Users tools.

Sean Comerford, Sun Microsystems, Inc., for investigating issues with remote systems and SMC.

Linda Gallops, Sun Microsystems, Inc., for helping identify technical resources at Sun.

Peter H. Gregory, author of *Solaris Security* and *Sun Certified System Administrator for Solaris 8 Study Guide*, for his excellent technical review comments.

Mary Lautman; Sun Microsystems, Inc.; Manager, SMC; for graciously answering questions and for referring other questions to members of her group.

Wil Mara, Prentice Hall PTR, for production support.

Douglas McCallum, Sun Microsystems, Inc., for answering questions about `fdisk` partitions and the SMC Disks tool.

Mary Lou Nohr for editing this manuscript with her usual skill and tact.

Ed Wetmore, Technical Support Engineer, Sun Microsystems, Inc., for help in troubleshooting problems with Solaris IA installation and identifying an appropriate Ethernet card.

Bob Yennaco, Sun Microsystems, Inc., for information on how to fix SMC server problems.

# CONTENTS

## Part Two: *System Status* *59*

## 5 Processes 61

## 6 Log Viewer 67

# Part Six: Devices and Hardware   219

# 1

# SMC
# INTRODUCTION

The Solaris Management Console 2.0 (SMC)—introduced in the Solaris 8 Update 3 (1/01) release—is a graphical user interface (GUI)-based application that you can use as the launching point for a variety of system management tools.

SMC software provides a consistent, easy-to-use interface for managing and administering a Solaris server, the clients of the server, and the applications running on the server. You can use the SMC console to monitor and tune applications and to administer user-written or third-party applications and tools.

With SMC, you can manage a Solaris server from almost anywhere—from a browser, from any Solaris workstation or server, from an NT server, or as a standalone system. You can also plug SMC into other systems' consoles.

With SMC, in addition to the base components of the Solaris Operating Environment, you can consolidate the management functions of Solaris-branded optional products. The interface provides a familiar X Windows look and feel, with point-and-click navigation, tab panels, and wizards.

# SMC Packages

Starting with the Solaris 8 1/01 release, the SMC packages are located in the `/cdrom/cdrom0/Solaris_8/Product` directory on the Solaris 8 Software 2 of 2 CD. The packages are listed in Table 1 in the order you should install them if they were not installed as part of the default system installation.

*Table 1      Solaris Management Console 2.0 Packages*

| Package | Description |
| --- | --- |
| SUNWmccom | Common components. |
| SUNWmcc | Client components. |
| SUNWmc | Server components. |
| SUNWwbmc | WBEM components. |
| SUNWmcex | Examples. |
| SUNWmcdev | Development kit. |
| SUNWmga | Solaris management applications. |
| SUNWdclnt | Solaris diskless client management application. |

# SMC Toolboxes

SMC uses a *toolbox* as a common user interface to provide a view of various system administration tools or applications. A toolbox enables you to group tools in a consistent hierarchy. An SMC toolbox is a hierarchical collection of folders, tools, legacy applications, and links to other toolboxes that have been registered with smcconf(1M). The root toolbox is called Management Tools. The default behavior of SMC is to look for a toolbox on the host system (This Computer) and link to it when you start SMC.

SMC comes with a default toolbox that contains the following tools.

- System Status
  - Processes—Use to suspend, resume, monitor, and control processes.
  - Log Viewer—Use to view application and command-line messages and manage log files.

- System Configuration
  - Users—Use to set up and maintain user accounts, user templates, groups, mailing lists, and administrative roles and rights. Grant or deny rights to users and to administrative roles to control the specific applications each user and role can work with and which tasks to perform.
- Services
  - Scheduled Jobs—Use to schedule, start, and manage jobs.
- Storage
  - Mounts and Shares—Use to view and manage mounts, shares, and usage information.
  - Disks—Use to create and view disk partitions.
- Devices and Hardware
  - Serial Ports—Use to configure and manage existing serial ports.

*NOTE. The Solaris Management Console 2.0 replaces functionality previously provided by AdminSuite 2.0 and Admintool.*

Refer to Parts Two through Six of this book for detailed information and examples of how to use the tools in the default toolbox.

You can use the SMC Toolbox Editor to modify existing toolboxes or to create additional toolboxes. You can add or delete tools from the default toolbox and create a new toolbox to manage a different set of tools. You can also manage multiple servers from one toolbox and group similar tools in a toolbox. See Chapter 4, "SMC Toolbox Editor," for information about how to use the SMC Toolbox Editor.

## SMC Commands

In addition to the SMC user interface and the smc(1M) command used to start SMC, SMC provides a set of commands, introduced in Table 2, that you can use to administer SMC from the command line and in scripts.

*Table 2    SMC Commands*

| Description | Command |
| --- | --- |
| Populate security-attribute databases in a name service. | smattrpop(1M) |
| Configure SMC. | smcconf(1M) |
| Manage jobs in the crontab database. | smcron(1M) |

*Table 2*      *SMC Commands (Continued)*

| Description | Command |
|---|---|
| Manage diskless clients. Available only through the command line. | smdiskless(1M) |
| Manage entries in the exec_attr database. | smexec(1M) |
| Manage group entries. | smgroup(1M) |
| Manage e-mail alias entries. | smmaillist(1M) |
| Batch user operations. | smmultiuser(1M) |
| Manage OS services, including those for diskless clients. | smosservice(1M) |
| Manage profiles (rights) in the prof_attr and exec_attr databases. | smprofile(1M) |
| Manage roles and users in role accounts. | smrole(1M) |
| Manage user entries. | smuser(1M) |

For complete descriptions and examples of each command, see Appendix A, "SMC Commands."

# SMC Components

SMC has three primary components.

- The SMC client—Called SMC or the Console. Used for routine system administration tasks.
- The SMC server—The back-end SMC process. The SMC server—started automatically at boot time—provides tools that the console uses to download and perform common services for the console and its tools; services include authentication, authorization, logging, and persistence.
- The SMC Toolbox Editor—Used to create or edit an SMC toolbox.

Refer to Part One of this book for more information about each of these components.

# SMC Software Development Kit

In addition to providing a consistent, easy-to-use interface, Sun provides an SMC software development kit (SDK) to enable independent software vendors (ISVs) to develop interfaces that integrate with Solaris Management Console.

The SMC development environment uses Java and Java-related technologies. The SDK includes an application GUI toolkit that enables ISVs to match the look and feel of existing SMC tools. A consistent interface enables system administrators to quickly learn and become proficient at managing a new application. The SDK also includes a set of communication service routines that enable the application to be managed from any remote instance of SMC.

Starting with the Solaris 8 1/01 release, the SMC SDK is available in the `SUNWmcdev` package in the `/cdrom/cdrom0/Solaris_8/Product` directory on the Solaris 8 Software 2 of 2 CD.

# Part One

# SMC Overview

This part introduces the three primary components of Solaris Management Console (SMC) in three chapters.

- The SMC client, also called SMC or the Console.
- The SMC server.
- The SMC Toolbox Editor.

Refer to the chapters in this part for information about the graphical user interface and for an overview of SMC components.

# 2

# *SMC CONSOLE*

The SMC Console—also called SMC or the Console—provides you with a view of various system administration tools or applications, possibly on different servers. You use the Console to perform routine system administration tasks. With the SMC Console, you can manage servers from almost anywhere on the network.

## Starting SMC

You can start SMC in any one of the following ways.

- By choosing Solaris Management Console from the Tools menu of the CDE front panel.
- By double-clicking on the SMC icon in CDE Applications Manager or File Manager.
- From a command line by typing **/usr/sadm/bin/smc&** and pressing Return.

*NOTE. You can start SMC as a normal user, but some tools or applications may not load unless you log in as root, have Primary Administrator rights, or assume a role during SMC server login.*

## Describing the Console

Figure 1 shows the elements of the default console.

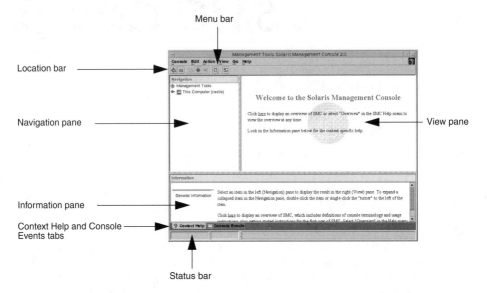

*Figure 1    Elements of the Default SMC Console*

## Navigation Pane

The Navigation pane on the left side of the SMC Console works like a frame in a Web page. Clicking on an item in the Navigation pane specifies what is displayed in the View pane. The icon that is displayed next to groups of items is called a *turner*. Click on the turner icon or double-click on the text next to the icon to expand or collapse the group.

Figure 2 shows the turner icon in the Navigation pane expanded to show the default items for This Computer.

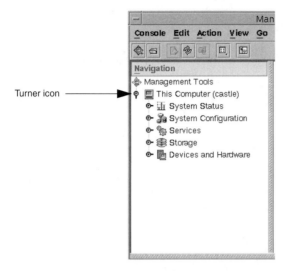

Turner icon ──────▶

*Figure 2      The Turner Icon in the Navigation Pane*

The View menu has a Show item, shown in Figure 3, that you can use to specify whether the Navigation pane is displayed. The Show menu also enables you to control display of the Tool bar, Location bar, Status bar, and Information pane.

*Figure 3      View Menu Show Item*

## View Pane

The View pane on the right of the SMC Console displays the contents of the node selected in the Navigation pane. The contents can be a file folder or a tool. If you selected a folder in the Navigation pane, the contents of that folder are displayed in the View pane.

Figure 4 shows the tools in the System Status folder displayed in the View pane. Note that the names of the tools are also displayed in the Navigation pane.

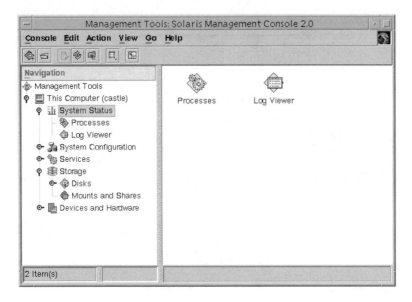

*Figure 4     Selected System Status Folder in the Navigation Pane*

When the node selected in the Navigation pane is a complex tool like User Manager, the contents displayed in the View pane are subtools for user accounts and e-mail accounts, as shown in Figure 5.

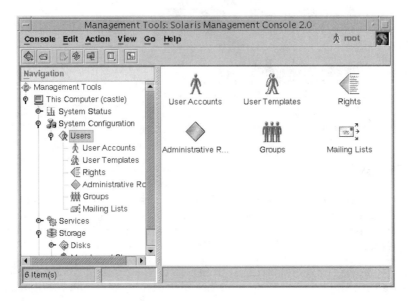

*Figure 5     Selected Users Folder in the Navigation Pane*

Double-clicking on one of the tools, such as the User Accounts, displays a list of available user accounts in the View pane, as shown in Figure 6.

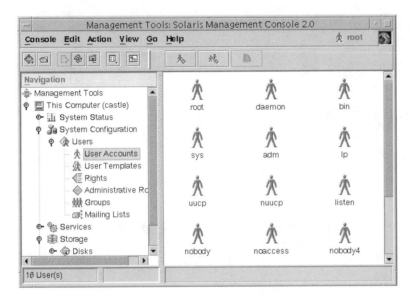

*Figure 6    Viewing User Accounts*

## Information Pane

The Information pane at the bottom of the Console window displays information specified by either the Context Help or Console Events tabs. The View menu has a Show item that you can use to specify whether the Information pane is to be displayed.

When the Information pane is displayed, if the Context Help tab is selected, context help for the object selected in the Navigation pane is displayed, as shown in Figure 7.

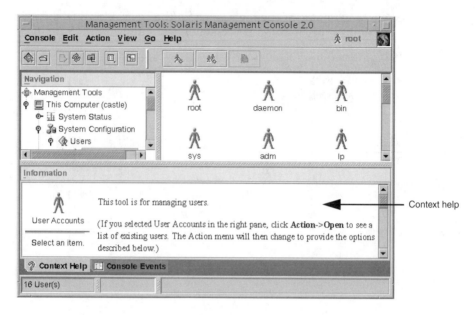

*Figure 7     Context Help for User Accounts*

When the Console Events tab is selected, the Information pane displays a list of events and alarm types for the object selected in the Navigation pane, as shown in Figure 8.

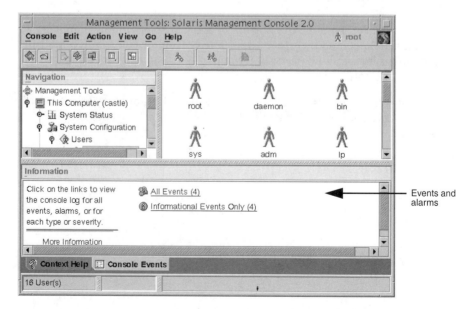

*Figure 8     Console Events for User Accounts*

## Menu Bar

The Console menu bar, with the Console menu displayed, is shown in
Figure 9.

*Figure 9*    *Console Menu Bar and Console Menu*

The Console menu bar contains the following items.

- Console
    - New Console—Open a new Console with the startup preferences
      defined in the Preferences dialog (Console tab).
    - Open Toolbox—Open an existing toolbox in the current Console
      window.
    - Preferences—Display the Preferences window with tabs for
      changing Console, Appearance, Tool bar, Fonts, Tool Loading, and
      Authentication.
    - Console Events—Display the SMC Console Events log, which
      provides a comprehensive list of all events and alarms that occur
      within the Console. Click on the Console Events tab at the bottom
      of the Console to list the types of events in the Information pane.
    - Close—Close the current Console instance. If the instance is the
      last one, exit from SMC.
    - Exit—Exit from SMC.
- Edit
    - Select All—Select all of the objects in the View pane.
- Action
    - Properties—Display the properties for the selected tools if that tool
      has properties. Note that Properties is inactive for many tools.
- View
    - Show—Display the Show submenu, which has toggles for
      displaying the Tool bar, Location bar, Status bar, Navigation pane,
      and Information pane.

- View As—Display the View As submenu that you can use to choose Large icon, Small icon, List, or Details view in the View pane. You can also toggle between Web Style (single-click) and Classic Style (double-click) actions in the View pane.
- Columns—For some tools you can display or suppress any of the columns available for the tool by clicking on a check box next to the item.
- Sort By—For some tools, you can sort columns in ascending or descending order for various categories.
- Filter—Display the Filter window to filter the information that is is displayed in the View pane.
- Refresh—Refresh and redraw the Console.

- Go
  - Up Level—Move up one level in the toolbox hierarchy and display the results in the navigation and View panes. This item is useful if the Navigation pane is not displayed because you have turned the display off in the View > Show menu.
  - Home Toolbox—Display the home toolbox, as defined in the Console tab of the Preferences window.

- Help
  - Overview—Display help viewer with Overview in the topic pane. Overview provides a general description of the Solaris Management Console.
  - Contents—Display help viewer with the table of contents in the Navigation pane.
  - Index—Display help viewer with the index in the Navigation pane.
  - Search—Display help viewer with the Find function in the help viewer Navigation pane.
  - About Console—Display the SMC version number, copyright, and trademark information.

## Tool Bar

The default tool bar is shown in Figure 10.

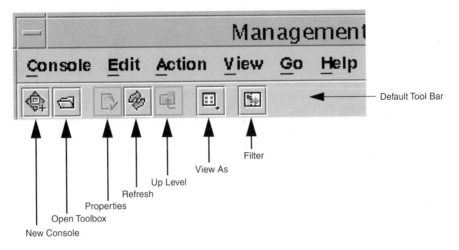

*Figure 10    Default Tool Bar*

The following list describes each of the toolbar icons and indicates, in parentheses, the menu where the tool is located. Clicking on one of the tools in the tool bar produces the same action as choosing the equivalent item from a Console menu. Some of the tools in the tool bar are active only for specific tools in the Console.

- New Console (Console menu)—Open a new Console window with the startup preferences defined in the Preferences dialog (Console tab).

- Open Toolbox (Console menu)—Open an existing toolbox in the current Console window.

- Properties (Action menu)—Display the properties for the selected tools if that tool has properties. Note that the Properties item is inactive for many tools.

- Refresh (View menu)   Refresh and redraw the Console.

- Up Level (Go menu)—Move up one level in the toolbox hierarchy and display the results in the Navigation and View panes. This item is useful if the Navigation pane is not displayed because you have turned the display off in the View > Show menu.

- View As (View menu)—Display the View As submenu that you can use to choose Large icon, Small icon, List, or Details view in the View pane. You can also toggle between Web Style (single-click) and Classic Style (double-click) actions in the View pane.

- Filter (View menu)—Display the Filter window to filter the information that is displayed in the View pane.

- Cut (Edit menu; optional)—Remove selected objects from the View pane and put them on the clipboard.

- Copy (Edit menu; optional)—Copy selected objects from the View pane and put them on the clipboard.
- Paste (Edit menu; optional)—Paste objects from the clipboard.
- Delete (Edit menu; optional)—Delete selected objects from the View pane.

Applications can add other icons to the right end of the tool bar. In the example shown in Figure 11, the Users application adds three icons that, from left to right, represent Add Users With Wizard, Add Multiple Users, and Copy to Group or Mailing List.

Figure 11    Users Application Icons at the Right End of the Tool Bar

## Location Bar

The location bar, by default, is not displayed. To display the location bar, from the View menu, choose Show, Location Bar. The location bar is shown in Figure 12.

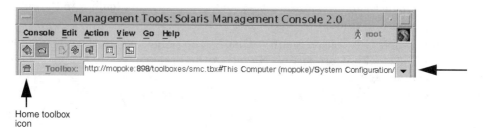

Figure 12    Location Bar

The location bar includes a Home Toolbox icon. You can click on the Home Toolbox icon to open your home toolbox. The Toolbox field shows the current toolbox and the item selected in the toolbox. The arrow at the right is a pulldown menu with a list of recent toolboxes visited. To open a recently visited toolbox, choose a toolbox from the pulldown menu.

## Status Bar

The status bar at the bottom of the Console contains three panes, as shown in Figure 13. The left pane of the status bar indicates the number of items (nodes) beneath the node that is selected in the Navigation pane. The center pane indicates Console activity with a back and forth "shade" movement. This pane is active when the console is performing an action such as loading a tool. The right pane displays progress information during some Console tasks such as opening a toolbox file.

*Figure 13   Status Bar*

The View menu has a Show item that you can use to specify whether the status bar is displayed.

## Console Help and Console Events Tabs

You can use the Context Help and Console Events tabs to specify what is displayed in the Information pane.

Context Help is displayed by default. The Console Events log displays the types of log events that you can view in the Console Events log. Only those types of events that have been logged are displayed. Click on any of the links in the Information pane to view the log for the selected event type. Click on the individual events in the log to view a brief description of the event.

Figure 14 shows an example of a Console Events log.

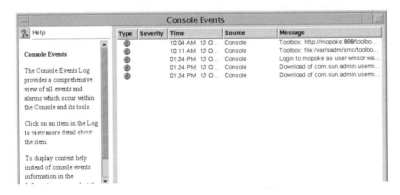

*Figure 14   Console Events Log*

# Specifying SMC Console Preferences

You can set preferences for six aspects of the SMC Console.

- Console.
- Appearance.
- Toolbar.
- Fonts.
- Tool Loading.
- Authentication.

To open the Preferences window, from the Console menu, choose Preferences.

## Console Preferences

The default Console preferences are shown in Figure 15.

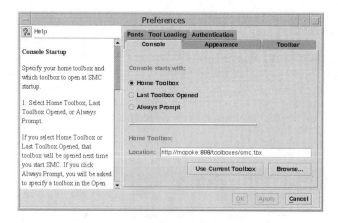

*Figure 15    Default Console Preferences*

Use Console preferences to specify a home toolbox and the startup behavior of the SMC Console. You can choose to have the console start in the following ways.

- Always start with the home toolbox.
- Always start with the last toolbox opened.
- Always prompt to ask you which toolbox you want to open when the SMC Console starts.

## Appearance Preferences

The default Appearance preferences are shown in Figure 16.

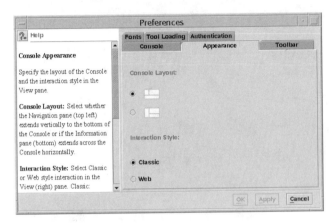

*Figure 16    Default Appearance Preferences*

Use Appearance preferences to specify two Console layout formats. You can also specify the interaction style. With classic interaction style, you double-click to load a tool. With Web interaction style, a single click loads a tool.

> *NOTE. Regardless of the interaction style preference you choose, a single click in the Navigation pane always loads a tool. The interaction style controls the behavior of icons only in the View pane.*

## Toolbar Preferences

The default Toolbar preferences are shown in Figure 17.

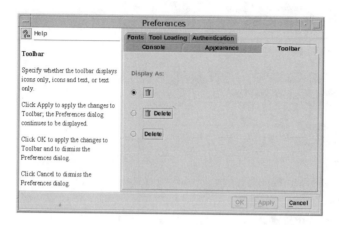

*Figure 17   Default Toolbar Preferences*

   Use Toolbar preferences to specify whether the tool bar displays only icons, icons and text, or text only.

## Fonts Preferences

The default Font preferences are shown in Figure 18.

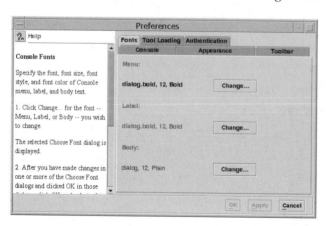

*Figure 18   Default Fonts Preferences*

   Use Font preferences to specify the font, point size, style, and color of the Console menu, label, and body text.

## Tool Loading Preferences

The default Tool Loading preferences are shown in Figure 19.

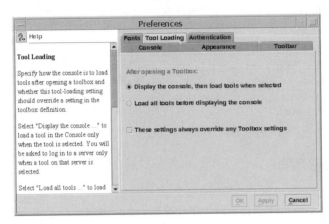

*Figure 19    Default Tool Loading Preferences*

Use Tool Loading preferences to specify how the console loads tools after opening a toolbox and whether the tool loading setting should override a setting in the toolbox definition.

## Authentication Preferences

The default Authentication preferences are shown in Figure 20.

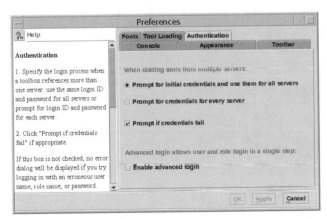

*Figure 20    Default Authentication Preferences*

Use Authentication preferences to specify how you want to authenticate users when they are loading tools from multiple servers. You can prompt for credentials—for example, user ID and password—once and use the same credentials for all servers, or you can prompt for credentials for each server. You can also specify that you want to be prompted if credentials fail.

When you enable advanced login, the login window shows both user ID and user password and role login and role password fields in a single window. If you do not enable advanced login and a role is assigned to a user, the Log In window first asks for user ID and password and a second window asks for role login and role password.

# Logging In to a Server

The first administrator to log in to SMC should set up at least one account with the rights of Primary Administrator. See "Getting Started with User Tools" on page 78 for more information about Primary Administrator rights and for instructions on how to assign Primary Administrator rights.

When you click on a tool in the Console, a Log In window, shown in Figure 21, is displayed in these circumstances:

- The first time you load a tool during a session.

- When the selected tool is on a different server than previous loaded tools and if your Tool Loading preferences are set to prompt for credentials for each server.

- When the selected tool is on a different server than previously loaded tools, your Tool Loading preferences are set to prompt for initial credentials for each server, and you are not authorized to access this server with the same credentials.

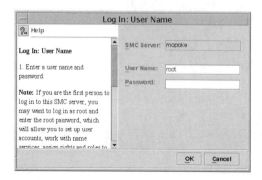

*Figure 21    Log In Window*

You are asked to log in with a user ID and password only when no roles have been assigned to you and the advanced login preference is not set.

*NOTE. A role is an account with all the attributes of a user account, including a name, user ID (UID), password, and home directory. A role also has a specific set of administrative rights. See Chapter 9, "Rights," and Chapter 10, "Administrative Roles," for information about rights and roles.*

When roles are assigned to you, you are asked to log in with both a user ID and password and a role login and password.

When roles are assigned to you and the advanced login preference is set, the Log In window includes both user and role login fields. When the advanced login preference is not set, the first Log In window asks for a user ID and password and the second Log In window asks for a role name and role password, as shown in Figure 22.

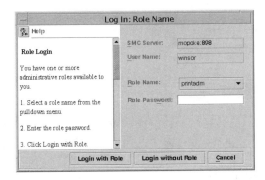

*Figure 22    Role Log In Window*

If you want to log in without a role, click on the Login without Role button. If you want to log in with a role, choose the name of the role from the Role Name drop-down menu, type the role password, then click on the Login with Role button.

# Opening a Toolbox

By default, the toolbox for the local server is loaded unless you specify a different toolbox as the default in the SMC Preferences window. See "Console Preferences" on page 20 for information on changing the default toolbox.

You can load a new toolbox at any time if you have the appropriate rights or role for that toolbox. See Chapter 4, "SMC Toolbox Editor," for information on how to create custom toolboxes.

## Server Toolbox

To open a new toolbox, from the Console menu, choose Open Toolbox. The Open Toolbox window is displayed with the Server Toolbox tab in front, as shown in Figure 23.

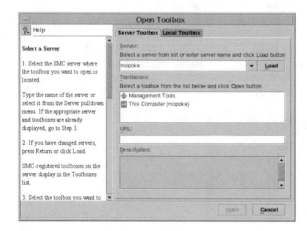

*Figure 23    Open Toolbox Window: Server Toolbox Tab*

Use the following steps to open a toolbox on a different server.

1.  Type the name of the toolbox in the top text field, or choose the name of a server from the drop-down menu to the left of the text field.

2.  Click on the Load button to load the toolboxes from the specified server.

    If the SMC server is not already running on the specified server, the SMC server is started automatically and the toolboxes on the specified server are displayed in the Toolboxes text field.

3.  Click on the toolbox you want to open.

    Alternatively, you can type the URL for the toolbox in the URL text field. Using the URL text field enables you to load an unregistered toolbox.

4.  Click on the Open button.

    The Open Toolbox window is closed. Depending on your Preferences setting, either the toolbox is opened in the SMC Console window or the Log In window is displayed on top of the Console.

## Local Toolbox

To open a local toolbox, after opening the Open Toolbox window from the
Console menu by choosing Open Toolbox, click on the Local Toolbox tab. The
Local Toolbox tab is displayed, as shown in Figure 24.

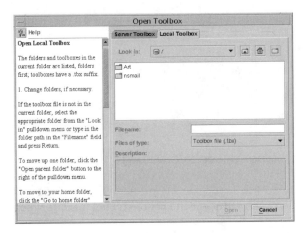

*Figure 24    Open Toolbox Window: Local Toolbox Tab*

The folders and toolboxes in the current folder are listed with the folders
first, then toolboxes. Toolbox files have a .tbx suffix. In the example shown
in Figure 24, the directories are in the user's home directory and no toolboxes
are located in this directory.

By default, toolboxes are located in the /var/sadm/smc/toolboxes
directory. To change to that directory, from the Look for menu, choose the root
directory. Then double-click on the var folder, the sadm folder, the
smc folder, and the toolboxes folder. The toolboxes for the local system
are displayed, as shown in Figure 25.

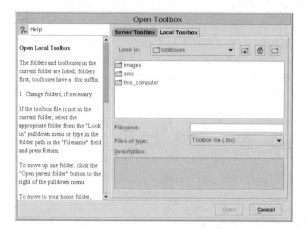

*Figure 25    Open Toolbox Window: Local Toolboxes*

Click on the toolbox you want to load. The file name and description are displayed in the Local Toolbox tab. To open the toolbox, click on the Open button.

# 3

# SMC SERVER

The Solaris Management Console (SMC) server is the back end to the SMC Console. The SMC server provides tools that the console uses to download and perform common services such as authentication, authorization, logging, and persistence.

## Starting the SMC Server Automatically

The system uses the `/etc/init.d/init.wbem` command to start both the SMC server and the Common Information Model Object Manager (CIMOM), both of which run combined in a single process.

`init.wbem` is run automatically during installation and each time a system is rebooted. The following scripts are linked to `/etc/init.d/init.wbem` to run the `start` and `stop` options, as appropriate for the specified init state.

- `/etc/rc2.d/S90wbem`
- `/etc/rc0.d/K36wbem`
- `/etc/rc1.d/K36wbem`
- `/etc/rcS.d/K36wbem`

The `init.wbem` command does not run the SMC server and CIMOM directly because the Java server process is too large to be run at system boot.

Instead, init.wbem runs a lightweight process that listens on the ports the SMC server and CIMOM normally use. The first time the lightweight process gets a connection on either port, it starts both server processes.

Because Java programs cannot inherit file descriptors, client connections may be dropped for the SMC server during the small period of time between the first connection request and the time when the server is fully operational.

## Determining SMC Server Status

If you have trouble running SMC, the SMC server may not be running or may be in a problem state.

To determine whether the SMC server is running, as root type **/etc/init.d/init.wbem status** and press Return.

The following example shows that the SMC server is running on port 898.

```
mopoke% su
Password:
# /etc/init.d/init.wbem status
SMC server version 2.0.0 running on port 898.
#
```

## Stopping the SMC Server

To stop the SMC server, as root, type **/etc/init.d/init.wbem stop** and press Return.

The following example stops the SMC server.

```
# /etc/init.d/init.wbem stop
Shutting down SMC server on port 898.
#
```

## Starting the SMC Server Manually

To start the SMC server, as root, type **/etc/init.d/init.wbem start** and press Return.

This command starts the CIM (Common Information Model) Boot Manager, `cimomboot`, which listens for connection requests from WBEM clients. When a client requests a connection, the `cimomboot` program starts the CIM Object Manager. You generally do not need to stop the CIM Object Manager. However, if you change an existing provider, you must stop and restart the CIM Object Manager before using the updated provider.

In the following example, `init.wbem` indicates that the SMC server is already running even though the `init.wbem stop` command has already been run and shows that the server is shut down.

```
# /etc/init.d/init.wbem start
removing /tmp/smc898 (not in use)
bind: Address already in use
#
```

## Troubleshooting the SMC Server

You may find occasions when `init.wbem stop` indicates that the server is not running but `/etc/init.d/init.wbem status` indicates that it already is running.

If you encounter this type of problem, try the following procedure.

1. Become superuser
2. Kill all instances of the `smcboot` process.
3. Kill all instances of the `cimomboot` process.
4. Kill all instances of SMC-related JVMs.

   These instances contain either `-Dviper.fifo.path=` or `-Djava.security.policy=` in their command paths.
5. Type `rm -rf /tmp/smc`*port* where *port* is usually `898`.
6. Type `/etc/init.d/init.wbem start`.

   The server should successfully start.

If the above procedure does not successfully start the SMC server, rebooting the system should clear the problem.

# 4

# SMC TOOLBOX EDITOR

Use the SMC toolbox editor to create or edit an SMC toolbox. You can create a toolbox that is shared by other toolboxes, or you can create a toolbox that includes all tools on a number of servers for a particular functionality.

You can use the toolbox to perform the following tasks.

- Edit toolbox properties.
- Add a folder to a toolbox.
- Add a toolbox URL to a toolbox.
- Add a legacy application to a toolbox.
- Add a toolbox to management tools.
- Create a toolbox.
- Create a nameservice domain toolbox.

## Starting the SMC Toolbox Editor

Use the following steps to start the SMC toolbox editor.

1. Become superuser.
   Although you can start the SMC Editor as a normal user, you cannot save a server toolbox unless you start the editor as root.
2. Type **/usr/sadm/bin/smc edit&** and press Return.

The SMC Editor splash screen is displayed, followed by the SMC Toolbox Editor window, as shown in Figure 26.

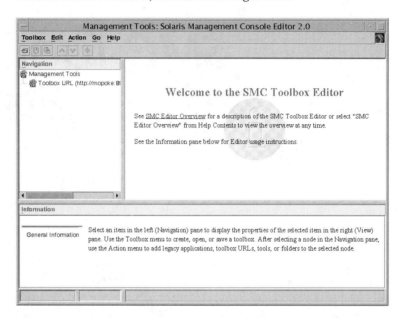

*Figure 26    SMC Toolbox Editor Window*

# Editing Toolbox Properties

You can use the SMC Toolbox Editor to modify the properties of tools, folders, toolbox URLs, and legacy applications.

1. If necessary, start the SMC Editor.

   Refer to "Starting the SMC Toolbox Editor" on page 33 for instructions on how to start the SMC Editor.

2. In the Navigation pane of the Editor, click on the object you want to modify.

   Its properties are displayed in the View pane of the editor, as shown in Figure 27.

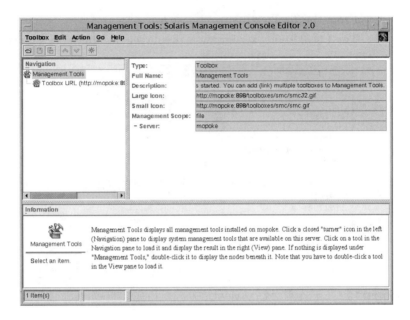

*Figure 27   Toolbox Properties*

3.   From the Action menu, choose Properties.

A wizard is displayed, as shown in Figure 28.

*Figure 28   Toolbox Wizard Editor Window*

4.   The wizard is slightly different for each type of objcct, but the process is the same. Modify the properties in the wizard.

Refer to the context help in each wizard window for instructions. Click Next in each panel except for the last one.

5.   In the last wizard panel, click Finish.

The wizard window closes and the Editor is displayed.

6.  From the Toolbox menu, choose Save As.

    The Local Toolbox window is displayed, as shown in Figure 29.

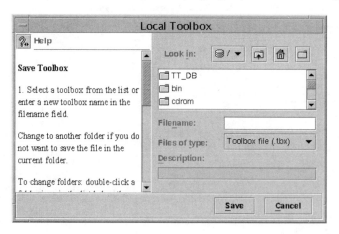

Figure 29    Local Toolbox Window

The first time the Local Toolbox window is displayed, the scrolling list starts at the root directory. Toolboxes are located in the /var/sadm/smc/toolboxes directory and have a .tbx suffix. The Management Tools toolbox is located in the /var/sadm/smc/toolboxes/smc directory and is named smc.tbx.

7.  Double-click on a folder to open it. To go up a level in the hierarchy, click on the folder icon with an arrow. When you reach the right place in the directory hierarchy, click on the name of the toolbox. The toolbox name is entered in the Filename text field.

8.  Click on the Save button to save the changes.

*NOTE. If you close the SMC Toolbox Editor without saving changes, an alert is displayed, as shown in Figure 30. If you click on Yes, the Save As window is displayed to enable you to save the toolbox. If you click on No, the changes to the toolbox are not saved.*

Figure 30    Save Current Toolbox Alert

# Adding a Folder to a Toolbox

You can use the SMC Editor to add a folder to an existing toolbox. You can add a folder to the top node of the toolbox or to another folder.

1. If necessary, start the SMC Editor.

   Refer to "Starting the SMC Toolbox Editor" on page 33 for instructions on how to start the SMC Editor.

2. From the Toolbox menu, choose Open.

   The Open Toolbox window is displayed, as shown in Figure 31.

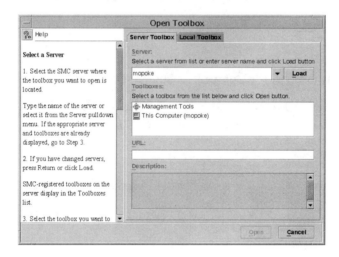

*Figure 31    Open Toolbox Window*

3. Double-click on the toolbox you want to edit.

   The toolbox is opened in the SMC Toolbox Editor window.

4. In the Navigation pane of the SMC Toolbox Editor, click on the node in the toolbox to which you want to add the folder.

   The node is highlighted.

5. From the Action menu, choose Add Folder.

   The Name and Description step in the Folder Wizard is displayed, as shown in Figure 32.

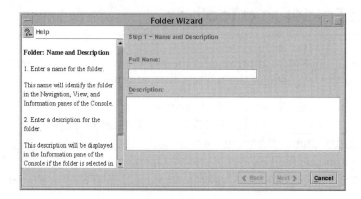

*Figure 32    Folder Wizard: Step 1*

6.  Type the name and description of the folder and click on Next.

    The Icons step is displayed, as shown in Figure 33.

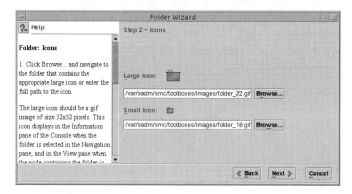

*Figure 33    Folder Wizard: Step 2*

7.  To use the default icons, click on Next. To use custom icons, click on
    the Browse button and navigate to the location of the icons you want
    to use, then click on Next.

    The Management Scope step is displayed, as shown in Figure 34.

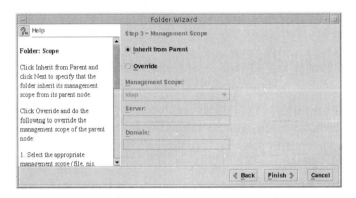

*Figure 34    Folder Wizard: Step 3*

8.  Specify the management scope. The default is Inherit from Parent. If you want to override the default, click on the Override radio button and specify the management scope.

9.  Click on the Finish button.

    The wizard is closed and the folder is added to the hierarchy in the Navigation pane at the bottom of the node you selected.

10. If you want to move the folder up in the hierarchy, highlight the folder in the Navigation pane and, from the Action menu, choose Move Up as many times as needed to move the folder to its new position in the hierarchy.

11. From the Toolbox menu, choose Save As.

12. Navigate to the toolbox location in the hierarchy.

    Toolboxes are located in the `/var/sadm/smc/toolboxes` directory.

13. Click on the toolbox and then click on Save.

    The changes to the toolbox are saved and the wizard is closed.

# Adding a Legacy Application to a Toolbox

A legacy application is an application that is not an SMC tool. A legacy application can be a command, an X application, or a URL. You can use the SMC Editor to add a legacy application.

*NOTE. The icon for a legacy application is not displayed in the Navigation pane hierarchy. The icon for a legacy application is displayed in the View pane when you have selected the application's*

*parent node in the Navigation pane or when you double-click on its
parent in the View pane.*

*When you load a legacy application by double-clicking in the View
pane, the legacy application spawns a separate window.*

1.  If necessary, start the SMC Editor.

    Refer to "Starting the SMC Toolbox Editor" on page 33 for
    instructions on how to start the SMC Editor.

2.  Open the toolbox to which you want to add the legacy application.

    Refer to the first four steps in "Adding a Folder to a Toolbox" on page
    37 if you need instructions.

3.  Choose the node in the toolbox where you want to add the legacy
    application.

    You can add a legacy application to the top node of a toolbox or to
    another folder.

4.  From the Action menu, choose Add Legacy Application.

    The first step of the Legacy Application Wizard is displayed, as shown
    in Figure 35.

*Figure 35    Legacy Application Wizard: Step 1*

5.  Choose the application type from the menu, type the full name,
    executable path or URL, and any command line arguments. Then
    click on Next.

    The Description and Icons step is displayed, as shown in Figure 36.

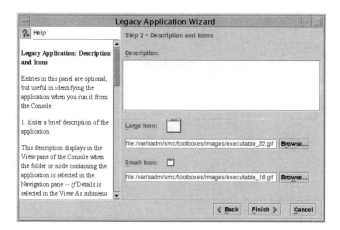

*Figure 36    Legacy Application Wizard: Step 2*

6. Type a description for the legacy application. Use the default icons or click on Browse to navigate to the location of alternate icons.

7. Click on Finish.

   The legacy application is added to the Navigation pane hierarchy at the bottom of the node you selected.

8. If you want, you can move the legacy application up in the hierarchy by selecting the legacy application and, from the Action menu, choosing Move Up.

9. From the Toolbox menu, choose Save As.

10. Navigate to the toolbox location in the hierarchy.

    Toolboxes are located in the `/var/sadm/smc/toolboxes` directory.

11. Click on the toolbox and then click on Save.

    The changes to the toolbox are saved and the wizard is closed.

# Adding a Toolbox to Management Tools

You can create a comprehensive view of the servers you want to manage by adding toolboxes from other servers to your list of Management Tools, which is the root toolbox on an SMC server.

1. If necessary, start the SMC Editor.

   Refer to "Starting the SMC Toolbox Editor" on page 33 for instructions on how to start the SMC Editor.

2. From the Toolbox menu, choose Open.

The Open Toolbox window is displayed, as shown in Figure 37.

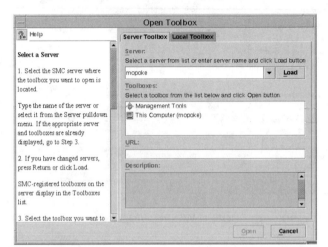

*Figure 37    Open Toolbox Window: Server Toolbox Tab*

3.  If you want to add a toolbox to Management Tools on a different server, type the server name in the Server text field and click on the Load button or press Return.

4.  In the Toolboxes list, click on Management Tools.

5.  Click on the Open button.

    The Editor displays Management Tools in the Navigation pane with each existing toolbox under Management Tools shown as a Toolbox URL, as shown in Figure 38.

*Figure 38    Management Tools Window*

6.  Click on Management Tools in the Navigation pane and from the Action menu, choose Add Toolbox URL.

    The Location step of the Toolbox URL wizard is displayed, as shown in Figure 39.

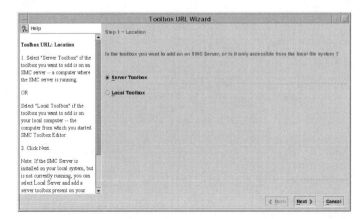

*Figure 39    Toolbox URL Wizard: Step 1*

7.  Select Server Toolbox or Local Toolbox and click on Next.

If you chose Local Toolbox, Step 2 is displayed, as shown in Figure 40.

*Figure 40    Toolbox URL Wizard: Step 2, Local Toolbox*

a.   Enter the name of the toolbox in the Toolbox File Name field and click on Next.

If you chose Server Toolbox, Step 2 is displayed, as shown in Figure 41.

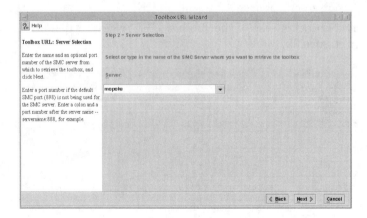

*Figure 41    Toolbox URL Wizard: Step 2, Server Toolbox*

b.   Type the server name and click on Next.

The Toolbox Selection panel is displayed, as shown in Figure 42.

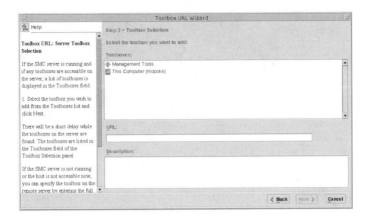

*Figure 42    Toolbox URL Wizard: Step 3*

*NOTE. Step 3 is skipped when you choose Local Toolbox.*

When the SMC server is running, any accessible toolboxes are listed in the Toolboxes field. Choose a toolbox from the list and click on Next. The Name and Description step is displayed, as shown in Figure 43.

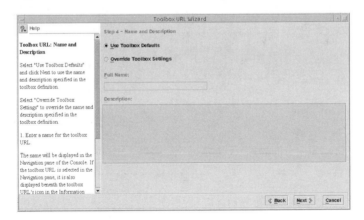

*Figure 43    Toolbox URL Wizard: Step 4*

8.  Use the toolbox defaults or click on Override Toolbox Settings to specify your own toolbox name and description. Then click on Next. The Icons step is displayed, as shown in Figure 44.

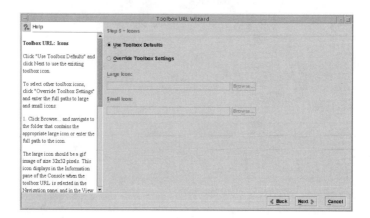

*Figure 44    Toolbox URL Wizard: Step 5*

9.  Use the default toolbox icons or click on Override Toolbox Settings to specify a path to custom icons. Then click on Next.

    The Management Scope step is displayed, as shown in Figure 45.

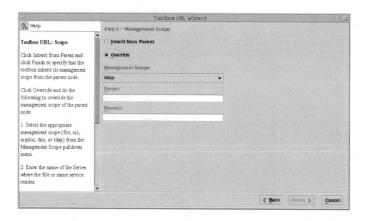

*Figure 45    Toolbox URL Wizard: Step 6*

10. Specify the management scope or click on Inherit From Parent. Then click on Finish.

    The toolbox URL is added to the hierarchy in the Navigation pane at the bottom of the node you selected, and the wizard is closed.

11. You can move the toolbox up in the hierarchy if you want. Select it in the Navigation pane and, from the Action menu, choose Move Up.

12. From the Toolbox menu, choose Save As.

13. Type **/var/sadm/smc/toolboxes/smc/smc.tbx** in the File Name field.

    Alternatively, you can navigate in the Look In menu to the appropriate directory.

14. Click on Save.

    The toolbox is saved.

15. Open the toolbox in SMC to see that the new toolbox has been added.

    In the example shown in Figure 46, the SMC Console on the system mopoke contains toolboxes for the systems mopoke and paperbark.

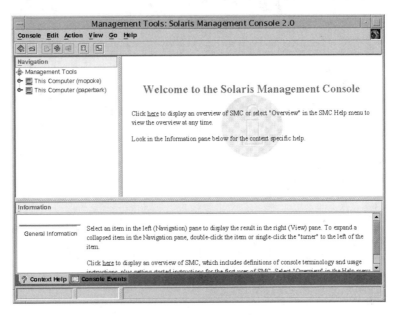

*Figure 46    Multiple Toolboxes on One SMC Server*

When you start a SMC Console that contains toolboxes for other servers and the SMC server is not running on any of the other servers, a message is displayed in the message area saying that the SMC server is not running on the system *systemname*.

Clicking on the toolbox for the system *systemname* starts the SMC server on that system.

If a remote server is down, the SMC Console loads only the toolboxes that are available. However, the time it takes to load the local toolbox may take substantially longer than usual.

# Adding a Toolbox URL to a Toolbox

Adding a toolbox URL to a toolbox is the same as adding a toolbox to
Management Tools except that you select a different node. You can add a
server toolbox URL or a local toolbox URL to the top node of a toolbox or to a
folder.

1.  Select the node in a toolbox to which you want to add a toolbox URL.

    Refer to the first four steps in "Adding a Folder to a Toolbox" on page
    37 if you need instructions.

2.  From the Actions menu, choose Add Toolbox URL.

    The Toolbox URL window is displayed, as shown in Figure 47.

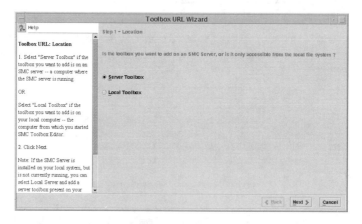

*Figure 47    Toolbox URL Window*

You can add a toolbox URL for either a server toolbox or a local
toolbox.

3.  Follow the instructions in the wizard.

    You can use the existing defaults or override the toolbox settings in
    subsequent steps.

4.  Click on the Finish button.

    The toolbox URL is added to the hierarchy in the Navigation pane at
    the bottom of the node you selected.

5.  If you want to move the toolbox URL up in the hierarchy, highlight
    the folder and, from the Action menu, choose Move Up as many times
    as needed to move the folder to its new position in the hierarchy.

6.  From the Toolbox menu, choose Save As.

7.  Navigate to the `/var/sadm/smc/toolboxes` directory.

8. Type the name you want to use for this toolbox in the Filename text field and then click on Save.

You do not need to add the .tbx suffix. The wizard automatically adds the suffix to the file name you specify. If you do add a .tbx suffix to the file name, it is ignored.

The changes to the toolbox are saved and the wizard is closed.

# Creating a Toolbox

Toolboxes are located in the /var/sadm/smc/toolboxes directory.

If you want to create a new toolbox, first create a directory with the mkdir command. Then use the SMC Toolbox Editor to create the toolbox.

1. Become superuser.

2. Type **cd /var/sadm/smc/toolboxes** and press Return.

By default the /var/sadm/smc/toolboxes directory contains two subdirectories: smc and this_computer.

3. Type **mkdir *toolboxname*** and press Return.

The following example creates a directory named NewToolbox.

4. Copy or move toolbox icons into the new directory.

The GIF icons are used to represent the toolbox in the SMC Console. The small icon is 16 x 16 pixels, and the large icon is 32 x 32 pixels. You can copy the icons from
/var/sadm/smc/toolboxes/this_computer.

```
mopoke% su
Password:
# cd /var/sadm/smc/toolboxes
# mkdir NewToolbox
# cp /var/sadm/smc/toolboxes/this_computer /var/sadm/smc/toolboxes/NewToolbox
#
```

5. Type **smc edit&** to start the toolbox editor (if necessary).

6. From the Toolbox menu, choose New.

The New Toolbox Wizard is displayed, as shown in Figure 48.

*Figure 48    New Toolbox Wizard—Step 1*

7. Type a toolbox name in the Full Name field.

   The name you enter is displayed in the Navigation pane tree and in the Console header if you open the toolbox from the SMC Console.

8. Type a description in the Description field and click on the Next button.

   Use the description to explain the use of the toolbox and its contents. The description is displayed in the Open Toolbox dialog when you select the toolbox for opening from the console. The description is also displayed in the Information pane of the Console when the toolbox is selected in the Navigation pane.

   The Icon window is displayed, as shown in Figure 49.

*Figure 49    New Toolbox Wizard—Step 2*

9. Enter the paths to a large and small icon and click on the Next button. Alternatively, you can click on the Browse button to navigate to the appropriate folder and select the GIF images.

   These icons are used to represent the toolbox in the SMC Console window. The small icon is displayed in the Navigation pane next to

the name of the toolbox, and the large icon is displayed in the
Information pane, as shown in Figure 50.

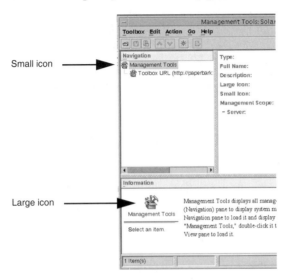

*Figure 50    Large and Small Toolbox Icons*

The Management Scope step is displayed, as shown in Figure 51.

*Figure 51    New Toolbox Wizard—Step 3*

10. Choose a management scope—ldap, dns, nisplus, nis, or file—from the
    Management Scope menu. If you choose file, skip the next two steps.

11. Type a server name in the Server text field.

12. Type a domain name in the Domain text field.

13. Click on the Finish button.

14. From the Toolbox menu choose Save As.

15. Navigate to the `/var/sadm/smc/toolboxes` directory.

16. Type the name for this toolbox in the Filename text field and then click on Save.

    You do not need to add the `.tbx` suffix. The wizard automatically adds the suffix to the file name you specify. If you do add a `.tbx` suffix to the file name, it is ignored.

    The changes to the toolbox are saved and the wizard is closed.

# Creating a Nameservice Domain Toolbox

Before you can create a nameservice domain toolbox, the following prerequisites must be met.

- A system must be set up to run a nameservice.
- The `smattrpop`(1M) command has been run to populate security attributes databases in a name service.
- Appropriate 32 x 32 pixel and 16 x 16 pixel GIF icons are available to represent the toolbox in the SMC Console on the server where you create the toolbox.

You perform the following steps to create a nameservice domain toolbox.

- Run the `smattrpop` command.
- Create the nameservice domain toolbox.
- Add the Users tool to the toolbox.
- Save the toolbox.

## The smattrpop Command

You use the `smattrpop` command to copy the information from a set of source RBAC (role-based access control) databases—`auth_attr`(4), `exec_attr`(4), `prof_attr`(4), and `user_attr`(4)—and merge each source entry field into the corresponding table entry in a target database. For example, before you create a nameservice domain toolbox, you must copy the information from the `file` databases to the `nis` or `nisplus` databases. If the source entry does not exist, the `smattrpop` command creates it. If the source entry exists in the target database, the fields are merged or replaced according to the specified command options.

The syntax for the `smattrpop` command used in the following example is shown below.

```
smattrpop -s type:/server/domain -t type:/server/domain database
```

The values for *type* are shown below.

| Type | Description |
|------|-------------|
| file | Local files. |
| nis | NIS nameservice. |
| nisplus | NIS+ nameservice. |
| ldap | LDAP nameservice. |

*server* is the name of the server and *domain* is the name of the domain.

The values for *database* are shown below.

| Type | Description |
|------|-------------|
| auth_attr | Processes the auth_attr database. |
| prof_attr | Processes the prof_attr database. |
| exec_attr | Processes the exec_attr database. |
| user_attr | Processes the user_attr database. |
| all | Processes all databases in the order shown above. |

Refer to "smattrpop" on page 238 or the `smattrpop(1M)` manual page for the complete syntax.

The following example uses the RBAC databases from `file` on the server `mopoke` to populate the `nisplus` tables on the server `mopoke` in the `wellard.com.` domain for `all` of the databases.

```
mopoke# /usr/sadm/bin/smattrpop -s file:/mopoke -t
  nisplus:/mopoke/wellard.com. all

Populating the auth_attr table...

Read 67 source entries; updated 67 target entries.
Populating the prof_attr table...

Read 28 source entries; updated 28 target entries.
Populating the exec_attr table...
```

```
Read 204 source entries; updated 204 target entries.

Populating the user_attr table...


Read 1 source entries; updated 0 target entries.
mopoke#
```

## New Toolbox for the Nameservice Domain

Use the following steps to create the new toolbox for the nameservice domain.

1.  If necessary, start the SMC Editor.

    Refer to "Starting the SMC Toolbox Editor" on page 33 for instructions on how to start the SMC Editor.

2.  From the toolbox, choose New.

    The Name and Description step of the New Toolbox Wizard is displayed, as shown in Figure 52.

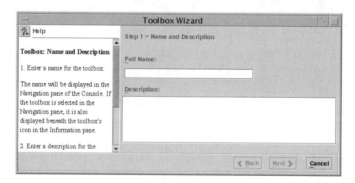

*Figure 52    New Toolbox Wizard*

3.  Type a toolbox name in the Full Name text field.

    This name is displayed in parentheses following the word Toolbox in the Navigation pane tree and in the Console header if you open the toolbox from the Console.

4.  Type a description in the Description text field and click on Next.

    Use the description to explain the contents and use of the toolbox.

5.  In the Icons step, path and file names for the default icons are displayed. Click on Next to use the default icons or click on Browse to navigate to the appropriate folder and select GIF images.

    These icons are used to represent the toolbox in the Console.

6.  Select a management scope from the pulldown menu.

You can choose ldap, dns, nisplus, nis, or file. The Users tool currently supports only nisplus, nis, or file.

7.  Type the domain name in the Domain field. If the management scope is nisplus, you do not need to include the trailing dot after the domain name.

    If you choose file as the management scope, you do not need to specify a domain name. Otherwise, enter the name of the domain to be managed—for example, `wellard.com`.

8.  Click on Finish.

    The full name of the new toolbox is displayed in parentheses in the window title of the SMC Editor in the Navigation pane.

## The Users Tool

After you create the nameservice domain toolbox, add the Users tool to that toolbox so that you can administer user accounts within that domain. Use the following step to add the Users tool to the domain toolbox.

1.  In the Navigation pane of the SMC Editor, select the toolbox you just created.

2.  From the Action menu, choose Add Tool.

    The first step of the Tool Wizard is displayed, as shown in Figure 53.

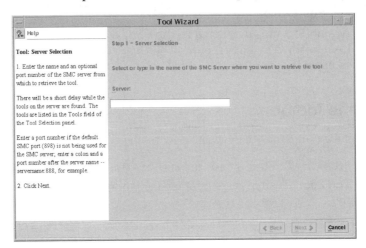

*Figure 53    Tool Wizard*

3.  Type the name of the server from which you plan to run the Users tool and click on Next.

If the server can be found and the SMC server is running on it, a list of tool class names is displayed in the Tools field.

4. From the list of tools, click on the Users tool.

   If the SMC server is not running on the selected server or if the Users tool is not displayed in the list of tools, type the name of the users tool in the Tool Class Name field and press Return. Type `com.sun.admin.usermgr.client.VUserMgr` and press Return. Then click on Next.

5. Click on Next to use the default name and description.

   To override the tool defaults, click on Override Tool Settings, type a new full name and description, and click on Next.

6. Click on Next to use the default icons.

   To override the default icons, click on Override Tool Settings, type the path to a new large and small icon, and click on Next.

7. Click on Next to inherit the management scope from the parent tool.

   To override the default management scope, click on Override Toolbox Settings, choose a new management scope, server, and domain, and click on Next.

8. Click on Next to load the tool when selected.

   Click on Load tool when toolbox is opened. Note that these settings can be overridden by Console preference settings.

9. Click on Finish.

   A generic tool is displayed in the SMC editor below the new toolbox item in the Navigation pane. The Users tool class name is displayed in parentheses after the word Tool.

## Save the Toolbox

Use the following steps to save the new toolbox.

1. From the Toolbox menu, choose Save As.

   The Local Toolbox save window is displayed, as shown in Figure 54.

*Figure 54    Local Toolbox Save Window*

2.  Navigate to the `/var/sadm/smc/toolboxes` directory.

3.  Type the name you want to use for this toolbox in the Filename text field and then click on Save.

    You do not need to add the `.tbx` suffix. The wizard automatically adds the suffix to the file name you specify. If you do add a `.tbx` suffix to the file name, it is ignored.

    The changes to the toolbox are saved and the wizard is closed.

# Part Two

# System Status

The System Status folder contains the Processes and Log Viewer tools, which are described in Chapter 5, "Processes," starting on page 61 and Chapter 6, "Log Viewer," starting on page 67.

# 5

# *PROCESSES*

Use the Processes tool to monitor and control processes in the current management domain. The Processes tool provides a graphical user interface to the `ps` command.

*NOTE. You can view processes only on the local system. This tool is not currently available for nameservice domains such as NIS, NIS+, and LDAP.*

Users can view all processes in the current management domain and can suspend, resume, and delete their own processes. Users with appropriate authorizations such as Primary Administrator and System Administrator can view, suspend, resume and delete all processes.

You can perform the following tasks with the Processes tool.

- Filter processes.
- Suspend a process and then resume running the process.
- Delete—or kill—one or more processes.
- View the properties of a process, including environment variables, resource limits, process DLLs, lightweight process stack trace, and file descriptors.
- View information about all processes.

# Starting the Processes Tool

Use the following steps to start the Processes tool.

1. Start SMC (if necessary) from the Tools menu by choosing Solaris Management Console.

2. If you want to open a different toolbox, from the Console menu, choose Open Toolbox.

   See "Opening a Toolbox" on page 25 for instructions on how to open server and local toolboxes.

3. In the Navigation pane, click on the System Status turner.

   The System Status tools are displayed in the Navigation pane.

4. Click on the Processes icon.

5. If necessary, log in with your user name or role name and appropriate passwords.

   After a few moments, the list of running processes is displayed in the right pane, as shown in Figure 55.

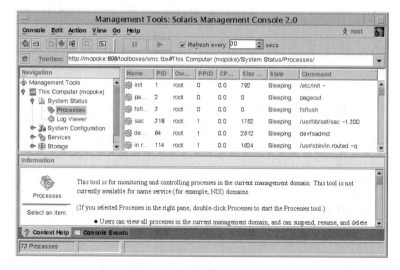

*Figure 55    Default Output of the Processes Tool*

The default columns are described in Table 3.

*Table 3*    *Default Processes Tool Columns*

| Column | Description | |
|---|---|---|
| Name | Name of the process. | |
| PID | Process ID. | |
| Owner | Owner of the process. | |
| PPID | Process ID of the parent process. | |
| CPU % | Percentage of the CPU used by this process. | |
| Size (KB) | Total size, in kilobytes, of the process in virtual memory. | |
| State | The current state of the process. | |
| | Running | Process is currently running. |
| | Sleeping | Process is waiting for an event to complete. |
| | Runnable | Process is on run queue. |
| | Zombie | Process terminated and the parent process is not waiting. |
| | Suspended | Process is stopped either because it is being traced or because it received a job control signal. |
| Command | Command that runs the process. | |

You can suppress display of any number of columns from the View > Columns menu. You can rearrange the width of the columns by dragging the right end of the label box. Existing columns are rearranged within the existing View pane.

The view is refreshed every 30 seconds, by default. You can turn off the refresh by clicking in the Refresh Every check box. You can change the default time by highlighting the number and typing a new one or by clicking on the up and down arrows to adjust the refresh time.

When the view is refreshed, the default column widths are used, any selected items are deselected, and the list is redisplayed from the top.

You may want to turn off refresh while you are scrolling through the list looking for a process to manage.

# Searching For a Process

You can search for an individual process through the View > Filter window, shown in Figure 56.

Figure 56     Filter Window

Select the filter criteria you want to use, type the information you want to search for, and click on the Filter button. You can filter by any element of the process: by process name, by process ID, by partial string, and so on.

Figure 57 shows all `csh` processes currently running.

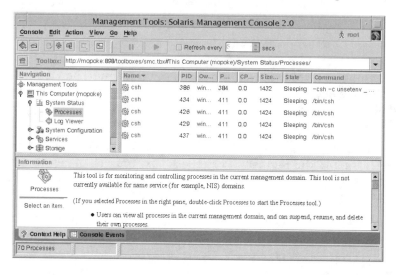

Figure 57     Filtered Output

When the display is filtered, refresh refreshes only the filtered items.

To display the complete list of processes, in the Filter window, click on Unfilter.

# Sorting Process Information

By default, processes are sorted by process ID. You can change the sort order by choosing View > Sort By to specify the column that is sorted. You can also sort any of the columns in descending order by choosing Descending at the bottom of the Sort By menu.

# Suspending and Resuming a Process

A suspended process is one that is temporarily stopped and that can be resumed at a future time. To suspend a process, click on the process to highlight it and, from the Action menu, choose Suspend.

The icon to the left of the process name changes and the state is changed to Suspended. In Figure 58, process 374 is suspended.

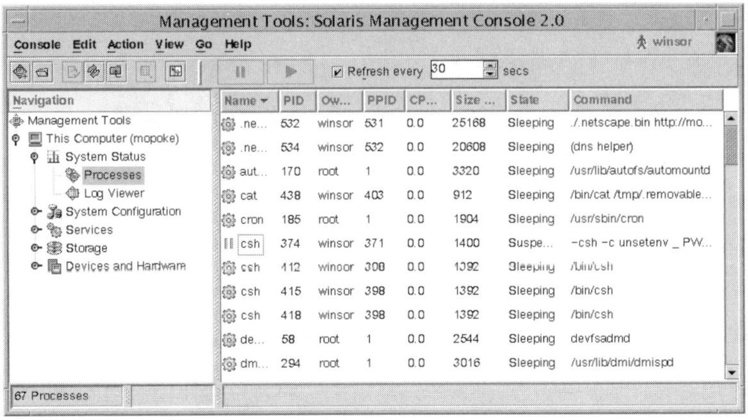

*Figure 58    Suspended Process*

To resume the process, select a suspended process and, from the Action menu, choose Resume. The process is resumed, the process icon changes, and the process returns to its previous state.

# Deleting a Process

To delete—or kill—one or more processes, select them and, from the Edit menu, choose Delete.

A warning is displayed, as shown in Figure 59, asking if you are sure you want to delete the processes.

*Figure 59    Delete Warning*

Click on Cancel to cancel the deletion or click on Delete to delete the selected processes.

# 6

# *LOG VIEWER*

You can use Log Viewer to view and manage log files for SMC Console tools and events.

*NOTE. Log Viewer entries are generated only by events logged to the WBEM logging service. Log Viewer entries differ from* syslog *entries.*

*Log Viewer also differs from the listings in the SMC Console Events tab, which provide information about events between SMC and its tools. The Console Events information is valid only for an individual SMC session.*

Log files are stored by default in /var/sadm/wbem/log. Log entries are generated for session open and close and for authentication success or failure.

SMC uses a single log file to log all SMC events for all management domains defined on a management server running SMC. By default, SMC displays log entries only for the currently active management domain—a single server or nameservice.

You can perform the following tasks with the Log Viewer tool

- Filter the list of log files.
- Open a log file.
- View log entry details.
- Change log file settings.

- Back up log files.
- Delete log files.

## Starting Log Viewer

Use the following steps to start the Log Viewer tool.

1. Start SMC (if necessary) from the Tools menu by choosing Solaris Management Console.

2. If you want to open a different toolbox, from the Console menu, choose Open Toolbox.

   See "Opening a Toolbox" on page 25 for instructions on how to open server and local toolboxes.

3. In the Navigation pane, click on the System Status turner.

   The System Status tools are displayed in the Navigation pane.

4. Click on the Log Viewer icon.

5. If necessary, log in with your user name or role name and appropriate passwords.

   When a large number of log files exist, the first time you open the Log Viewer during a session, the Set Initial View alert, shown in Figure 60, is displayed. The Set Initial View alert tells you how many log entries are available.

*Figure 60    Set Initial View Alert*

6. Click on Continue to load all of the log entries. Click on Filter to display the Log Filter window, shown in Figure 61, or click on Cancel to cancel opening of Log Viewer.

Figure 61    Log Filter Window

7.  You can filter by start and end date, by log properties, by computer or user identification, and by category.

*NOTE. Filter settings can prevent log entries from displaying in the log. If the Unfilter button in the Log Filter window is dimmed, no entries are filtered. If the Unfilter button is active, click on it to display all log file entries.*

Figure 62 shows unfiltered log entries.

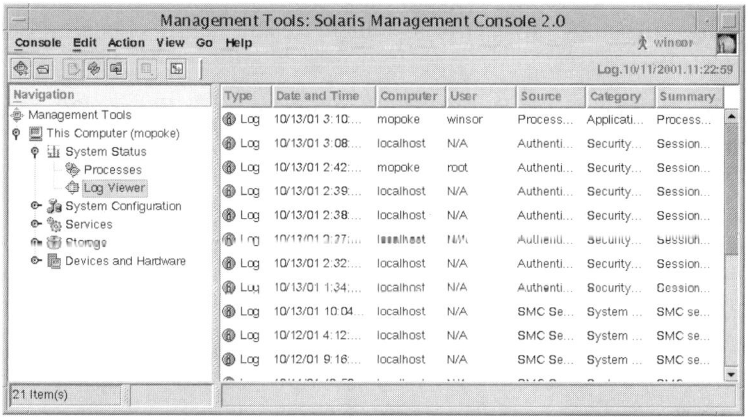

Figure 62    Log Viewer

The log viewer columns are described in Table 4.

Table 4     Log Viewer Columns

| Column | Description |
|---|---|
| Type | The type of file. For Log Viewer, the type is always Log. |
| Date and time | The date and time the log file was initiated. |
| Computer | The name of the computer that generated the log file. |
| User | The name of the user logged in to SMC when the log file was generated. |
| Source | The name of the tool that generated the log file. |
| Category | Possible categories are Application, Security log, and System log. |
| Summary | A summary of the contents of the log file. |

The default columns in Log Viewer are always visible. You cannot suppress display of any of the columns as you can in other tools. As with all SMC tools, you can rearrange the width of the columns by dragging the right end of the label box. You can refresh the display by choosing Refresh from the View menu.

## Viewing the Details of a Log Entry

You can view the details of a log entry in two ways.

- By double-clicking on the log entry in the Log Viewer.
- By highlighting a log entry and, from the Action menu, choosing Log Entry Details.

An example of a Log Entry Details window is shown in Figure 63.

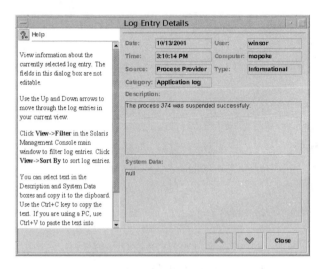

*Figure 63    Log Entry Details*

The top portion of the Log Entry Details window contains the information displayed in the Log Viewer list. The Description field contains a detailed description of the action logged. The System Data field contains any relevant system data.

You can select text in the Description or System Data field and copy and paste the text with keyboard shortcuts. Refer to the Help text in the Log Entry Details window for details about keyboard shortcuts.

You can use the up and down arrows at the bottom of the Log Entry Details window to move through the log entries in the current view.

*NOTE. After a log is generated, it is not displayed in the current view until you refresh the screen from the View menu by choosing Refresh.*

## Changing Log File Settings

You can change the default log file settings from the Action menu by choosing Log File Settings. The Log File settings window is displayed, as shown in Figure 64.

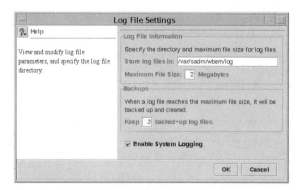

*Figure 64    Log File Settings Window*

From this window, you can specify the following information.

- The directory where log files are stored (default is `/var/sadm/wbem/log`).
- The maximum size for log files (default is 2 Mbytes).
- The number of backed-up log files to save (default is 3).
- Enable/disable system logging (default is enable).

# Backing Up Log Files

To back up log files before they reach the maximum file size, from the Action menu, choose Back Up Now. A Back Up Now warning is displayed, as shown in Figure 65.

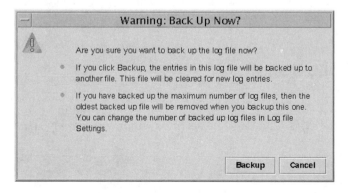

*Figure 65    Back Up Now Warning*

Click on Cancel to cancel the backup. Click on Backup to back up the current log file entries to a backup file. If you have backed up the specified maximum number of log files—three, by default—the oldest backed-up file is removed when the new backup file is created.

## Opening Backed-Up Log Files

To open a backed-up log file, from the Action menu, choose Open Log File. The Open Log File window is displayed, as shown in Figure 66.

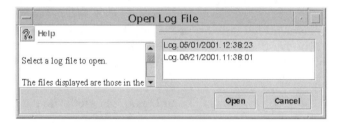

*Figure 66    Open Log File Window*

A list of available log files shows the date and time the log file was created. The oldest log files are listed first.

Highlight the log file you want to open and click on Open.

The entries from the log file are displayed in the Log Viewer pane.

## Deleting Log Files

You can delete the current log file. To delete an older log file from the Action menu, choose Open Log File and open the log file you want to delete. Then, from the Action menu, choose Delete Log File. The Delete Log File warning is displayed, as shown in Figure 67.

*Figure 67    Delete Log File Warning*

Deleting the file removes all log entries, including those generated outside the current domain. If the log file has been filtered, you can view all of the log entries that will be removed by choosing View > Filter and clicking on the Unfilter button.

Click on Cancel to retain the log file. Click on Delete to delete the log file.

# *Part Three*

# System Configuration

The System Configuration folder contains the following six chapters describing the tools that enable you to administer user accounts.

- Chapter 7, "User Accounts," starting on page 77—Use the User Accounts tool to add and maintain user accounts, assign rights to users, specify administrative roles, and set default user policies.
- Chapter 8, "User Templates," starting on page 111—Use the User Templates tool to add and maintain templates to use when adding new user accounts of a specific type.
- Chapter 9, "Rights," starting on page 119—Use the Rights tool to grant users the ability to perform specific administrative tasks. You can grant rights directly to a user or to a role the user can assume. SMC provides a comprehensive set of rights.
- Chapter 10, "Administrative Roles," starting on page 129—Use the Administrative Roles tool with predefined roles to make rights available to administrators.
- Chapter 11, "Groups," starting on page 141—Use the Groups tool to add user groups, maintain a list of group members for each, and delete obsolete groups.
- Chapter 12, "Mailing Lists," starting on page 149—Use the Mailing Lists tool to create and maintain mail aliases.

# 7

# USER ACCOUNTS

This chapter describes how to use the SMC User Accounts tool to perform the following tasks.

- Get started with user tools.
- Set user policies.
- Create a new user account with a wizard.
- Create multiple user accounts with a wizard.
- Create a new user account with a template.
- Create multiple user accounts with a template.
- Assign rights to a user.
- Copy a user account to a group or mailing list.
- Edit user properties.
- Delete user accounts.
- Disable user accounts.

You may find it useful to create a form from the following checklist to ensure that you have all the needed information about a user account before you crcatc it.

- User name.
- UID.
- Primary group.
- Secondary groups.

- Comment.
- Default shell.
- Password status and aging.
- Home directory server name.
- Home directory path name.
- Mounting method.
- Permissions on home directory.
- Mail server.
- Department name.
- Department administrator.
- Manager.
- Employee name.
- Employee title.
- Employee status.
- Employee number.
- Start date.
- Mail aliases to add account to.
- Desktop system name.

# Getting Started with User Tools

The Solaris 8 Operating Environment provides role-based access control (RBAC). RBAC is a new security feature that provides a flexible way to package certain superuser privileges for assignment to user accounts. You no longer need to give users all superuser privileges to enable them to perform one or more tasks that require superuser privileges.

With traditional security models, superuser has full superuser privileges and other users do not have enough privilege to fix their own problems. With role-based access control (RBAC), you now have an alternative to the traditional all-or-nothing security model.

With RBAC, those with Primary Administrator (one with root privileges) and User Security rights can divide superuser capabilities and assign them separately to individuals sharing administrative responsibilities. When you separate superuser privileges with RBAC, users can have granularity of privileges and you can control delegation of privileged operations to other users.

The suite of SMC System Configuration: Users tools integrates how you assign RBAC rights, create rights and roles, and administer rights and roles. See Chapter 9, "Rights," and Chapter 10, "Administrative Roles," for more information on creating and administering rights and roles.

The User Accounts tool contains a list of available rights, including Primary Administrator rights. The first administrator to log in to SMC on a specific server should set up at least one user account with the rights of Primary Administrator. Although the root account is automatically assigned Primary Administrator rights, Sun recommends that one or more key system administrators be assigned Primary Administrator rights to enable them to perform system administration tasks while logged in with their own user names.

## Primary Administrator Capabilities

With RBAC, the Primary Administrator can provide all other administrators with tools and commands to perform specific jobs and can restrict the other administrators' access to additional tools and commands.

A right is a named collection that includes three components.

- Commands.
- Authorizations to use specific applications or to perform specific functions within an application.
- Other, previously created rights.

SMC provides a comprehensive set of rights, described in Table 8 on page 103. The Primary Administrator can grant or deny rights to other administrators.

The Primary Administrator uses the Solaris Management Console (SMC) to grant rights in the following two ways.

- Assign the rights directly to users, who can then perform their administrative tasks. Assigning rights directly to users is recommended in small companies where system administrators perform a wide range of administrative tasks.
- Assign the rights to roles and associate users with those roles. To perform administrative tasks, users assume the role login and gain the rights assigned to that role. Assigning rights to roles is recommended for large organizations with many administrators, each with specific administrative tasks to perform.

By default, all users who can log in are granted the right of simply viewing any data that are accessible to those users with standard UNIX permissions.

Figure 68 illustrates the relationship of rights and roles. The Primary Administrator has assigned user ray rights to perform media backup and restore. The Primary Administrator has also created a role named printmgr that grants Device Management and Printer Management rights. User accounts ray and rob are assigned to the printmgr role. With this configuration, user ray can log in with his user name and perform media backup and restore. When he wants to perform printer administration, he logs in as the printmgr role and uses the role password. He can then perform printer administration tasks.

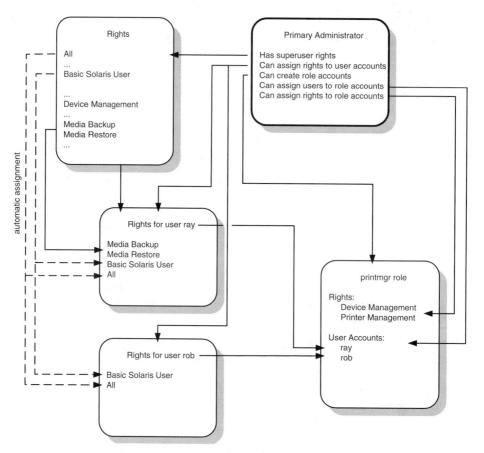

*Figure 68　Relationship of Rights and Roles*

When the Solaris Management Console (SMC) and User Management tools are installed, a comprehensive default set of rights is included. Only the special accounts included in the Solaris Operating Environment exist and no administrator has the rights needed to begin creating users, assigning roles, and administering RBAC.

To begin adding groups and users, assigning rights, and creating roles, the first administrator to log in to SMC must log in as root on the local system and then give himself or herself the right of Primary Administrator.

Use the following steps to assign Primary Administrator rights to a user.

1.  Start SMC (if necessary) from the Tools menu by choosing Solaris Management Console.

2.  If you want to open a different toolbox, from the Console menu, choose Open Toolbox.

    See "Opening a Toolbox" on page 25 for instructions on how to open server and local toolboxes.

3.  In the Navigation pane, click on the System Configuration turner. The list of System Configuration tools is displayed in the Navigation pane.

4.  Click on the Users turner.

    If you haven't already logged in to the SMC Console or if you have preferences set to always ask for authentication, the Log In: User Name window is displayed, as shown in Figure 69.

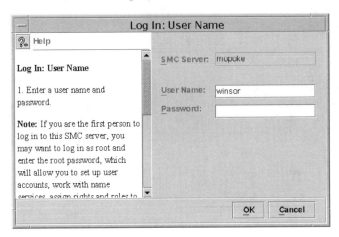

*Figure 69    Log In: User Name Window*

5.  Type **root** in the User Name text field and the root password in the Password field and click on the OK button.

    After a brief pause, the icons for the suite of Users tools are displayed in the View pane, as shown in Figure 70.

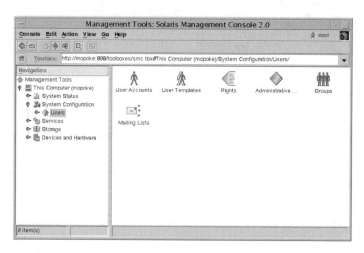

*Figure 70    Users Tools*

Notice that the login or role name is displayed at the right side of the menu bar.

6.  Double-click on the User Accounts icon.

The user accounts are displayed in the View pane, as shown in Figure 71.

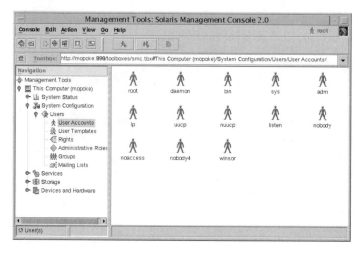

*Figure 71    User Accounts*

7.  Double-click on the icon for the user to whom you want to assign Primary Administrator Rights.

The User Properties window is displayed, as shown in Figure 72.

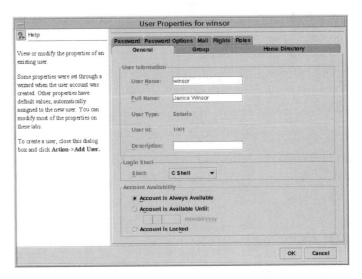

*Figure 72    User Properties Window*

8.  Click on the Rights tab.

    The Rights tab is displayed.

9.  In the Available Rights column, click on Primary Administrator, as
    shown in Figure 73.

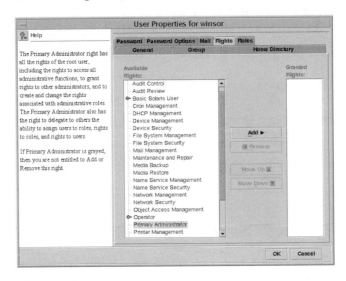

*Figure 73    Rights Tab*

10. Click on the Add button to move Primary Administrator to the
    Granted Rights column, then click on the OK button.

Primary Administrator rights are granted to the specified user.

11. You can verify the rights for the user in a Terminal window by typing **profiles *username*** and pressing Return.

In the following example, user winsor has been assigned Primary Administrator in addition to the default Basic Solaris User and All rights.

```
mopoke% profiles winsor
Primary Administrator
Basic Solaris User
All
mopoke%
```

# Setting User Policies

Before you start creating or deleting user accounts, it's a good idea to first set user policies. For the SMC User Accounts tool, policies include specifying the default user template, which you create with the User Templates tool. The template specifies a set of default values such as default shell, primary group, mail server, and password policies. See Chapter 8, "User Templates," for information on creating user templates. User Policies also includes specifying whether the home directory and mailbox are deleted by default when you use the User Accounts tool to delete a user account.

To set user policies, from the Action menu, choose User Policies. The User Policies window is displayed, as shown in Figure 74.

*Figure 74    Set User Policies Window*

You can specify a default user template and specify by clicking in the appropriate check box that users' home directories or mailboxes are removed by default when a user account is deleted.

Before you can specify a user template, you must create one with the User Templates tool.

When you specify a user template, that template is used as the default when you choose Add Users > From Template and Add Multiple Users > From Template. You can always choose another template from the Add Users and Add Multiple Users windows.

If you create more than one template and do not specify a default template from the User Policies window, the first template in the alphabetical list is automatically specified as the default template.

# Adding a Single User Account

Before you add users to the network, the users' systems must be installed and configured. When appropriate, NIS+ or NIS software should be installed and running on the network.

Adding users so that they can log in and start working has two parts: setting up the user account and providing the user with a working environment.

When you set up a user account with the User Accounts tool, you perform the following steps.

- Assign a login name and user ID.
- Define the user's primary group.
- Provide a home directory with a user initialization file.
- Define the user's environment.
- Create a password.

The next sections provide background information and describe how to do these tasks.

To create a single user account with the Wizard, from the Action menu, choose Add User > With Wizard. The wizard is displayed at the first step, as shown in Figure 75.

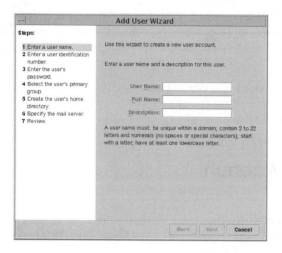

*Figure 75   Add User Wizard: Step 1*

## User Name

The first step in adding a user account is to assign a user name. A user name must be unique within a domain, start with a letter, and contain 2 to 32 letters and numerals with no spaces or special characters. The user name must have at least one lowercase letter.

The User Name field is the only required field. Enter a user name and a full name and description if desired. Then, click on the Next button.

## User ID Number

The next step is assigning a user ID (UID). A UID is always associated with each user name and is used by systems to identify the owners of files and directories and to identify the user at login. If you create user accounts for a single individual on more than one system, always use the same user name and UID. In that way, the user can easily move and copy files between systems without ownership problems.

A UID must be a whole number less than or equal to 2147483647. The maximum UID was increased from 60000 to 2147483647 starting with the Solaris 2.5.1 release.

UIDs are required for both regular user accounts and special system accounts. Table 5 lists the UIDs that are reserved for user accounts and system accounts.

*Table 5*     *Reserved UIDs*

| UIDs | Login Accounts | Description |
|---|---|---|
| 0 | root | Root account. |
| 1 | daemon | Daemon account. |
| 2 | bin | Pseudo-user bin account. |
| 3-99 | sys, uucp logins, who, tty, and ttytype | System accounts. |
| 100-60000 | Regular users | General-purpose accounts. |
| 60001 | nobody | Unauthenticated users. |
| 60002 | noaccess | Compatibility with previous Solaris and SVR4 releases. |
| 60003-2147483647 | Regular users | General-purpose accounts. |

*CAUTION. Be careful when using UIDs in the 60000 to 2147483647 range. These numbers do not have full functionality and are incompatible with many Solaris features. See Table 6 for more information.*

Even though UIDs 0 through 99 are reserved for use by system accounts, you can add a user with one of these UIDs. You should not, however, use these UIDs for regular user accounts. Use the numbers 0 through 99 to assign system accounts, uucp logins, and pseudo-user logins.

## Large User IDs and Group IDs

Previous Solaris Operating Environments used 32-bit data types to contain UIDs and GIDs. UIDs and GIDs were constrained to a maximum useful value of 60000. The limit on UID and GID values has been raised to the maximum value of a signed integer, or 2147483647 starting with the Solaris 2.5.1

release. Table 6 lists the interoperability issues with the Solaris Operating Environment products and commands.

*Table 6     Interoperability Issues for UIDs and GIDs over 60000*

| Category | Product/Command | Issues/Cautions |
|---|---|---|
| NFS Interoperability. | SunOS 4.x NFS software. | SunOS 4.x NFS server and client code truncates large UIDs and GIDs to 16 bits. This truncation can create security problems if SunOS 4.x systems are used in an environment where large UIDs and GIDs are being used. SunOS 4.x and compatible systems require a patch. |
| Name Service Interoperability. | NIS name service. File-based name service. | Users with UIDs above 60000 can log in and use the su command on systems running the Solaris 2.5 Operating Environment and compatible versions; however, their UIDs and GIDs are set to 60001 (nobody). |
| | NIS+ name service. | Users with UIDs above 60000 are denied access on systems running the Solaris 2.5 Operating Environment, compatible versions, and the NIS+ name service. |
| Printed UIDs/GIDs. | OpenWindows File Manager. | Large UIDs and GIDs are not displayed correctly if the OpenWindows File Manager is used with the extended file listing display option. |

Table 7 summarizes the limitations of using large UIDs and GIDs.

*Table 7     Limitations of Using UIDs and GIDs over 60000*

| UID/GID Number | Limitation |
|---|---|
| 60003 or greater. | A UID and GID of nobody are assigned to users who log in to systems running the Solaris 2.5 Operating Environment and compatible releases and the NIS or files name service. |

*Table 7*    *Limitations of Using UIDs and GIDs over 60000 (Continued)*

| UID/GID Number | Limitation |
|---|---|
| 65536 or greater. | Solaris 2.5 Operating Environment and compatible release systems running the NFS version 2 software truncate UIDs in this category to 16 bits, creating possible security problems. |
|  | Using the `cpio` command with the default archive format to copy files displays an error message for each file, and the UID and GID are set to `nobody` in the archive. |
|  | SPARC-based systems: Systems running SunOS and compatible applications display `EOVERFLOW` messages from some system calls, and the UID and GID are set to `nobody`. |
|  | IA-based systems: SVR3-compatible applications on an IA system are likely to display `EOVERFLOW` messages from system calls. |
|  | IA-based systems: If users create a file or directory on a mounted System V file system, the System V file system returns an `EOVERFLOW` error. |
| 100000 or greater. | The `ps -l` command displays a maximum five-digit UID, so the printed column is not aligned when it includes a UID or GID greater than 99999. |
| 2622144 or greater. | Using the `cpio` command with `-H odc` format or the `pax -x cpio` command to copy files returns an error message for each file, and the UIDs and GIDs are set to `nobody` in the archive. |
| 10000000 or greater. | Using the `ar` command sets UIDs and GIDs to `nobody` in the archive. |
| 2097152 or greater. | UIDs and GIDs are set to `nobody` when the `tar` command, the `cpio -H ustar` command, or the `pax -x tar` command is used. |

The Add User ID step is shown in Figure 76.

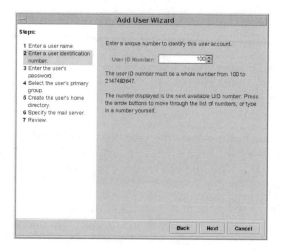

*Figure 76    Add User Wizard: Step 2*

Type the user ID number in the text field or click on the up and down arrows to choose a number. Then, click on the Next button.

## Password Policy

Passwords are an important part of system security. Each user account should be assigned a password of 6 to 10 characters as a combination of letters and numbers. See the passwd(1), yppasswd(1), or nispasswd(1) manual pages for information about changing passwords and password attributes.

In the Solaris 8 Operating Environment, the encrypted password and associated password aging information are stored in the Shadow field of the NIS+ Passwd database (or in the local /etc/shadow file). Permissions on the Shadow field are restricted. Permissions for the /etc/shadow file are -r--------. Only root can read the /etc/shadow file, and only the passwd, yppasswd, nispasswd commands, and the User Accounts tool used with appropriate rights can write to this file.

The password policy step is shown in Figure 77.

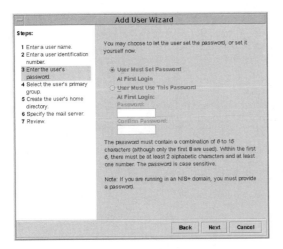

*Figure 77    Add User Wizard: Step 3*

You can ask users to specify a password the first time they log in, or you can specify a password that users must use the first time they log in. Choose the password policy, as appropriate. Then, click on the Next button.

## User's Primary Group

The next step is to specify the primary group for the user, as shown in Figure 78.

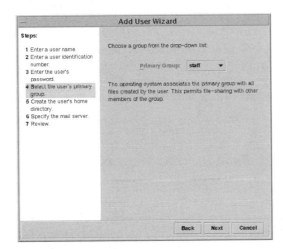

*Figure 78    Add User Wizard: Step 4*

The default primary group is `staff` with a group ID of `10`. You can choose a different group from the Primary Group drop-down menu. When you have specified the primary group, click on the Next button.

## Home Directory Location

The next step is to specify the home directory location, as shown in Figure 79.

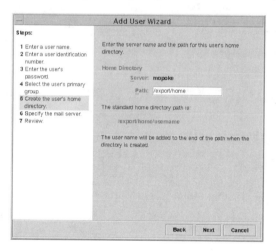

*Figure 79    Add User Wizard: Step 5*

*NOTE. The SMC User Accounts tool automatically copies to the user's home directory the* `local.cshrc` *as* `.cshrc`, `local.profile` *as* `.profile`, *and* `local.login` *as* `.login`. *Ownership is set to the user name. The Wizard does not enable you to set the user's default login shell. If you want to change the shell, after you finish creating the user account, edit the user account properties and change the default (Bourne) shell or use Add Multiple Users > With Wizard.*

*If you have created custom initialization files for your users, replace the default files in the* `/etc/skel` *files with your own files to automatically copy your own initialization files to the users' home directory.*

The standard home directory is `/export/home/username`. To use the default location, click on the Next button. Otherwise, type the path to the home directory and then click on the Next button. The home directory is created, and the user initialization files are copied from the `/etc/skel` directory into the user's new home directory with appropriate ownership and permissions.

## User's Mail Account

Each user has a mailbox either on a local system or on a mail server and a mail alias in the `/etc/mail/aliases` file that points to the location of the mailbox. The mail server step is shown in Figure 80.

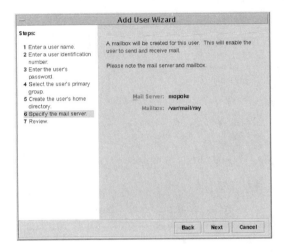

*Figure 80    Add User Wizard: Step 6*

The mail server and mailbox name are specified by the User Accounts tool. You cannot edit these settings. Simply note them for future reference.

## Review

The final step is to review the settings for the user account, as shown in the example in Figure 81.

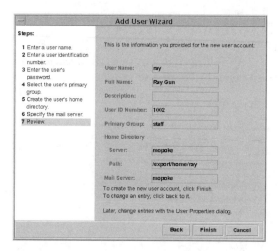

*Figure 81    Review Settings*

If you want to change any of the settings, click on the Back button until you get to the step you want to change. Then click on Next until you reach the Review screen. When the information is correct, click on the Finish button. The account is created.

Use the View > Refresh menu item to display the new user account in the View pane.

# Creating Multiple User Accounts with a Wizard

You can create multiple user accounts at the same time with the User Accounts tool from the Action menu by choosing Add Multiple Users > With Wizard. The Add Multiple Users wizard is displayed, as shown in Figure 82.

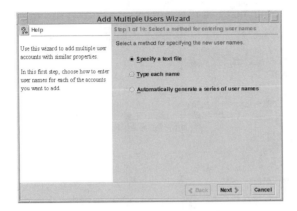

*Figure 82    Add Multiple Users Wizard*

You can specify a list of user names in the following ways.

- In a text file in which each line specifies a user name, full name, and description as a colon-separated list. For example `winsor:Janice Winsor:Paperbark Designs`.

- Type each name individually.

- Automatically generate a series of user names with a prefix and starting number that you specify, as shown in Figure 83.

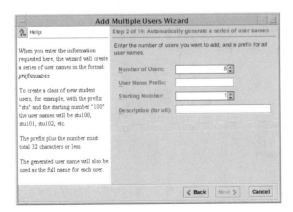

*Figure 83    Add Multiple Users with Prefix and Starting Number*

Once you specify the way to enter the list of user names, click on the Next button.

When you create multiple user accounts, you can specify a login shell. The login shell must be the same for all accounts. You also specify whether the account is always available or when the account is no longer to be available, as shown in Figure 84. You can specify that the account is always available (the default), or specify an expiration date for the account by *mm / dd / yyyy*.

*Figure 84    Specify Login Shell and Availability*

The next step sets password policy, as shown in Figure 85. You can specify that user assigns a password the first time he logs in, or you can assign a password to the user.

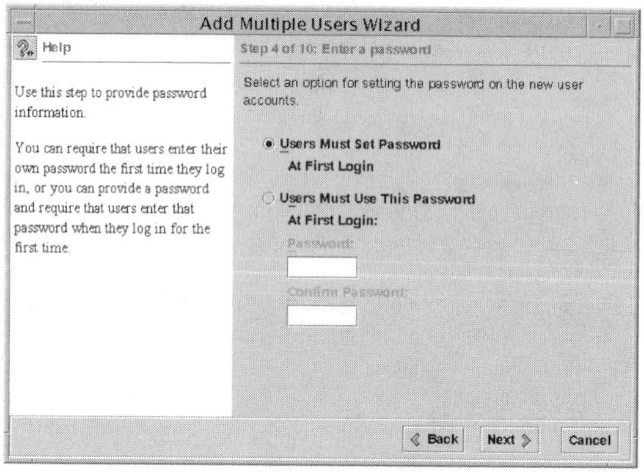

*Figure 85    Set Password Policy*

The next step specifies additional password options, as shown in Figure 86. You can specify time limits and time requirements for keeping, changing, and expiring passwords.

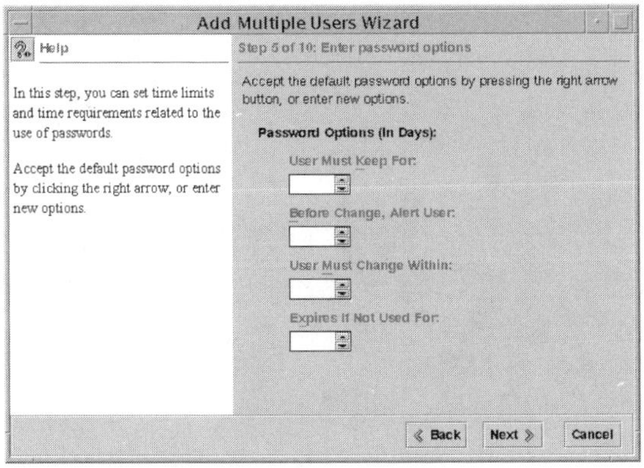

*Figure 86    Set Password Options*

The next step specifies the starting user ID number, as shown in Figure 87. The ID numbers are added in the order you specified: by listing the names in the text file, by typing the names individually, or by using the prefix and numeric automatic assignment method.

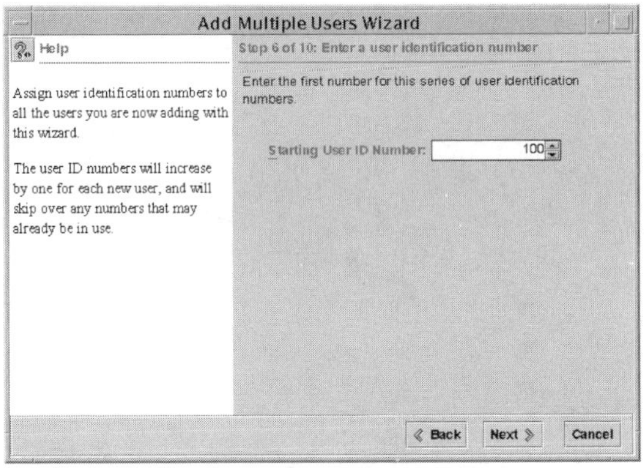

*Figure 87    Specify Starting UID Number*

The next step specifies the primary group for the users, as shown in Figure 88.

*Figure 88    Specify Primary Group*

The next step specifies the user's home directory, as shown in Figure 89. The default is to automatically mount the home directory. If you uncheck the check box, you must specify the home directory in the Path text field.

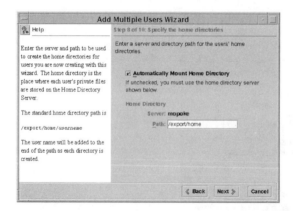

*Figure 89    Specify the Home Directory Path*

The next step shows the mail server and mailbox for this set of users, as shown in Figure 90.

*Figure 90    Note Mail Server and Mailbox Locations*

The next step is to review the settings for this set of users, as shown in Figure 91.

*Figure 91    Add Multiple Users Wizard*

When the settings are correct, click on Finish.

A warning might be displayed, as shown in Figure 92, notifying you that an SMC tool wants to read a file.

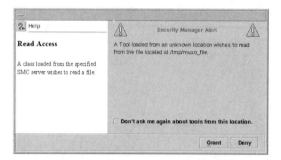

*Figure 92    Read Access Warning*

If you don't want to be warned again, click the check box, then click on the Grant button to grant permission. Click on the Deny button to deny access.

The accounts are created in the background, as shown by the message in Figure 93, which is displayed at the end of the process.

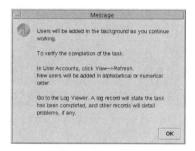

*Figure 93    Completion Message*

When the accounts have been created, choose View > Refresh to display them in the View pane of the SMC Console.

# Creating a New User Account with a Template

Refer to Chapter 8, "User Templates," for information on how to use the User Templates tool to create templates that specify a set of defaults for different types of user accounts. The following instructions assume that at least one template already exists.

From the Action menu, choose Add User > From Template. The Add User From Template window is displayed, as shown in Figure 94.

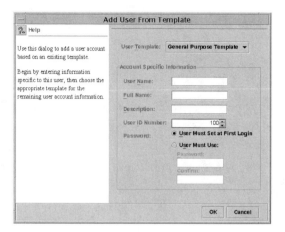

*Figure 94    Add User From Template Window*

If you want to use a template other than the default, choose the template from the User Template drop-down menu. Then, type the user name, full name, and description, specify the user ID number and password policy, and click on the OK button. The rest of the properties are set from the template you specify.

# Creating Multiple User Accounts with a Template

To create multiple user accounts from a template, from the Action menu, choose Add Multiple Users > From Template. The Add Multiple Users From Template window is displayed, as shown in Figure 95.

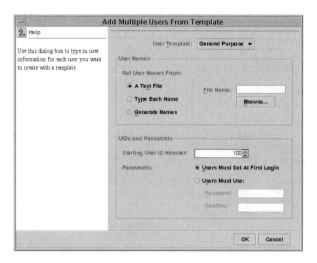

*Figure 95     Add Multiple Users From Template Window*

If you want to use a template other than the default, choose the template from the User Template drop-down menu. Specify the method for assigning user names, choose the starting user ID, and set the password policy. Then, click on the OK button. The user accounts are created with the properties from the template you specify.

## Assigning Rights to a User

Table 8 describes the rights you can assign to users. For convenience in assigning rights, three sets of rights contain a group of rights.

- Basic Solaris User.
- Operator, System Administrator.
- Primary Administrator.

You can assign any set of rights individually.

*Table 8    Available Rights*

| Right | Description |
|-------|-------------|
| All | Automatically assigned to each user. It grants the right for a user or role to use any command when working in an administrator's shell such as Administrator's Korn or Administrator's C shells. The All right should always be the last right in the list. If All is first, no other rights are consulted when command attributes are looked up. |
| Audit Control | Grants the right to read the audit subsystem but not the right to read audit files. |
| Audit Review | Grants the right to read the audit trail but not to manage the audit subsystem. |
| Basic Solaris User | Assigned to every user who logs in to SMC. Provides read permissions to users of applications and enables users to add cron jobs to their own crontab files. The Basic Solaris User right always includes the All right. |
| Device Management | Grants the right to allocate and deallocate devices and to correct error conditions relating to those devices. |
| Device Security | Grants the right to manage and configure devices and volume manager. |
| DHCP Management | Grants the right to manage the DHCP service. |
| File System Management | Grants the right to manage file system mounts and shares. |
| Mail Management | Grants the right to configure sendmail, modify mailing lists, and check mail queues. |
| Maintenance and Repair | Grants the right to use commands needed to maintain or repair a system. |
| Media Backup | Grants the right to back up files but not the right to restore them. |
| Media Restore | Grants the right to restore backed-up files but not the right to perform system backup. |
| Name Service Management | Grants the right to control the nameservice daemon. |

*Table 8     Available Rights (Continued)*

| Right | Description |
|---|---|
| Name Service Security | Grants the right to manage nameservice properties and table data. |
| Network Management | Grants the right to manage the host and network configuration. |
| Network Security | Grants the right to manage network and host security with authorizations for modifying trusted network databases. |
| Object Access Management | Grants the right to file ownership and permissions. |
| Operator | Contains Printer Management, Media Backup, and All rights. Operator rights also include Process Management, Rights Delegation, and Software Installation rights. |
| Primary Administrator | Assigns all the rights of the root user and is responsible for assigning rights to users, assigning users to roles, creating new roles, and changing the rights associated with administrative roles. The Primary Administrator can designate other users as a Primary Administrator. The Primary Administrator can also grant Rights Delegation, which gives other administrators the limited ability to grant to others only rights the delegators already have or rights to roles to which the delegators are already assigned. |
| Printer Management | Grants the right to manage printer devices, daemons, and spooling. |
| Process Management | Grants the right to manage current processes and daemons. |
| Rights Delegation | Grants the user or role limited ability to assign to other users or roles those rights and roles already assigned to the user with the Rights Delegation right. |
| Software Installation | Grants the right to add and remove application software. |

*Table 8     Available Rights (Continued)*

| Right | Description |
|---|---|
| System Administrator | Contains Audit Review, Printer Management, Cron Management, Device Management, File System Management, Mail Management, Maintenance and Repair, Media Backup, Media Restore, Name Service Management, Network Management, Object Access Management, Process Management, Software Installation, User Management, and All rights. |
| User Management | Grants the right to create and modify user accounts—except for its own user account. It does not grant the right to modify user passwords. |
| User Security | Grants the right to create and modify user passwords. |

Assigning rights to users is similar to granting Primary Administrator rights except that you first log in as a user who has Primary Administrator rights instead of as root. See "Getting Started with User Tools" on page 78 for illustrations of the screens.

Use the following steps to grant rights to a user.

1. From the Tools menu, choose Solaris Management Console.
2. Open the toolbox you want to use if it is not the default toolbox.
3. Click on the turner control next to the This Computer toolbox.

   The list of tools is displayed.
4. Click on the turner control to the left of the System Configuration item in the Navigation pane.

   The Users tool is displayed.
5. Double-click on the Users icon.

   The Users Login window is displayed.
6. Log in as a user who has Primary Administrator rights, type your password, and click on the OK button.

   After a few moments, the Users tools are displayed in the View pane.
7. Click on the icon for the user account to which you want to assign rights.
8. From the Action menu, choose Assign Rights to User.

   The Assign Rights to User window is displayed, as shown in Figure 96.

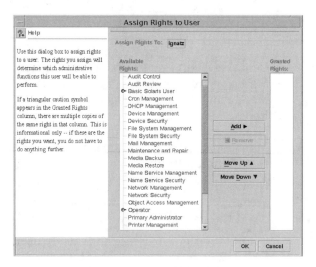

*Figure 96    Assign Rights to User Window*

9.  Click on each right you want to assign and click on the Add button to move the right to the Granted Rights column.

10. When you have chosen all the rights you want to add, click on the OK button.

    The rights are granted. The order of rights in the hierarchy is important because rights are searched in a way similar to the search path for files and directories. See "Rights Hierarchies" on page 126 for more detailed information. The All Rights should always be last in the list.

11. If necessary, highlight a right in the Granted Rights column and click on the Move Up or Move Down button to rearrange the rights hierarchy.

12. You can verify the rights for the user in a Terminal window by typing **profiles** *username* and pressing Return.

# Copying a User Account to a Group or Mailing List

Use the following steps to copy a user account to a group or mailing list.

1.  Click on the user account(s) you want to add to a group or mailing list.

2.  From the Actions menu, choose Copy to Group or Mailing List.

3.  Click on the Group or Mailing List icon in the Navigation pane.

4. In the View pane, click on the icon for the group or mailing list to which you want to add the users.

5. From the Action menu in the Group or Mailing List tool, choose Paste Users.

   The user accounts are added to the group or mailing list that you specified.

# Editing User Account Properties

When information about a user changes, use the User Accounts, User Properties window to edit information about the user. Unless you define a user (login) name or UID that conflicts with existing ones, you probably do not need to modify a user account's login name or UID.

To edit user properties, double-click on the icon for the user account you want to modify. The User Properties window for that user is displayed, as shown in Figure 97.

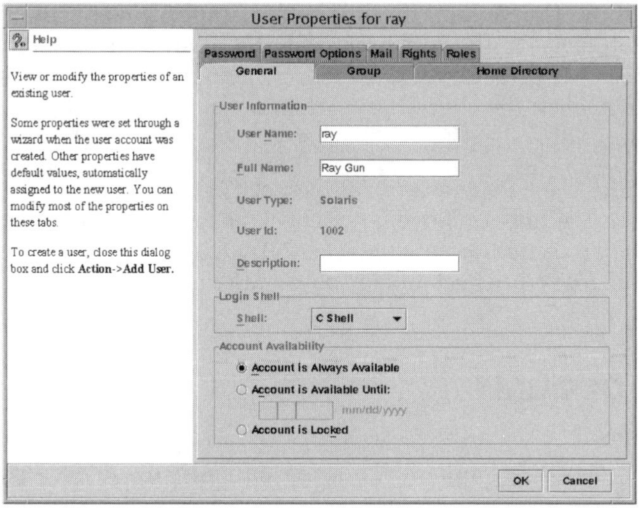

*Figure 97    User Properties Window*

Click on the tab for each property you want to modify and make the changes. When you have completed all the changes, click on the OK button. The properties for the user account are changed.

# Deleting User Accounts

To delete a user account, click on the icon for the user account(s) you want to delete. From the Edit menu, choose Delete.

A warning window is displayed, as shown in Figure 98.

*Figure 98    Warning: Delete User? Window*

When you click on the Delete button, all user account entries in the directory services databases and group accounts are removed. The default is that the Remove the home directory and Remove the mailbox check boxes are unchecked. When you check the check boxes, the user's home directory and mailbox are also removed.

If the User Accounts User Policies are set to specify that the home directory and mailbox are to be removed, the check boxes in the Warning: Delete User? window are automatically checked. If you want, you can override the user policies to uncheck one or both of the check boxes.

# Disabling User Accounts

Occasionally, you may need to temporarily or permanently disable a login account. You should have good reason for taking such action. For example, the user may be on leave of absence or you may have strong evidence that the account is being misused or that security is being violated.

The easiest way to disable a login account is to change the password for an account. Use the following steps to change a user's password.

1.  Double-click on the user account you want to disable.
    The User Properties window is displayed.
2.  Click on the Password tab.

3. Click on the radio button next to User Must Use This Password at Next Login setting.

4. Type the new password twice.

5. Click on the OK button.

You can also control access to a user's account from the Password Options tab by requiring password aging, by setting an expiration date for the login account, or by requiring that a user access the account at regular intervals.

# 8

# *USER TEMPLATES*

Use the User Templates tool to create templates for creating user accounts with the SMC Console User Accounts tool. The user templates enable you to construct specific profiles for a group of user accounts that share the same characteristics such as login shell, home directory server, and mail server.

With this tool you can perform the following tasks.

- Create new templates.
- Clone an existing template.
- Change the properties of an existing template.

Within the Users tools, click on the User Templates icon in the Navigation pane or double-click on the User Templates icon in the View pane to display the User Templates tool.

## Starting the User Templates Tool

Use the following steps to start the User Templates tool.

1. Start SMC (if necessary) from the Tools menu by choosing Solaris Management Console.
2. If you want to open a different toolbox, from the Console menu, choose Open Toolbox.

See "Opening a Toolbox" on page 25 for instructions on how to open server and local toolboxes.

3. In the Navigation pane, click on the System Configuration turner.

The System Configuration tools are displayed in the Navigation pane.

4. Click on the Users icon.

5. If necessary, log in with your user name or role name and appropriate passwords.

The Users tools are displayed in the Navigation pane.

6. Click on the User Templates icon.

When no templates exist, the View pane is blank, as shown in Figure 99.

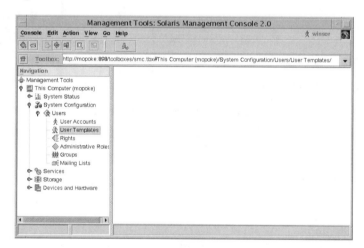

*Figure 99    User Templates Tool*

# Creating a New Template

To create a new template, from the Action menu, choose Add User Template. The Add User Template window is displayed, as shown in Figure 100.

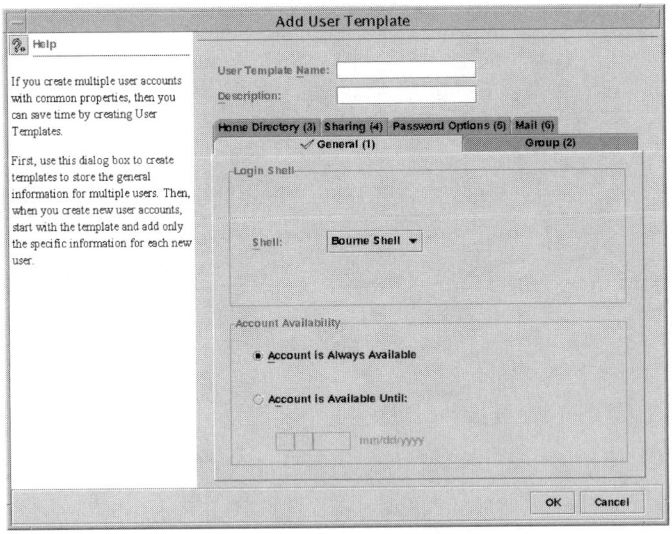

*Figure 100　Add User Template Window: General Tab*

Type the name of the template and a description of what the template is to be used for, for example, "Accounts Payable User."

In the General tab, specify the login shell (default is Bourne Shell), and the account availability policy (default is Account is Always Available.

Click on the Group tab, shown in Figure 101, to specify the primary group and additional groups for this template.

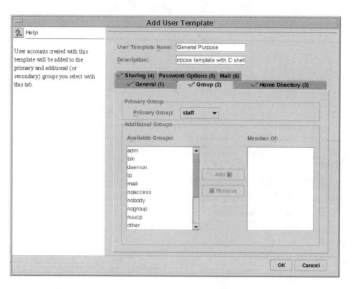

*Figure 101  Add User Template Window: Group Tab*

Click on the Home Directory tab, shown in Figure 102. Specify the home directory server, home directory path, and path to the initialization files. If you do not want to automatically mount the home directories, click to turn off the Automatically Mount Home Directory check box.

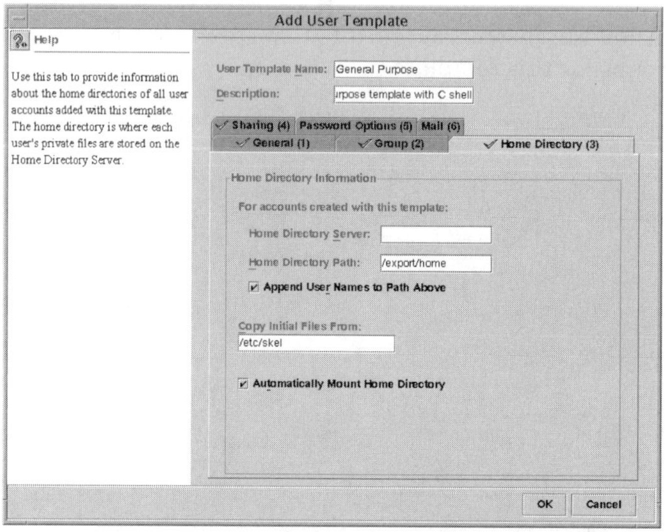

*Figure 102  Add User Template Window: Home Directory Tab*

Click on the Sharing tab to specify the sharing policy for this user template. Figure 103 shows the default settings.

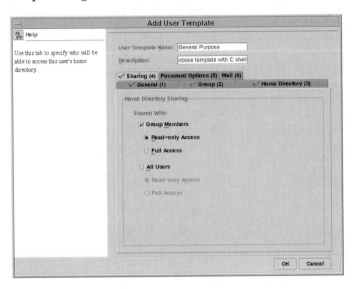

*Figure 103  Add User Template Window: Sharing Tab*

Click on the Password Options tab to specify the password policy. The default settings are shown in Figure 104.

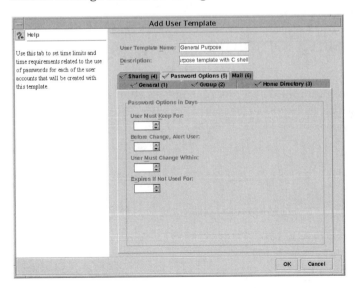

*Figure 104  Add User Template Window: Password Options Tab*

Set the password options, if desired, then click on the Mail tab, shown in Figure 105, to specify the mail server. The mail server can be on the same server as the home directory or on a different server.

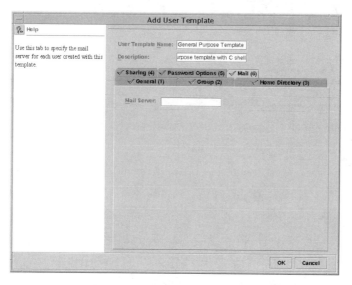

*Figure 105  Add User Template Window: Mail Tab*

When the template is complete, click on the OK button.

# Cloning an Existing Template

To clone an existing template and modify some or all of its properties, from the Action menu choose Clone User Template. The Clone User Template window is opened, as shown in Figure 106.

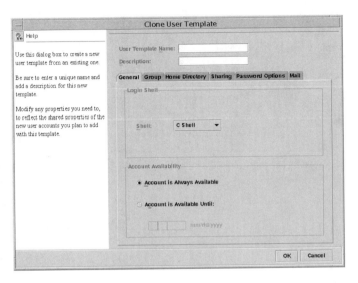

*Figure 106  Clone User Template Window*

Type a new, unique template name in the User Template Name text field. Modify properties as necessary, and click on the OK button. The cloned template is added to the User Templates View pane.

## Changing Template Properties

You can change the properties for a template at any time.

*NOTE. Changing the properties of a template affects only accounts created in the future. It does not affect existing user accounts that were created with this template.*

Double-click on the template you want to modify. Alternatively, click on the template you want to change and, from the Actions menu, choose Properties. The User Template Properties window for the template you chose is displayed, as shown in Figure 107.

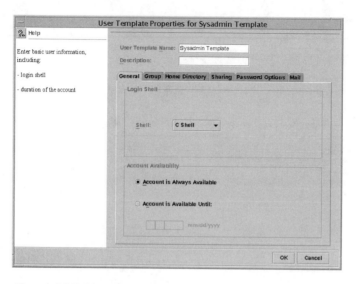

*Figure 107  User Template Properties Window*

Make the changes you require and click on the OK button. The template is updated to use the new properties.

# Setting User Policies

From the User Accounts tool, you can use the User Policies window to set a default template. See "Setting User Policies" on page 84 for more information.

# 9

# RIGHTS

Rights are groups of role-based access control (RBAC) authorizations and commands with special attributes. See "Getting Started with User Tools" on page 78 for an introduction to RBAC and rights.

*NOTE. You assign rights to user accounts from the Rights tab of the User Accounts tool. See "Assigning Rights to a User" on page 102 for information on how to assign rights to a user account. See Chapter 10, "Administrative Roles," for information about administrative roles and how to assign rights to a role.*

The Rights tool enables someone with Primary Administrator rights to perform the following tasks.

- Add new rights.
- View and edit the properties of existing rights.
- Delete rights.

## Starting the Rights Tool

Use the following steps to start the Rights tool.

1. Start SMC (if necessary) from the Tools menu by choosing Solaris Management Console.

2.  If you want to open a different toolbox, from the Console menu, choose Open Toolbox.

    See "Opening a Toolbox" on page 25 for instructions on how to open server and local toolboxes.

3.  In the Navigation pane, click on the System Configuration turner.

    The System Configuration tools are displayed in the Navigation pane.

4.  Click on the Users icon.

5.  If necessary, log in with your user name or role name and appropriate passwords.

    The Users tools are displayed in the Navigation pane.

6.  Click on the Rights icon.

    Available rights are displayed in the View pane, as shown in Figure 108.

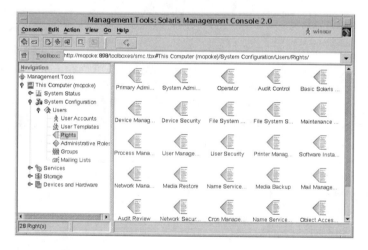

*Figure 108  Rights Window*

# Adding New Rights

You can create new rights to combine your own specified collection of commands, authorizations, and existing supplementary rights.

To create a new right, from the Action menu, choose Add Right. The Add Right window is displayed, as shown in Figure 109.

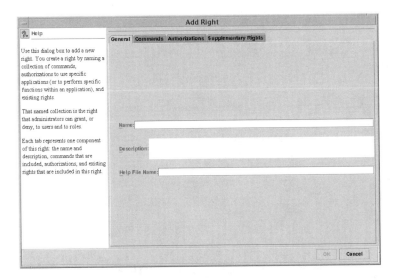

*Figure 109  Add Right: General Tab*

The Add Right window has four components—General, Commands, Authorizations, and Supplementary Rights—each represented by a tab. Click on each tab to configure the new right. When you have added all of the commands, authorizations, and supplementary rights, click on the OK button to create the right. The contents of each tab are described in the following sections.

## General Tab

Use the General tab to add the unique name of a new right and a description. You must also specify an HTML help file name. Help files must have an `.html` suffix. After you have created the right, use a text editor to create the HTML help file in the `/usr/lib/help/profiles/locale/C/` directory.

## Commands Tab

To add commands to the new right, click on the Commands tab, shown in Figure 110.

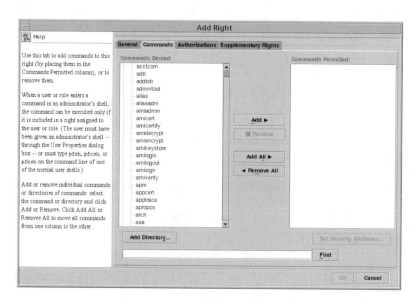

*Figure 110  New Right: Commands Tab*

In the Commands Denied list, click on each command that you want to permit and then click on the Add button. You can remove commands from the Commands Permitted list by highlighting the command and clicking on the Remove button. If you are adding many commands from the same directory, you can click on the Add All button to add all the rights and then remove the individual commands you do not want to include. Click on the Remove All button if you want to remove all commands from the Command Permitted list.

> *NOTE. Before you start adding individual commands, check the Authorizations and Supplementary Rights tabs to see if the commands you want are already grouped as part of an existing authorization or supplementary right. See "Authorizations Tab" on page 124 and "Supplementary Rights Tab" on page 125.*

## Adding a Directory

You can specify the name of a directory to be added to the Commands Denied list for the current session. Click on the Add Directory button. The Add Directory window is displayed, as shown in Figure 111.

*Figure 111  Add Directory Window*

Type the name of a directory that contains commands you want to add to the right and click on the OK button. The directory name and its contents are added to the Commands Denied list. You can then either add individual commands from that directory or add the whole directory, commands and all, to the Commands Permitted column.

## Finding a Command

In lieu of scrolling through the long list of available commands, you can type the name of the command in the Find text field at the bottom of the Add Right window and then click on the Find button. The command is highlighted, and you can then click on the Add or Remove button to add or remove the command from the list. The Find function first searches the Command Denied list and then searches the Commands Permitted list. The Find function matches the text string even if it is embedded in another string. For example, if you search for date, the Find function first matches the ckdate command, then date, rdate, nsupdate, and so on.

## Setting Security Attributes

If the user has been associated with a role and its attendant rights, all commands affected by these rights have two types of user IDs (UIDs) and group IDs (GIDs)—effective and real. See Chapter 10, "Administrative Roles," for more information about roles.

Effective UIDs and GIDs are used to control access to protected resources. Real UIDs and GIDs are used to establish ownership and responsibility (for logging purposes). For example, when users create files, the files are created with the real UID and GID; however, the ability to open a file is based on the effective UID and GID.

In most cases, effective IDs are sufficient to grant access to restricted system resources. In other cases, the real IDs are required.

Commands are executed under the real or effective UID and GID established for the command, whether launched by SMC or executed in an administrator's shell.

Try effective IDs first; if the command does not perform as expected, real IDs are probably necessary. You can change the real and effective UID and GID from the SMC Rights tool.

Use the following steps to change the real and effective UID and GID for a command.

1. In the Add Rights window, click on the Commands tab.
2. Click on the command you want to change and then click on the Set Security Attributes button.

   The Set Security Attributes window is displayed, as shown in Figure 112.

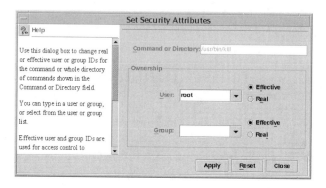

Figure 112  Set Security Attributes Window

3. Click on the settings you want for the command and then click on the Apply button.

   The security attributes are set for the command.

## Authorizations Tab

An authorization permits the use of a specific application or of specific functions within an application. For example, Audit Management is divided into Configure Auditing and Read Audit Trail authorizations. To enable a right access to the complete functionality of audit management, the right should grant access to both authorizations.

Use the authorizations tab, shown in Figure 113, to add authorizations to the new right.

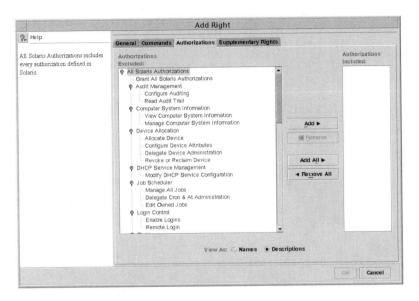

*Figure 113  Add Right: Authorizations Tab*

Click on each authorization that you want to grant to the new right and then click on the Add button. You can remove commands from the Authorizations Included list by highlighting the command and clicking on the Remove button. If you are adding many authorizations, you can click on the Add All button to add all the rights; then remove the individual commands you do not want to include. Click on the Remove All button to remove all authorizations from the Command Permitted list.

## Supplementary Rights Tab

Use the Supplementary Rights tab, shown in Figure 114, to include existing rights. Using existing rights can streamline the process of creating a new right by enabling you to add commands and authorizations in groups instead of adding them individually.

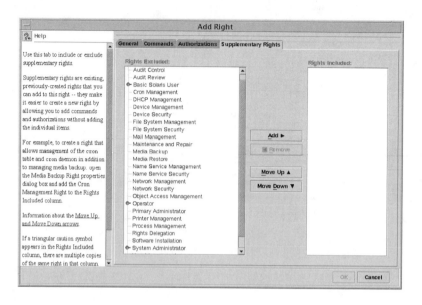

*Figure 114  New Right: Supplementary Rights Tab*

> *NOTE. Refer to Table 8 on page 103 for a description of the set of available rights, or click on an individual right to view its description in the Help pane.*

Click on each supplementary right you want to add to the new right and then click on the Add button. You can remove rights from the Rights Included list by highlighting the right and clicking on the Remove button.

## Rights Hierarchies

With the Rights tool, you can add a right to a right, which means you can include the same command more than once in a right. The order of rights is important. Just as with searches for the PATH variable, searches for commands in a right use the first occurrence of the command they find. For example, you might specify the /usr/bin/date command in one right with an effective UID of root but specify it in another right to run as the normal user. Always list the most specific and powerful rights first, followed by subordinate rights. Any wildcard entries should be at the end of the list.

> *NOTE. The All right, which is a wildcard entry, should always be the last item in the list because no other rights that are after All in the list are consulted when command attributes are looked up.*

You can change the order of rights within rights from the Rights tool.

1. Click on the Supplementary Rights tab.
2. Click on a right and use the Move Up and Move Down buttons to change the order of the supplementary rights.
3. When the supplementary rights are in the correct sequence, click on the OK button.

   The supplementary rights hierarchy is set.

## Viewing and Editing Properties of Existing Rights

To view and edit the properties of an existing right, double-click on the icon for the right in the View pane. Alternatively, you can highlight a right and, from the Action menu, choose Properties. The properties for that right are displayed. The Properties window has the same four tabs—General, Commands, Authorizations, and Supplementary Rights—as shown in "Adding New Rights" on page 120. Refer to the descriptions in that section for information about each of the tabs.

## Deleting Rights

You can delete rights, although it is recommended that you do not delete rights from the default set provided in the Solaris release.

Deleting a right removes all entries in the local databases and removes the right from all user accounts and administrative roles.

To delete a right, highlight the right in the View pane and, from the Edit menu, choose Delete Right.

The Delete Rights warning is displayed, as shown in Figure 115.

*Figure 115  Delete Right Warning*

Click on Cancel to retain the rights. Click on Delete to delete the highlighted rights.

# 10

# ADMINISTRATIVE ROLES

A role is an account with all the attributes of a user account, including a name, user ID (UID), password, and home directory. A role also has a specific set of administrative rights. Instead of a login shell, a role has a *role shell* (for example, Administrator's Bourne instead of Bourne shell). The root account is a role with all rights, whereas other roles have more limited rights.

When a user is associated with a role, that user first logs in as usual, with the individual's user name and password. The user can log in to the SMC Users tools with the role ID and role password. Alternatively, from a command line, the user can type **su** **rolename** and then type the role password to assume the rights of the specific role.

When SMC is installed, all authenticated users can run the Administrative Roles tool and read data. Initially, the Primary Administrator can add roles and assign them to users. Once the Primary Administrator assigns a user to a role, any user or role that has the User Security right can use the Administrative Roles tool to add, modify, and delete roles.

You can use the Administrative Roles tool to perform the following tasks.

- Create a role.
- Assign an administrative role.
- Assign rights to a role.
- Edit the properties of a role.
- Delete a role.

# Starting the Administrative Roles Tool

Use the following steps to start the Administrative Roles tool.

1. Start SMC (if necessary) from the Tools menu by choosing Solaris Management Console.

2. If you want to open a different toolbox, from the Console menu, choose Open Toolbox.

   See "Opening a Toolbox" on page 25 for instructions on how to open server and local toolboxes.

3. In the Navigation pane, click on the System Configuration turner.

   The list of System Configuration tools is displayed in the Navigation pane.

4. Click on the Users icon.

   If you haven't already logged in to the SMC Console or if you have preferences set to always ask for authentication, the Login window is displayed.

5. Log in as a user who has solaris.role.write authorization rights, type your password, and click on the OK button.

   By default, Primary Administrator and User Security have solaris.role.write rights.

   The list of Users tools is displayed in the Navigation pane.

6. Click on the Administrative Roles icon.

   The Administrative Roles window is displayed. If the Primary Administrator has not created any roles, the right pane of the Administrative Roles window contains no entries, as shown in Figure 116.

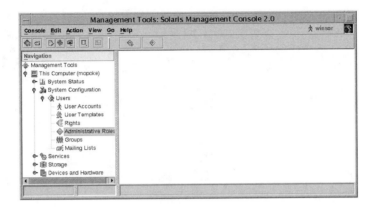

*Figure 116  Administrative Roles Window*

# Creating a Role

You create a role when you want to enable members of that role to be granted a specific set of rights.

The following example creates a role named `printadm` and assigns a set of users to it.

1.  In the Administrative Tools window, from the Action menu, choose Add Administrative Role.
    The Add Administrative Role window is displayed, as shown in Figure 117.

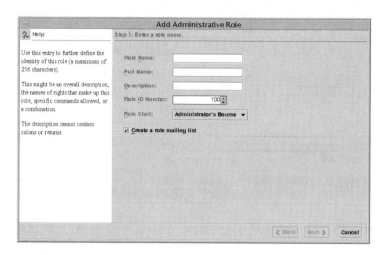

*Figure 117  Add Administrative Role Window: Step 1*

2.  Type a unique role name (2 to 32 alphanumeric characters, no spaces, dashes, or other special characters), the unique full name of the role (no limitations on length or characters), a longer description of the role (no colons or returns), and choose a role shell. The default is to create a role mailing list. If you do not want to create a mailing list, click to turn off the check box.

    Administrators can use the role mailing list to communicate with all of the members of the role to notify them of changes to the members of the role and of any other relevant information, such as changes in company policy.

    Review the information in the Help pane on the left if you need more details for each of the entries.

3.  When the information is complete, click on the Next button.

    The password screen is displayed, as shown in Figure 118.

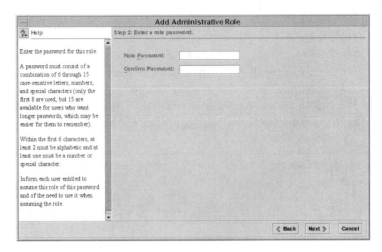

Figure 118  *Add Administrative Role: Step 2*

Role passwords must have a minimum of six characters. Although only the first eight characters are recognized, the password can contain up to 15 characters for users who want to use longer passwords that are easier to remember. Passwords can contain case-sensitive letters, numbers, and special characters. Within the first six characters, two must be alphabetic and at least one must be a number or a special character.

4. Type the password for the role once in each of the text fields and click on the Next button.

   The Select Role Rights screen is displayed, as shown in Figure 119.

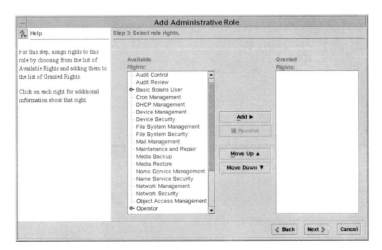

Figure 119  *Add Administrative Role: Step 3*

Refer to Table 8 on page 103 for a description of the set of available rights, or click on an individual right to view its description in the Help pane.

5. Click on the right you want to add to the role and then click on the Add button. Repeat the process as many times as needed until all of the rights you want to grant are listed in the Granted Rights pane.

In Figure 120, Printer Management rights are granted to the `printadm` role.

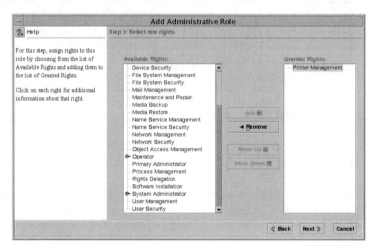

*Figure 120  Add Administrative Role: Step 3*

6. When you have granted the appropriate rights, click on the Next button.

The Select a Home Directory screen is displayed, as shown in Figure 121. The default is to create the home directory for the role on the current server in the `/export/home` directory.

Figure 121  Add Administrative Role: Step 4

7.  Change the server or path if necessary, and click on the Next button.

The Assign Users to This Role screen is displayed, as shown in
Figure 122.

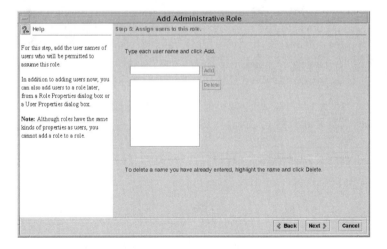

Figure 122  Add Administrative Role: Step 5

8.  For each user you want to assign to this administrative role, type the
user name in the top text field and click on the Add button.

Each user name is added to the list. If you want to delete a user,
highlight the user name in the list and click on the Delete button.

9.  When all users are assigned, click on the Next button.

A summary screen displays the settings for the role, as shown in Figure 123. The list of users assigned to the role is not displayed on this screen.

*Figure 123  Add Administrative Role: Summary Screen*

10. If you want to change any of the information, click on the Back button to go back to the appropriate screen and enter the correct information. If the information is correct, click on the Finish button.

The role is created, the users are assigned, and the role is listed in the Administrative Role screen, as shown in Figure 124.

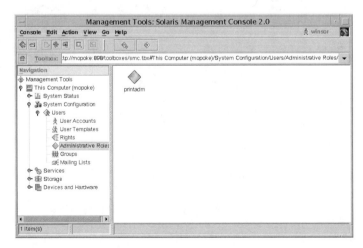

*Figure 124  Administrative Role Window with printadm Role*

11. You can verify the rights granted to the role by typing **profiles *rolename*** and pressing Return.

    The following example shows the rights granted to the printadm role. The rights include the default Basic Solaris User and All rights as well as the Printer Management rights.

```
paperbark% profiles printadm
Printer Management
Basic Solaris User
All
paperbark%
```

# Assigning an Administrative Role

You can review the users assigned to an existing administrative role and add and delete users from the Assign Administrative Role window.

Use the following steps to add to and remove users from an existing administrative role.

1. From the Action menu choose Assign Administrative Role.

   The Assign Administrative Role window is displayed, as shown in Figure 125.

*Figure 125  Assign Administrative Role Window*

2. From the Role menu, choose the role you want to administer.

3. To assign user names to the role, type the user name in the top text field and click on the Add button.

4. To remove user names from the role, click on the user name in the bottom list to highlight it and then click on the Delete button.

5. When you have completed editing the user names for the role, click on the OK button.

   If you choose a different role to administer without first clicking on the OK button, the changes to the previous role are not saved.

## Assigning Rights to a Role

Use the following steps to administer the rights for an existing role.

1. Click on a role icon in the View pane to select it.

2. From the Action menu, choose Assign Rights to Role.

   The Assign Rights to Role window is displayed, as shown in Figure 126.

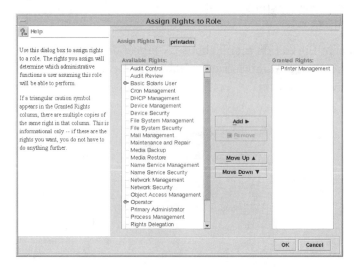

*Figure 126  Assign Rights to Role Window*

Refer to Table 8 on page 103 for a description of the set of available rights or click on an individual right to view its description in the Help pane.

3. Click on each right you want to assign in the Available Rights scrolling list and click on the Add button.

   The right is added to the Granted Rights list.

4. If you want to remove rights from this role, click on the right in the Granted Rights list and click on the Remove button.

5. To change the hierarchy of granted rights, click on the right and then click on the Move Up or Move Down button until the right is in the appropriate position.

6. When you have completed modifying the rights for this role, click on the OK button.

# Editing the Properties of a Role

You can use the Properties window to view the properties of a role and to edit all of the properties of an existing role except its role ID number. To display the properties of a role, double-click on the role in the View pane. The Role Properties window for that role is displayed, as shown in Figure 127.

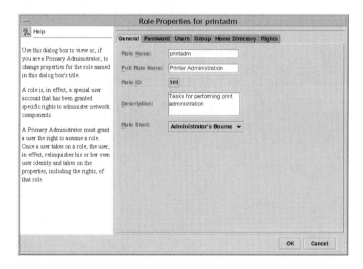

*Figure 127  Role Properties Window*

Alternatively, you can click on the role icon and, from the Action menu, choose Properties.

If you change the existing role name, the mailing list name for the role is automatically changed. Make the changes to the role and click on the OK button. Refer to "Creating a Role" on page 131 for information about each of the tabs.

# Deleting a Role

When you delete a role, you remove all entries in the directory services databases and remove the role name from all groups. You also have the option of removing or retaining the home directory for the role.

To delete a role, click on the role in the View pane and, from the Edit menu, choose Delete. The Delete Administrative Role warning is displayed, as shown in Figure 128.

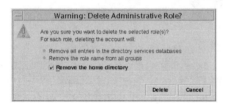

*Figure 128  Delete Administrative Role Warning*

Click on Cancel to retain the role. Click on the Remove the home directory check box if you want to retain the home directory for the role. Click on the Delete button to delete the administrative role.

# 11

# *G*ROUPS

This chapter provides information about UNIX groups—a collection of user accounts that can access common data—and describes how to use the Groups tool to perform the following tasks.

- Add new groups.
- Paste user accounts into a group.
- View and edit the properties of a group.
- Delete groups.

## About Groups

The *Group database* (NIS maps, NIS+ tables, or local /etc/group file) stores information about user groups, traditionally called *UNIX groups*. A *user group* is a collection of user accounts that can share files and other system resources. For example, a set of users who are working on the same project could be formed into a user group

Each group has a GID (group ID) that identifies it internally to the system. A group should have a name and a list of user names. You can define user groups in two ways.

- Implicitly, by the GID for the user's primary group, which is defined in the user account. Whenever a new GID appears in the Group field of the Passwd database, a new group is defined.

- Explicitly, by name, GID, and user list, as entered into the Group database.

*NOTE. It's best to explicitly define all groups so every group has a name.*

All users belong to at least one group—their primary group—which is indicated by the Group field of their user account. Although it is not required by the operating system, you should add the user to the member list of the group you've designated as his or her primary group. Optionally, users can belong to up to 16 secondary groups. To belong to a secondary group, the user must be added to the member list for that group.

You can use the SMC Groups tool or the groups command to show the groups to which a user belongs. For any user, only one group at a time can be considered the primary group. However, users can temporarily change the primary group (with the newgrp command) to any other group they belong to.

Some applications and the file system look only at the user's primary group. For example, ownership of files created and accounting data recorded reflect only the primary group. Other applications may take into account a user's membership across groups. For example, a user has to be a member of the sysadmin group to use Admintool to make changes to a database, but it doesn't matter if sysadmin is the current primary group.

User groups are probably best known as the groups referred to by the read-write-execute permissions for the user, group, and other on files and directories. These permissions are a cornerstone of file system access control. You cannot access others' files (if they do not allow world access) unless your primary or a secondary group has permission to access the files. For example, a group called techwrite could be created for technical writers, and a central directory of document files could be set up with write permission for the techwrite group. That way, only writers who are members of this group would be able to access or change the files.

User groups can be local to a workstation or defined by a network service. Across the network, user groups enable a set of users on the network to access a set of files on a workstation or file server without making those files available to everyone.

*NOTE. NIS+ supports another, unrelated, kind of group, called a netgroup, which is a group of systems.*

By default, all Solaris workstations and servers have the following groups.

```
root::0:root
other::1:
bin::2:root,bin,daemon
sys::3:root,bin,sys,adm
adm::4:root,adm,daemon
uucp::5:root,uucp
mail::6:root
tty::7:root,tty,adm
lp::8:root,lp,adm
nuucp::9:root,nuucp
staff::10:
daemon::12:root,daemon
sysadmin::14:
nobody::60001:
noaccess::60002:
nogroup::65534
```

*NOTE. The* sysadmin *group with a GID of 14 is part of the default set of groups. This group specifies the users who have access to all functions of Admintool.*

# Starting the Groups Tool

Use the following steps to start the Groups tool.

1. Start SMC (if necessary) from the Tools menu by choosing Solaris Management Console.

2. If you want to open a different toolbox, from the Console menu, choose Open Toolbox.

   See "Opening a Toolbox" on page 25 for instructions on how to open server and local toolboxes.

3. In the Navigation pane, click on the System Configuration turner.

   The System configuration tools are displayed in the Navigation pane.

4. Click on the Users icon.

5. If necessary, log in with your user name or role name and appropriate passwords.

   The Users tools are displayed in the View pane.

6. Double-click on the Groups icon in the View pane.

   After a few moments, the list of groups is displayed in the right pane. as shown in Figure 129.

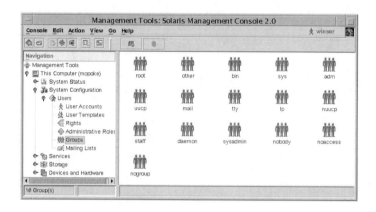

*Figure 129   Groups Tool*

The user or role name is displayed to the right of the menu bar, and
the number of groups is displayed in the status bar at the bottom of
the window.

# Adding New Groups

As a system administrator, you may frequently create new group accounts.
You must create a group and assign it a GID before you can assign users to it.

Use the Groups tool to create and maintain groups.

You need the following information to create a new group.

- Login names of users who will belong to the group.
- UIDs of users who will belong to the group.
- Group name.
- GID.

The SMC Groups tool does not support group passwords.

Use the following steps to add groups.

1.  From the Action menu, choose Add Group.
    The Add Group window is displayed, as shown in Figure 130.

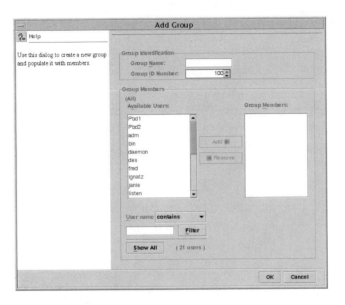

*Figure 130  Add Group Window*

2. Type the name of the group.

   Group names must be unique within the domain, start with a letter, contain no spaces or special characters, and contain between 2 and 32 letters and numbers.

3. Specify the group ID number.

   Either type the group number in the text field or click on the up or down arrow to display the group ID number.

4. Click on the name of each user you want to add to the group and click on the Add button.

   The list displays available user names. You can use the controls below the list of user names to filter the list of user names.

5. If you want to remove a name from the Group Members list, highlight the name and click on the Remove button.

6. Click on the OK button to create the group.

# Pasting User Accounts into a Group

You can add users to an existing group with cut-and-paste by following the steps below.

1.  In the User Accounts tool, select a set of user account icons.
2.  In the User Accounts tool, from the Actions menu, choose Copy to Group or Mailing List.
3.  Open the Groups tool.
4.  In the View pane, click on the group to which you want to add users.
5.  From the Groups tool Actions menu, choose Paste User(s) into Group.

    The user accounts are added as members of the group.

# Modifying Groups

Membership in group accounts can change frequently as new employees are hired and other employees change job responsibilities. Consequently, you have to modify existing group accounts to add or remove users. If you choose to have a user belong to secondary groups, you must modify those groups to add the user to the user lists. When adding groups, you may make a mistake. The ability to modify or delete groups helps you correct such mistakes.

*NOTE. When projects finish, groups set up for them may no longer be needed and you can delete these groups. Be careful to avoid conflicts if you reuse GIDs from deleted groups.*

Use the following steps to modify a group entry.

1.  In the View pane, double-click on the icon for the group you want to modify. Alternatively, you can highlight the group icon and, from the Action menu, choose Properties.

    The Properties window for the group is displayed, as shown in Figure 131.

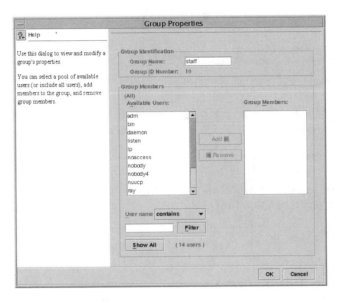

*Figure 131   Group Properties Window*

2. Make the changes to the group.

   Refer to "Adding New Groups" on page 144 for detailed instructions.

3. When the changes are complete, click on the OK button.

# Deleting a Group

If a group account is no longer needed, you can delete it. When you delete a group, the entry is removed from the group directory service database. For user accounts that have the deleted group as their primary group, the Groups tool changes the primary group to `staff`. User accounts that are members of this group are otherwise unaffected.

Use the following steps to delete a group.

1. In the View pane of the Groups tool, click on the group you want to delete.

   The item is highlighted.

2. From the Edit menu, choose Delete.

   A warning window is displayed, as shown in Figure 132, asking if you want to delete the group.

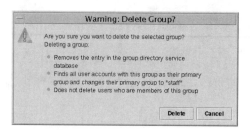

*Figure 132   Delete Group Warning*

3.   To retain the group, click on the Cancel button. To delete the group, click on the Delete button.

# 12

# MAILING LISTS

This chapter provides information about mailing lists and describes how to use the Mailing Lists tool to perform the following tasks.

- Add a new mailing list.
- View or modify the contents of an existing mailing list.
- Delete a mailing list.

## About Mailing Lists

Mailing lists are a way to create an *alias*—an alternative name. For electronic mail, you can use aliases to assign additional names to a user, to route mail to a particular system, to define mailing lists, to send e-mail through programs for processing, and to append e-mail messages to a file for later use. Mail aliases in SMC are called Mailing Lists.

Providing a mailing list alias is like providing a mail stop as part of the address for an individual at a large corporation. If you do not provide the mail stop, the mail is delivered to a central address. Extra effort is required to determine where the mail is to be delivered within the building, and the possibility of error increases. For example, if two people named Kevin Smith work in the same building, the probability is high that each Kevin will receive mail intended for the other.

When you create a user account with the SMC User Accounts tool, a mailing list is automatically created for each user name. The mailing list contains one entry: *username@systemname*. See Chapter 7, "User Accounts," for more information about creating user accounts.

When you create a role with the SMC Administrative Roles tool and assign user names to that role, SMC automatically creates a mailing list for the name of the role and adds each user name to the distribution list. See Chapter 10, "Administrative Roles," for more information about creating roles.

Mailing lists are also a convenient way to handle multiple e-mail addresses. When a user specifies the name of a mailing list, the message is sent to all of the members of that mailing list.

Use domains and location-independent addresses as much as possible when you create mailing lists. To enhance the portability and flexibility of alias files, make your alias entries as generic and system independent as possible. For example, if you have a user named `ignatz` on system `oak` in domain `Eng.sun.com`, create the alias as `ignatz` instead of `ignatz@Eng` or `ignatz@oak`. If the user `ignatz` changes the name of the system but remains within the engineering domain, you do not need to update any alias files to reflect the change in his system name.

When creating mailing lists that include users outside your domain, create the alias with the user name and the domain name. For example, if you have a user named `smallberries` on system `privet` in domain `Corp.sun.com`, create the alias as `smallberries@Corp`.

## E-mail Recipient Formats

You can specify four types of recipients of e-mail messages in an SMC mailing list.

- Individual e-mail addresses.
- A file name to which messages are appended.
- A file containing additional addresses.
- A program that acts as an e-mail message addressed to the mailing list.

One mailing list can contain all four types of e-mail recipients.

## An Individual Address

You can specify an individual address as a local user name— winsor—or as a complete e-mail address— winsor@wellard.com. You can include user names from the User Manager tool as local addresses in a list of mailing list recipients.

## File with Appended Messages

You can specify the name of a file to which messages are appended. Specify the recipient as a path and file name, starting with a slash (/). Each e-mail message addressed to that recipient's mailing list is appended to the end of the file.

For example, you can create an archive of all files sent to a mailing list named project. Specify /usr/share/projects.txt (or some other path and file name) as a recipient in the project mailing list.

## File with Additional Addresses

You can specify a file containing additional addresses as a recipient of a mailing list. Specify the recipient as :include: followed by a path and file name that contains a list of e-mail recipients.

For example, to create a file containing the e-mail addresses of all the members of a project team, create a file named projectlist.txt that contains a separate e-mail address on each line or a comma-separated list of addresses all on one line.

If the projectlist.txt file is located in /usr/share, in the project mailing list, specify the :include:/usr/share/projectlist.txt recipient.

Any message sent to the project mailing list is mailed to each of the e-mail addresses in the projectlist.txt recipient list. The person responsible for maintaining the mailing list for the project can simply edit the projectlist.txt file to keep the list of recipients current.

## Name of a Program to Run

You can specify the name of a program that runs when a mailing list receives an e-mail message. The program might, for example, sort by subject all e-mail sent to the mailing list or use the notify program to send e-mail to root@mailhost. The program has the contents of the e-mail message as its standard input.

You can specify the program and its arguments with the following syntax. The program name must begin with a pipe ( | ).

- |*program*
- "|*program args*"
- "|*program*"
- |"*program*"
- |"*program args*"

You must specify each program with a fully qualified name, starting with a slash (/), for example, |"/usr/local/bin/notify root@mailhost".

# Special Mailing Lists

Mailing Lists must contain the following two special mailing lists.

- Postmaster
- MAILER-DAEMON

You cannot delete either of these mailing lists. Each special mailing list must contain at least one e-mail recipient.

## Postmaster

Postmaster is the mailing list users can write to when they have problems with e-mail. The default recipient is root, but you can substitute or add the e-mail address of the person responsible for managing e-mail problems.

postmaster is the default recipient for the MAILER-DAEMON mailing list, so the postmaster mailing list, by default, receives messages when undeliverable e-mail messages are returned.

## MAILER-DAEMON

MAILER-DAEMON is the e-mail address that users see when undeliverable e-mail is returned. Users often request assistance from MAILER-DAEMON for problems with undeliverable e-mail. The default recipient is postmaster, so that the Postmaster mailing list, by default, handles all e-mail delivery problems and questions from users. You can substitute or add the e-mail address of the person responsible for managing e-mail problems. You can discard all e-mail addressed to MAILER-DAEMON by specifying /dev/null as the recipient for the MAILER-DAEMON mailing list.

# Starting the Mailing Lists Tool

Use the following steps to start the Mailing Lists tool.

1.  Start SMC (if necessary) from the Tools menu by choosing Solaris Management Console.

2.  If you want to open a different toolbox, from the Console menu, choose Open Toolbox.

    See "Opening a Toolbox" on page 25 for instructions on how to open server and local toolboxes.

3.  In the Navigation pane, click on the System Configuration turner.

    A list of the System Configuration tools is displayed in the Navigation pane.

4.  Click on the Users icon.

5.  If necessary, log in with your user name or role name and appropriate passwords.

    A list of the Users tools is displayed in the Navigation pane.

6.  Click on the Mailing Lists icon.

    The list of mailing lists for the toolbox is displayed in the View pane, as shown in Figure 133.

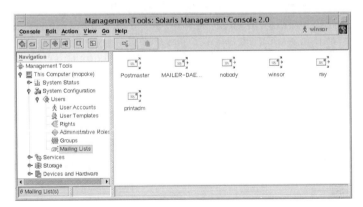

Figure 133   Mailing Lists Tool

# Adding a New Mailing List

Use the following steps to add a new mailing list.

1.  From the Action menu, choose Add Mailing List.
    The Add Mailing List window is displayed, as shown in Figure 134.

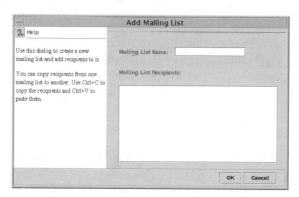

Figure 134   Add Mailing List Window

2.  Type the unique name of the mailing list and type a
    comma-separated list of e-mail recipients.

    See "E-mail Recipient Formats" on page 150 for information about the
    format of e-mail recipients. You can also copy recipients from one
    mailing list to another. Use Control+C to copy the recipients and
    Control+V to paste them.

3.  When the mailing list is complete, click on the OK button.
    The new mailing list is added to the mailing lists in the View pane.

# Viewing or Modifying the Contents of an Existing Mailing List

You can view or modify the contents of an existing mailing list by
double-clicking on the mailing list icon in the View pane. Alternatively, you
can highlight the mailing list and, from the Action menu, choose
Properties. The Properties window for the mailing list is displayed, as
shown in Figure 135.

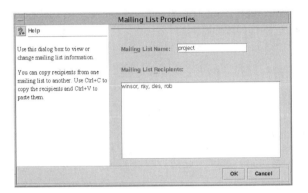

*Figure 135  Properties for Mailing List*

From the Properties window, you can view or change information for the mailing list.

# Deleting a Mailing List

When you delete a mailing list, the SMC Mailing Lists tool removes the mailing list entry from the directory services database. It leaves any user accounts that were members of this mailing list unaffected.

Use the following steps to delete a mailing list.

1. Click on the icon for the mailing list in the View pane.
2. From the Edit menu, choose Delete.

   A Warning window is displayed, as shown in Figure 136, asking if you're sure you want to delete the mailing list.

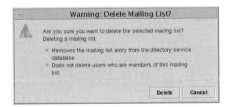

*Figure 136  Delete Mailing List Warning*

3. Click on the Cancel button to retain the mailing list. Click on the Delete button to delete the mailing list.

The mailing list is removed from the directory services database and the View pane of the Mailing Lists tool.

# *Part Four*

# Services

The Services folder contains the Scheduled Jobs tool, described in Chapter 13, "Scheduled Jobs," starting on page 159.

# 13

# *SCHEDULED JOBS*

Scheduled jobs are commands or batch files that are run at predetermined times. These jobs are the well-known UNIX `cron` jobs. Use the Scheduled Jobs tool as a convenient way to create, schedule, and review `cron` jobs in the current management domain.

*NOTE. This tool is not currently available for nameservice domains such as NIS, NIS+, and LDAP.*

The authorizations granted to the user determine the jobs that are displayed in the Scheduled Jobs tool.

- The root login and users with Primary Administrator and System Administrator rights can view, modify, and delete jobs owned by any user, including the default system user accounts `adm`, `lp`, `root`, `sys`, and `uucp`. Users with these rights can also create new jobs and assign ownership of these jobs to any user account. Both Primary and System Administrators have root privileges when using the Scheduled Jobs tool.

- Users with other rights can create, view, modify, and delete only jobs that they own.

In addition to using the Scheduled Jobs tool, you can use the `smcron`(1M) command to perform operations from the command line. See "smcron" on page 260 for information on how to use the `smcron` command.

You can perform the following tasks with the Scheduled Jobs tool.

- Add a scheduled job.
- Set scheduled job logging policies and search path.
- View the properties of a scheduled job.
- Delete a scheduled job.

The Scheduled Jobs tool uses or modifies the files listed in Table 9.

*Table 9     Files Used by the Scheduled Jobs Tool*

| File | Description |
|------|-------------|
| `/etc/default/cron` | |
| | Sets `cron` policies that execute commands at specific dates and times. For example, this file sets the PATH for user's `cron` jobs and sets the CRONLOG variable to `disable` or `enable` logging in the `/var/cron/log` file. |
| `/var/cron/log` | |
| | Contains logging information when the CRONLOG variable is set to `enable`. |
| `/var/spool/cron/crontabs` directory | |
| | Contains files that are created as jobs are added by specific users. This directory can contain `adm`, `lp`, `root`, `sys`, and *username* files. |

# Starting the Scheduled Jobs Tool

Use the following steps to start the Scheduled Jobs tool.

1. Start SMC (if necessary) from the Tools menu by choosing Solaris Management Console.
2. If you want to open a different toolbox, from the Console menu, choose Open Toolbox.

   See "Opening a Toolbox" on page 25 for instructions on how to open server and local toolboxes.
3. In the Navigation pane, click on the Services turner.

   A list of the Services tools is displayed in the Navigation pane.
4. Click on the Scheduled Jobs tool.

5. If necessary, log in with your user name or role name and appropriate passwords.

The list of scheduled jobs for the toolbox is displayed in the View pane, as shown in Figure 137.

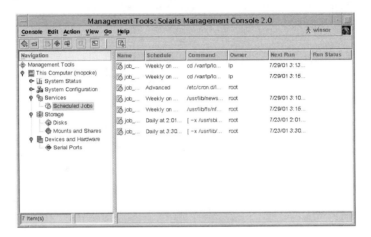

*Figure 137  Scheduled Jobs Window*

The default columns are described in Table 10.

*Table 10    Default Scheduled Jobs Columns*

| Column | Description |
| --- | --- |
| Name | Name of the job. |
| Schedule | Day, time, and frequency of when the job is run. |
| Command | The command run by `cron`. |
| Owner | The owner or user name of the person who scheduled the job. |
| Next Run | Date and time when the job will be next run. |
| Run Status | Status of the job. |

You can suppress display of any number of columns from the View > Columns menu. You can rearrange the width of the columns by dragging the right end of the label box. Existing columns are rearranged within the existing View pane.

You can also choose View > Refresh to refresh the view.

When the view is refreshed, the default column widths are used, any selected items are deselected, and the list is redisplayed from the top.

# Adding a Scheduled Job

Use the following steps to add a scheduled job.

1. From the Action menu, choose Add Scheduled Job.

   The Add Scheduled Job window is displayed, as shown in Figure 138.

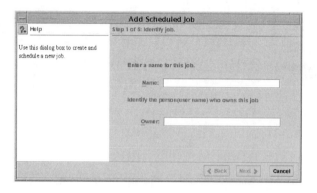

*Figure 138   Add Scheduled Job Window: Step 1*

2. Enter a job name.

   You cannot begin the name of a job with the string job_. This string is reserved for use by the Job Scheduler.

3. Identify the owner of the job. Make sure the owner of the job has the appropriate rights to run the job. Then click on Next.

   Step 2 is displayed, as shown in Figure 139.

*Figure 139   Add Scheduled Job Window: Step 2*

4. Enter the command to be run by the job and click on Next.

   Step 3 is displayed, as shown in Figure 140.

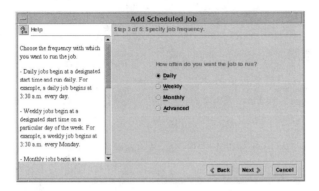

*Figure 140   Add Scheduled Job Window: Step 3*

5.  Specify the job frequency and click on Next.
    Step 4 is displayed, as shown in Figure 141.

*Figure 141   Add Scheduled Job Window: Step 4*

6.  Specify the time and day you want to run the job and click on Next.
    Step 5 is displayed, as shown in Figure 142.

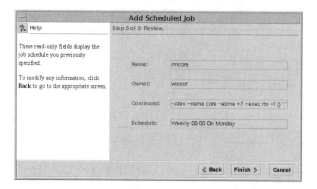

*Figure 142   Add Scheduled Job Window: Step 5*

7.  Review the information for the scheduled job. If you need to make any corrections, click on the Back button to return to the step you want to change. When the information is correct, from the Review step, click on Finish.

    The job is added to the appropriate `crontab` and is displayed in the View pane of the Scheduled Jobs window, as shown in Figure 143.

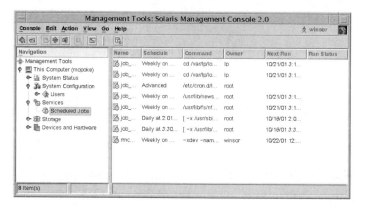

*Figure 143   Scheduled Job Window*

# Setting Scheduled Job Policies

You can set the logging policy and search path for root and non-root user jobs from the Action menu by choosing Scheduled Job Policies. The Scheduled Job Policies window is displayed, as shown in Figure 144.

*Figure 144   Scheduled Job Policies Window*

Changes to scheduled job policies affect any jobs that you schedule after you set the policy. To disable or enable job logging, click on the Enable Job Logging check box. The default is to enable job logging.

The Scheduled Jobs tool uses the path designated in the Scheduled Job Policies window to search for and run scheduled jobs. The default search path for root is /usr/sbin:/usr/bin. The default search path for nonroot user jobs is /usr/bin. Modify these search paths as appropriate and click on the OK button.

# Viewing and Editing Properties of a Scheduled Job

You can view and edit the properties of a scheduled job by double-clicking on the icon to the left of the job name in the View pane. Alternatively, you can highlight the job and, from the Action menu, choose Properties. The Properties window for the scheduled job is displayed, as shown in Figure 145.

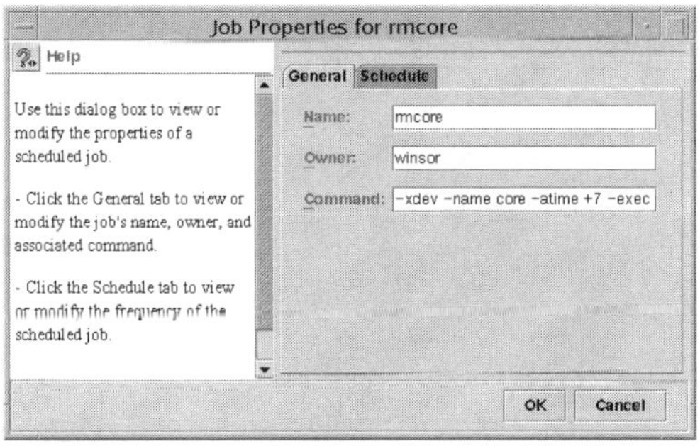

*Figure 145   General Job Properties*

The General tab shows the name, owner, and command for the job. Click on the Schedule tab to display the schedule information, as shown in Figure 146.

*Figure 146   Schedule Job Properties*

If you have changed any information for the scheduled job, click on OK to register the changes. If you have not made any changes, click on Cancel to dismiss the window.

# Deleting a Scheduled Job

Use the following steps to remove a job from the list of scheduled jobs.

1.  Click on the job to highlight it, then from the Edit menu, choose Delete.

    A Delete Selected Job warning is displayed, as shown in Figure 147.

*Figure 147   Delete Scheduled Job Warning*

2.  Click on Cancel to retain the job. Click on Delete to remove the entry from the list of scheduled jobs.

# *Part Five*

# Storage

The Storage folder contains the following chapters describing the tools that enable you to administer storage devices.

- Chapter 14, "Disks," starting on page 169—Use the Disks tool to view properties of disks, create Solaris disk partitions, and copy disk layout.
- Chapter 15, "Mounts and Shares," starting on page 193—Use the Mounts and Shares tool to create and maintain information about mount points and shared file systems.

# 14

# *D*ISKS

This chapter provides information about disks and disk formats and describes how to use the Disks tool to perform the following tasks.

- View disk partitions.
- View properties of disks and change the disk label.
- Create Solaris disk partitions.
- Copy the layout of one disk to another disk of the same type.
- Create `fdisk` partitions on an IA computer.
- Change the active `fdisk` partition on an IA computer.

## Disk Formats

You format disks to improve disk performance. The formatting specifies the layout in a way that groups information to reduce the movement required by the heads to read and write information.

The smallest unit on a platter is a 512-byte sector (also called a block). A track is a series of contiguous sectors. Tracks on each platter are concentric. The read/write heads can read or write to each track as the disk rotates without moving the heads.

A cylinder is made up of all of the tracks that occupy the same position on all of the platters. The most efficient way for the heads to read and write to the disk is to locate all blocks containing related information in a single cylinder to enable the read/write heads to move as a unit on the constantly spinning disk.

Cylinders are grouped into partitions (also called slices). On Sun systems, a disk can contain up to eight partitions, labeled 0 through 7. On IA systems, a disk can contain up to ten partitions, labeled 0 through 9. Each partition contains a single file system, and no file system can span multiple partitions.

# Disk Partitions

The most common disk partitions are listed in Table 11.

*Table 11    Commonly Used Disk Partitions*

| Partition | Description |
|---|---|
| unassigned | A partition with no named function. |
| boot | Stores information used to boot the computer. |
| root | Contains operating system files and directories. Partition 0 usually contains the root file system. |
| swap | Reserved disk space for swapping program components in and out of memory when the programs are too big to fit entirely in memory. Partition 1 is often used as the swap partition. |
| usr | Contains system commands. Partition 6 usually contains the usr file system. |

## Setting Up Disk Partitions

Files are stored within file systems. Each disk partition is treated as a separate device both by the operating system and by the system administrator. When setting up partitions, be aware of the following constraints.

- Each disk partition holds only one file system.
- No file system can span multiple partitions.

You set up partitions differently on SPARC and IA platforms, as described in Table 12.

*Table 12    Partitions Differences on Platforms*

| SPARC Platform | IA Platform |
|---|---|
| Entire disk is used for Solaris environment. | Disk is divided into `fdisk` partitions, one per operating environment. |
| Disk is divided into eight slices, numbered 0–7. | The Solaris `fdisk` partition is divided into 10 slices, numbered 0–9. |

## SPARC Disk Partitions

On SPARC-based systems, you define eight disk partitions and assign each to a conventional use, as described in Table 13.

*Table 13    SPARC Disk Partition Conventions*

| Partition | File System | Client/ Server | Description |
|---|---|---|---|
| 0 | `root` | Both | Holds files and directories that make up the operating system. |
| 1 | `swap` | Both | Provides virtual memory or swap space. |
| 2 | – | Both | By convention, refers to the entire disk. The entire disk is defined automatically by the `format` command and the Solaris installation programs. Do not change the size of this slice. |
| 3 | `/export` | Server | Holds alternative versions of the operating system that are required by client systems whose architecture differs from that of the server. Clients with the same architecture type as the server obtain executables from the `/usr` file system, usually slice 6. |
| 4 | `/export/swap` | Server | Provides virtual memory/swap space for client systems. |

*Table 13    SPARC Disk Partition Conventions (Continued)*

| Partition | File System | Client/ Server | Description |
|---|---|---|---|
| 5 | /opt | Both | Holds application software added to a system. If a slice is not allocated for this file system during installation, the /opt directory is put in slice 0. |
| 6 | /usr | Both | Holds operating system commands—also known as *executables*—designed to be run by users. This slice also holds documentation, system programs such as init and syslogd, and library routines. |
| 7 | /home or /export/home | Both | Holds files created by user accounts. |

## IA Disk Partitions

On IA-based systems, you divide disks into fdisk partitions. Each fdisk partition is a section of the disk reserved for a particular operating environment. For a Solaris fdisk partition, you define 10 slices, numbered from 0 through 9 and assign each to a conventional use. The uses for slices 0 through 7 are the same as on Solaris systems, described in Table 13. Table 14 describes slices 8 and 9.

*Table 14    IA Conventions for Partitions 8 and 9*

| Partition | File System | Client/ Server | Description |
|---|---|---|---|
| 8 | — | Both | Contains the boot partition information at the beginning of the Solaris partition that enables Solaris to boot from the hard disk. |
| 9 | — | Both | Provides an area reserved for alternate disk blocks. Partition 9 is known as the alternate sector partition. |

## Determining Which Partitions to Use

When you set up file systems for a disk, you choose which partitions to use. Your decisions depend on the configuration of the system and the software you want to install on the disk. System types are defined by how they access the root (/) and /usr file systems, including the swap area. For example, stand-alone and server systems mount these file systems from a local disk; other clients mount the file system remotely.

With the Solaris 8 release, system configurations are servers, stand-alone systems, and JavaStations. The JavaStation is a client designed for zero administration. It optimizes Java technology and takes full advantage of the network to deliver everything from Java applications and services to complete, integrated system and network management. You do no local administration for a JavaStation. The server handles booting, administration, and data storage.

Table 15 summarizes the three system types.

*Table 15   System Configurations and Partition Requirements*

| System Type | Local File Systems | Local Swap | Remote File Systems | Network Use |
|---|---|---|---|---|
| Server | root (/) | Yes | None | High |
| | /usr | | | |
| | /home | | | |
| | /opt | | | |
| | /export/home | | | |
| | /export/root | | | |
| Stand-alone | root (/) | Yes | None | Low |
| | /usr | | | |
| | /export/home | | | |
| JavaStation | None | No | /home | High |

# Starting the Disks Tool

1. Start SMC (if necessary) from the Tools menu by choosing Solaris Management Console.
2. If you want to open a different toolbox, from the Console menu, choose Open Toolbox.

See "Opening a Toolbox" on page 25 for instructions on how to open server and local toolboxes.

3.  In the Navigation pane, click on the Storage turner.

A list of the Storage tools is displayed in the Navigation pane.

4.  Click on the Disks icon.

5.  If necessary, log in with your user name or role name and appropriate passwords.

The list of available disks for the system is displayed in the View pane and the number of available disks is shown in the status bar, as shown in Figure 148.

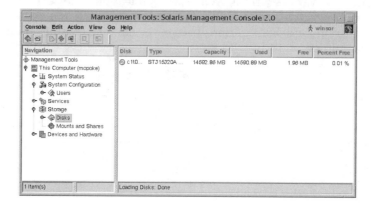

*Figure 148  Disks Window*

The default columns are described in Table 16.

*Table 16    Default Disks Columns*

| Column | Description |
| --- | --- |
| Disk | Name of the disk. |
| Type | Type of disk. |
| Capacity | Size of the disk in megabytes. |
| Used | Amount of megabytes used. |
| Free | Amount of free space on the disk in megabytes. |
| Percentage Free | Percentage of free space on the disk. |

You can suppress display of any number of columns from the View > Columns menu. You can rearrange the width of the columns by dragging the right end of the label box. Existing columns are rearranged within the existing View pane.

You can also choose View > Refresh to refresh the view.

When the view is refreshed, the default column widths are used, any selected items are deselected, and the list is redisplayed from the top.

# Viewing Disk Partitions

To view the partitions (slices) of a disk, double-click on one of the disks listed in the View pane. The partitions for the disk are displayed in the View pane, as shown in Figure 149.

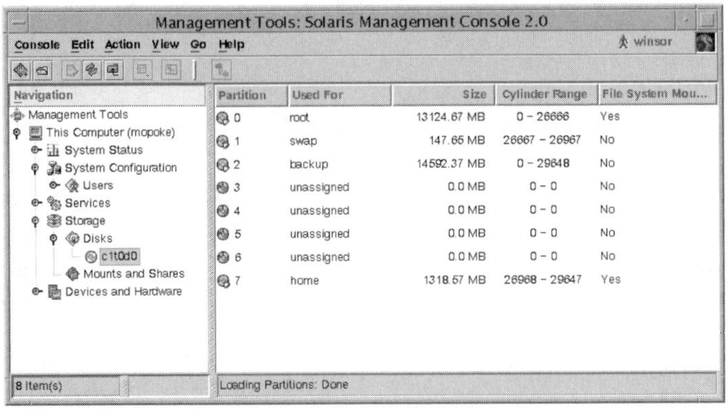

*Figure 149　Disk Partitions*

You can view and change the properties of a disk partition by double-clicking on the partition. Partition properties are displayed. You can move the mouse over the cylinder information to see information specific to that cylinder, as shown in Figure 150.

*NOTE. When you move the mouse over a cylinder, it takes a few seconds for the cylinder information to display.*

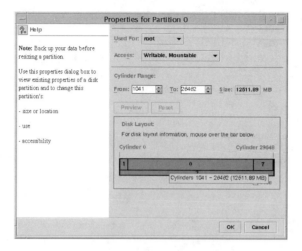

*Figure 150   Disk Partition Properties*

*WARNING. Be sure to back up all data on a disk before you change the size of a partition or create a file system on an existing partition.*

You can change the following partition properties.

- The use of the partition.
- Accessibility of the partition.
- The starting and ending cylinder.

## Creating a File System

To create a UFS file system, highlight the partition and, from the Action menu, choose Create File System. The Create File System window is displayed, as shown in Figure 151.

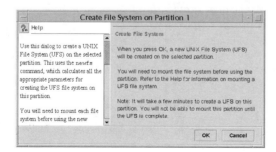

*Figure 151   Create File System on Partition Window*

Click on OK to create a new UFS file system on the selected partition. After a few minutes, the file system is created. After you create the file system, you need to mount it. Refer to Help in this window for instructions on mounting file systems.

# Viewing Properties of Disks

To view the properties of a disk, highlight a disk and, from the Action menu, choose Properties. The disk properties are displayed, as shown in Figure 152.

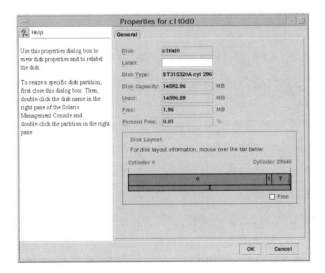

*Figure 152   Disks Properties*

The Properties window for a disk shows the disk name, type, label, capacity, used megabytes, free megabytes, and percent free. It also shows the disk layout. You can move the mouse over a cylinder to view information about each cylinder. A few seconds after you move the mouse over a cylinder, the layout information for that cylinder is displayed.

You can use the disk properties window to assign a label to the disk or to change the label.

# Creating Solaris Disk Partitions

Use the following steps to create Solaris partitions on a disk.

1.  Click on the disk you want to partition and, from the Action menu, choose Create Solaris Partitions. The Create Solaris Partitions window is displayed, as shown in Figure 153.

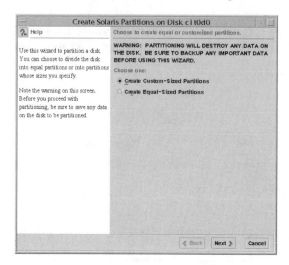

*Figure 153   Create Solaris Partitions Window*

*WARNING. Partitioning destroys all data on the disk. Be sure to back up any data on the disk before partitioning it.*

2.  Choose whether you want to create custom-sized or equal-sized partitions and then click on the Next button.

    The window displayed depends on the choice you made in the previous step. Figure 154 shows the step for specifying number of partitions for custom-sized partitions.

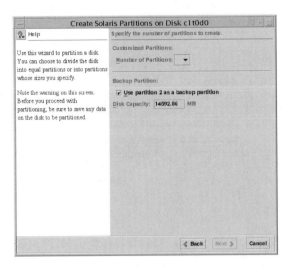

*Figure 154   Custom-Sized Partitions: Specify Number of Partitions*

Figure 155 shows the  step for specifying number of partitions for equal-sized partitions.

*Figure 155   Equal-Sized Partitions: Specify Number of Partitions*

3.  Choose the number of partitions and the backup partition and click on the Next button.

    The next step for custom-sized partitions is to specify the size of each partition and assign a use for each, as shown in Figure 156.

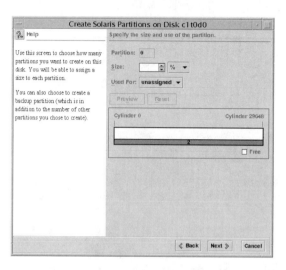

*Figure 156   Custom-Sized Partitions: Specify Number of Partitions*

4.  Starting with partition 0, specify the size either in megabytes or as a percentage, and assign the use. You can click on Preview to view the assignment in the Cylinder portion of the window. Click on Next to go to the next partition.

    Figure 157 shows the size of equal partitions and enables you to assign the use for each partition by choosing from the Used For menu for each partition.

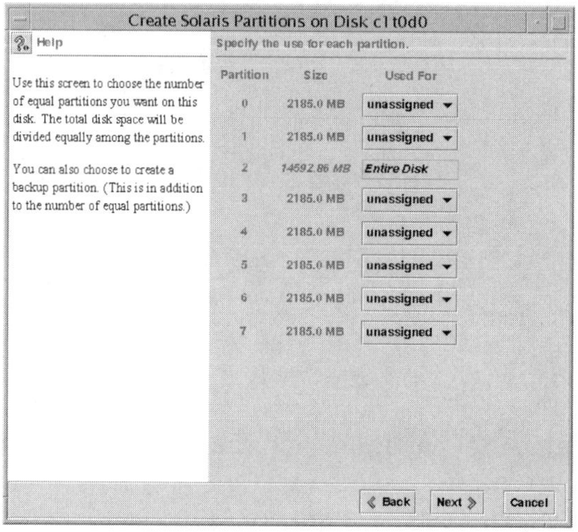

*Figure 157   Equal-Sized Partitions: Specify Number of Partitions*

5.  After you have assigned the use for each partition, click on Next.

    You next specify in which partitions to create file systems, as shown in Figure 158. Refer to Table 13 on page 171 for information about Solaris disk partitions.

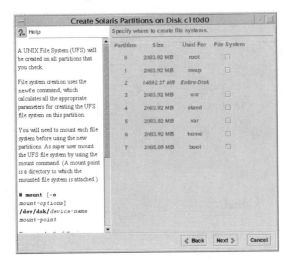

*Figure 158   Create File Systems*

6.  Click next to each partition in which you want to create a file system—don't create a file system on the swap partition—and click on Next.

    A summary screen is displayed, as shown in Figure 159.

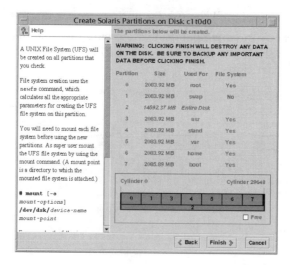

*Figure 159   Summary Screen*

> *WARNING. Clicking on the Finish button will destroy all data on the disk. Be sure you back up your data before proceeding with the next step.*

7.  Review the information on the summary screen. Click on the Back button to revise any of the information. When the information is correct, click on Finish.

    The disk is partitioned and any file systems are created.

8.  Mount each file system before using the new partitions.

    Refer to the help text in the window for instructions on mounting file systems.

## Copying Disk Layout

You can use the Disks tool to copy the disk layout of one disk to another disk of the same manufacturer and size. From the Action menu, choose Copy Disk Layout. Follow the instructions in the wizard to copy the disk layout.

# Creating fdisk Partitions on an IA Computer

On IA computers, you can create up to four `fdisk` partitions for each hard disk. Each `fdisk` partition is reserved for a particular operating system, for example, Solaris or EXT-DOS. You can use the Disks tool to create `fdisk` partitions.

*NOTE. An `fdisk` partition might be the entire disk or a portion of a disk. An `fdisk` partition used for the Solaris Operating Environment is subsequently divided into Solaris partitions, also called slices.*

Use the following steps to create `fdisk` partitions on an IA computer.

1. Click on the Disks tool.

   The available disks are displayed, as shown in Figure 160.

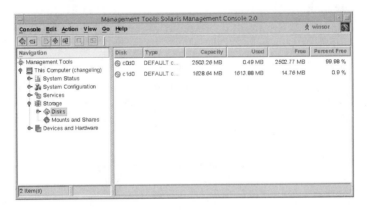

*Figure 160   IA Disks Tool*

2. Select a disk and, from the Action menu, choose Create Fdisk Partitions.

   *NOTE. The Disk tool does not warn you if you select the active `fdisk` partition for formatting.*

   The Create Fdisk Partitions window is displayed, as shown in Figure 161.

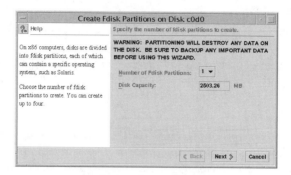

*Figure 161   Create Fdisk Partitions Window*

3.  You can create from 1 to 4 `fdisk` partitions. However, the Solaris Operating Environment supports only one Solaris `fdisk` partition per disk.

4.  Choose the number of `fdisk` partitions you want to create on the disk and click on Next.

    Partitions are identified by numbers starting with 0.

    Next, you specify the size and use for each `fdisk` partition. Figure 162 shows the next step and the types of use you can assign to an `fdisk` partition: Solaris, Unix, Linux, BSD, PCIX, Other, EXT-DOS, Huge-DOS.

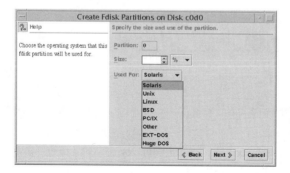

*Figure 162  Specify Size and Use for Fdisk Partitions Window*

    If you created one `fdisk` partition, use 100% as the size. Otherwise, decide what percentage or how many megabytes you want to assign to each `fdisk` partition on the disk.

5.  For each `fdisk` partition, assign the size and use and click on Next.

    A review screen is displayed, as shown in Figure 163.

*Figure 163   Review fdisk Partition Information*

6.  Review the information. Click on the Back button to go back and make any required changes.

*WARNING. When you click on the Finish button, all data on the disk will be destroyed. Be sure you have backed up your data before clicking on Finish.*

7.  When the `fdisk` partition information is correct, click on Finish.

    The `fdisk` partitions are created.

# Creating Solaris Partitions on an fdisk Partition

After you have created a Solaris `fdisk` partition, you can use the Action > Create Solaris Partitions menu item to create one or more Solaris partitions on the `fdisk` partition. You might use this option, for example, to create one or more Solaris partitions on a new disk that has been added to a system that is already running the Solaris Operating Environment.

Creating Solaris partitions destroys all data on the `fdisk` partition. Be sure you have backed up your data before creating Solaris partitions on an `fdisk` partition.

1.  Select the `fdisk` partition on which you want to create Solaris partitions and, from the Action menu, choose Create Solaris Partitions.

    The Create Solaris Partitions window is displayed, as shown in Figure 164.

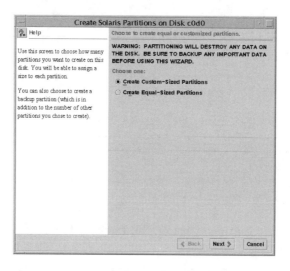

*Figure 164  Creating Solaris Partitions Window*

You can create custom partition sizes or partitions of equal size.

2.  Choose the method you want to use to create disk partitions.

Figure 165 shows the screen for creating partitions of equal sizes.

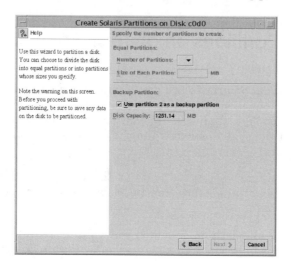

*Figure 165  Creating Solaris Partitions of Equal Sizes*

3.  Choose the number of partitions you want to create, from 1 to 7.
    When you choose the number of partitions, the partition size is
    displayed in the Size of Each Partition menu. By default, partition 2
    is used as a backup partition.

*NOTE. In a future release, additional IA Solaris partitions will be added to the Number of Partitions menu.*

If you choose not to use the default, click on the check box. Then click on Next. Skip to step 6.

Figure 166 shows the screen for creating custom partition sizes.

*Figure 166   Creating Custom Solaris Partition Sizes*

4.  Choose the number of partitions and click on Next.

    The screen for partition 0 is displayed, as shown in Figure 167.

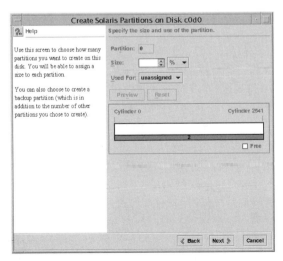

*Figure 167   Assign Partition Information*

5. For each partition, assign its size as a percentage or in megabytes. Assign a use for the partition: unassigned, boot, root, swap, usr, stand, var, or home.

*NOTE. In a future release, additional IA Solaris partition types will be added to the Used For menu (Bug ID 4508018).*

You can preview the partition allocation by clicking on the Preview button. Click on Reset to reset the allocation to 0. Click on Next. Skip to step 7.

6. If you chose equal-sized partitions, you must choose the use for each partition, as shown in Figure 168.

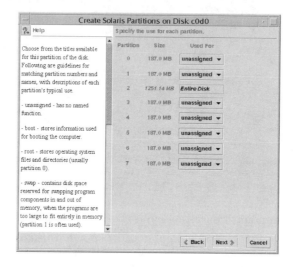

*Figure 168   Assign Use for Each Partition*

7. Assign the use for each partition and click on Next.

The screen for creating file systems is displayed, as shown in Figure 169.

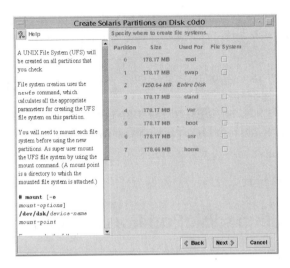

*Figure 169   Create File Systems*

8.   Click in the check box next to the partitions for which you want to
     create file systems. Do not create a file system for the swap partition.
     Then click on Next.

     The summary screen is displayed, as shown in Figure 170.

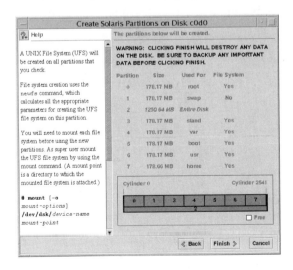

*Figure 170   Review Solaris Partition Information*

9.   Review the information on the screen. Click on the Back button to go
     back and change information as required.

*WARNING. All data on the* fdisk *partition will be destroyed when you click on the Finish button. Be sure that all data is backed up before clicking on Finish.*

10. When the partition information is correct and complete, click on Finish.

    The partitions and specified file systems are created.

11. Mount each file system before using the new partitions.

    Refer to the help text in the window for instructions on mounting file systems.

# Changing the Active fdisk Partition on an IA Computer

On IA computers, you can use the Disks tool to change the active fdisk partition. The active fdisk partition is the one the computer uses as the boot partition.

1. Select a Disk and, from the Action menu, choose Change Active Fdisk Partition.

   The Change Active Fdisk Partition window is displayed, as shown in Figure 171.

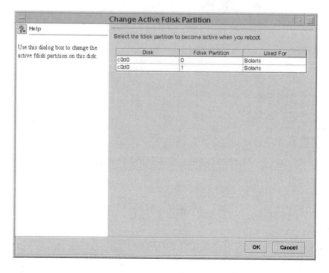

*Figure 171   Change Active Fdisk Partition Window*

Highlight the partition you want to use as the active `fdisk` partition and click on OK.

The `fdisk` partition you chose becomes the active `fdisk` partition.

# 15

# MOUNTS AND SHARES

This chapter describes how to use the Mounts and Shares tool to view, create, and manage mounts and shares. Sharing makes a directory on one computer available to other computers on the network. Mounting connects a shared directory to a mount point.

> *NOTE. Because you mount and share file systems from a single system, you use the Mounts and Shares tool only on single servers, not for a nameservice management domain.*

## Starting the Mounts and Shares Tool

Use the following steps to start the Mounts and Shares tool.

1. Start SMC (if necessary) from the Tools menu by choosing Solaris Management Console.
2. If you want to open a different toolbox, from the Console menu, choose Open Toolbox.

   See "Opening a Toolbox" on page 25 for instructions on how to open server and local toolboxes.
3. In the Navigation pane, click on the Storage turner.

   A list of the Storage tools is displayed in the Navigation pane.
4. Click on the Mounts and Shares icon.

5. If necessary, log in with your user name or role name and appropriate passwords.

Mounts and Shares tool has three components: Mounts, Shares, and Usage, as shown in Figure 172.

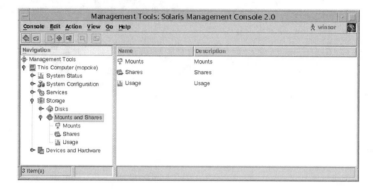

*Figure 172   Mounts and Shares Window*

# Mounts

Use the Mounts tool to perform the following mount tasks.

- Display a list of mounted file systems.
- Display or modify the properties of mounted file systems.
- Add a new NFS mount.
- Unmount a mounted file system.

## Making File Systems Available for Other Systems to Mount

When you have created a file system, you need to make it available; you do this by mounting it. A mounted file system is attached to the system directory tree at the specified mount point and becomes available to the system. The root file system is always mounted. Any other file system can be connected to the root file system or disconnected from it.

You can mount a local file system in the following ways.

- By creating an entry in the /etc/vfstab (virtual file system table) file. The /etc/vfstab file contains a list of file systems that are automatically mounted when the system is booted in multiuser state.
- From a command line with the mount command.
- From the SMC Console with the Mounts tool.

File systems on disk partitions must always be mounted on the server system and shared (exported) before other systems can access them. See "Sharing Files from a Server" on page 207 for information about sharing file systems. When file systems are shared from a server, a client can mount them as NFS file systems in any of the following three ways.

- By adding an entry to the /etc/vfstab file so that the file system is automatically mounted when the system is booted in multiuser state.
- By using the automount program to automatically mount or unmount the file system when a user changes into (mount) or out of (umount) the automounting directory.
- By using the mount command at a command line.
- From the SMC Console by using the Mounts tool.

## Understanding Mounting and Unmounting

File systems can be attached to the hierarchy of directories available on a system. This process is called *mounting*. To mount a file system, you need the following things.

- To be superuser or have rights or be the member of a role that grants permission to mount file systems.
- A mount point on the local system. The mount point is a directory to which the mounted file system is attached.
- The resource name of the file system to be mounted (for example, /usr).

As a general rule, local disk partitions should always be included in the /etc/vfstab file. Any software from servers, such as CDE, OpenWindows, or manual pages, and home directories from a server can either be included in the /etc/vfstab file or be automounted, depending on the policy at your site.

When you mount a file system, any files or directories that might be present in the mount point directory are unavailable as long as the file system is mounted. These files are not permanently affected by the mounting process and become available again when the file system is unmounted. However, mount directories usually are empty because you usually do not want to obscure existing files.

The system tracks the mounted file systems in the /etc/mnttab (mount table) file. Whenever you mount or unmount a file system, the /etc/mnttab file is modified to show the list of currently mounted file systems. You can display the contents of the mount table with the cat or more command, but you cannot edit the mount table as you would the /etc/vfstab file. The following example shows a mount table file.

```
paperbark% more /etc/mnttab
/dev/dsk/c0t0d0s0        /        ufs
  rw,intr,largefiles,onerror=panic,suid,de
v=2200000        1002508460
/proc   /proc   proc    dev=4180000     1002508459
fd      /dev/fd fd      rw,suid,dev=4240000     1002508461
mnttab  /etc/mnttab     mntfs   dev=4340000     1002508462
swap    /var/run        tmpfs   dev=1   1002508463
swap    /tmp    tmpfs   dev=2   1002508465
/dev/dsk/c0t0d0s7        /export/home    ufs
  rw,intr,largefiles,onerror=panic
,suid,dev=2200007       1002508465
-hosts  /net    autofs  indirect,nosuid,ignore,nobrowse,dev=4400001
  10025084
86
auto_home       /home   autofs  indirect,ignore,nobrowse,dev=4400002
  10025084
86
-xfn    /xfn    autofs  indirect,ignore,dev=4400003      1002508486
paperbark:vold(pid240)  /vol    nfs     ignore,dev=43c0001      1002508492
/export/home/winsor     /home/winsor    lofs    rw,suid,dev=2200007
  10025087
78
paperbark%
```

## Files Used by the Mounts and Shares Tool

The Mounts and Shares tool uses the files listed in Table 17 to display information. The tool updates these files when you use the SMC Mounts and Shares windows to modify information for existing file systems or to create new NFS mounts.

*Table 17    Files Used by the Mounts and Shares Tool*

| File | Description |
|------|-------------|
| /etc/mnttab | Current mount properties and dynamic mount information generated by the mount command. |
| /etc/dfs/sharetab | Current share properties and dynamic information generated by the share command. |
| /etc/nfssec.conf | Authorization parameters specified on an NFS client. |
| /etc/vfstab | UFS and NFS file systems mounted at boot time. |
| /etc/dfs/dfstab | Resources shared at boot time by an NFS server. |

## Displaying a List of Mounted File Systems

To display a list of mounted file systems, double-click on the Mounts icon. Alternatively, you can highlight the Mounts icon and, from the Action menu, choose Open. The list of mounts on the server is displayed, as shown in Figure 173.

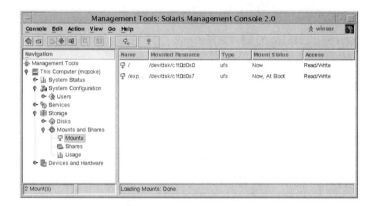

*Figure 173   Mounts View*

The default columns are described in Table 18.

*Table 18      Default Mounts Columns*

| Column | Description |
| --- | --- |
| Name | Name of the mounted file system. |
| Mounted Resource | The name of the partition (slice) for the mounted file system. |
| Type | The type of mounted file system: UFS or NFS. |
| Mount Status | Status of the mounted file system. |
| Access | Access permissions of the mounted file system. |

You cannot suppress display of columns in the Mounts view.

## Displaying or Modifying the Properties of Mounted File Systems

Use the following steps to display or modify the properties of a UFS-mounted file system.

*NOTE. When you modify properties and click on the OK button, the properties are applied only to the current tab and the Properties window is dismissed. If you want to modify properties in more than one of the Properties tabs, redisplay the Properties window for each relevant tab.*

1. In the View pane, double-click on the UFS file system you want to view. Alternatively, you can highlight the file system and, from the Action menu, choose Properties.

   The default mount properties are shown in Figure 174.

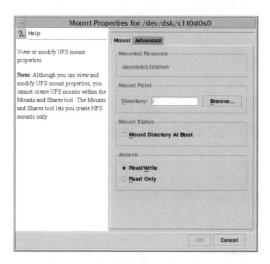

*Figure 174   UFS Mounts Properties Window: Mount Tab*

2. From the Mount tab you can view or change the mount point directory, the mount state, and access. Click on the OK button to register any changes.

   When you click on the OK button, a warning is displayed, as shown in Figure 175.

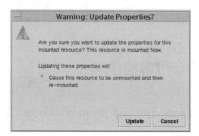

*Figure 175   UFS Mount Properties Warning*

3.   Click on Cancel to cancel the changes. Click on Update to change the properties, unmount and remount the file system, and dismiss the Properties window.

    If you update the properties, the Properties window is closed. If you have changed properties in the Mount tab, double-click on the Mounts icon to redisplay the Mount Properties window before you proceed to the next step.

4.   Click on the Advanced tab to view or modify advanced properties.

    The default Advanced properties are shown in Figure 176.

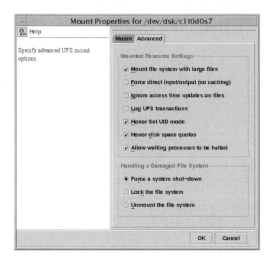

*Figure 176   UFS Mounts Properties Window: Advanced Tab*

5.   From the Advanced tab, click the check box to specify the mounted resource settings and the policy for handling a damaged file system. When you click on a check box, help text describing the mount setting is displayed in the Help pane.

6.   Click on the Cancel button to dismiss the Mounts Properties window without making any changes. Click on the OK button to change the Advanced properties.

    The Mount Properties Warning is displayed, as shown in Figure 175 on page 198.

7.   Click on Cancel to retain the current mount properties. Click on Update to change the properties, unmount and remount the file system, and dismiss the Properties window.

Use the following steps to display or modify the properties of an NFS mounted file system.

1. In the View pane, double-click on the NFS file system you want to view. Alternatively, you can highlight the file system and, from the Action menu, choose Properties.

   The default mount properties for the directory are shown in Figure 177.

*Figure 177   NFS Mounts Properties Window: Mount Tab*

2. From the Mount tab you can view or change the mount point directory, the mount state, and access. Click on the OK button to register any changes.

   When you click on the OK button, a warning is displayed, as shown in Figure 178.

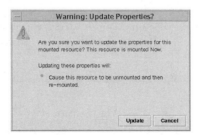

*Figure 178   NFS Mount Properties Warning*

3. Click on the NFS tab to view or modify NFS properties.

The default NFS properties are displayed, as shown in Figure 179.

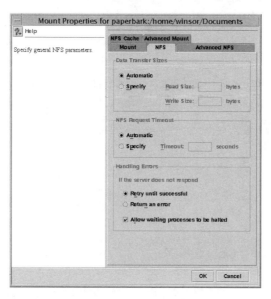

*Figure 179   NFS Mounts Properties Window: NFS Tab*

4. Click on the Advanced NFS tab to view or modify advanced NFS
   properties.

   The default Advanced NFS properties are shown in Figure 180.

*Figure 180  NFS Mounts Properties Window: Advanced NFS Tab*

5.  Click on the NFS Cache tab to view or modify NFS cache properties.
    The default NFS Cache properties are shown in Figure 181.

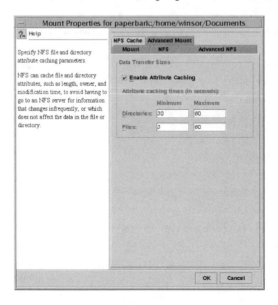

*Figure 181  NFS Mounts Properties Window: NFS Cache Tab*

6.  Click on the Advanced Mount tab to view or modify advanced mount properties.

    The default Advanced Mount properties are shown in Figure 182.

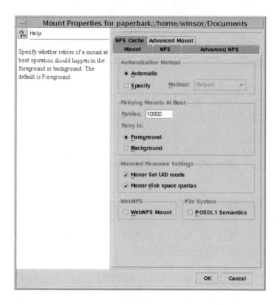

*Figure 182  NFS Mounts Properties Window: Mount Tab*

7.  Click on Cancel to retain the current mount properties. Click on Update to change the properties, unmount and remount the file system, and dismiss the Properties window.

## Adding a New NFS Mount

Before you can add a new NFS mount, the file system must be shared from its server. See "Sharing Files from a Server" on page 207 for instructions on using the Shares tool to share file systems.

When the file system is shared from the system, use the following steps to add a new NFS mount to the current server.

1.  In the Mounts view, from the Action menu, choose Add NFS Mount.

    The Add NFS Mount window is displayed, as shown in Figure 183.

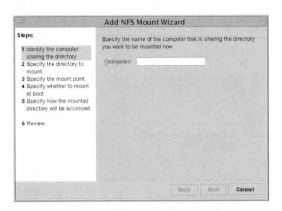

*Figure 183   Add NFS Mounts Window: Step 1*

2.  Type the name of the computer from which you want to add an NFS
    mount and click on Next.

    For the next step, a list of shared directories on that server is
    displayed, as shown in Figure 184.

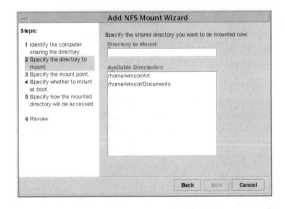

*Figure 184   Add NFS Mounts Window: Step 2*

3.  Click on the directory you want to NFS-mount and click on Next.
    You next specify the mount point, as shown in Figure 185.

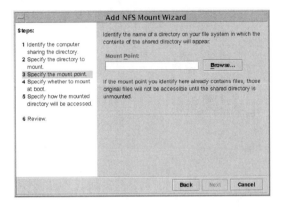

*Figure 185   Add NFS Mounts Window: Step 3*

4.  Specify the mount point and click on Next.

    If the mount point directory you specify contains files and directories, those files and directories will be obscured while this directory is NFS-mounted.

    The next step is to specify whether this directory is to be mounted at boot, as shown in Figure 186.

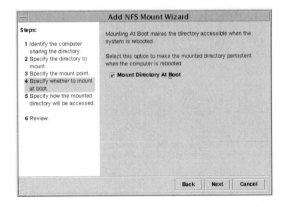

*Figure 186   Add NFS Mounts Window: Step 4*

5.  The default is to enable the mounted directory to persist when the system is booted. If you want the file to be NFS-mounted only for this session, click on the check box to remove the check. Click on Next.

    The next step specifies the access for the NFS-mounted directory, as shown in Figure 187.

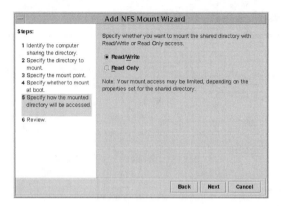

*Figure 187   Add NFS Mounts Window: Step 5*

6.  Specify whether the directory is to be mounted Read/Write or Read Only and click on Next.

    The summary screen is displayed for the final step, as shown in Figure 188.

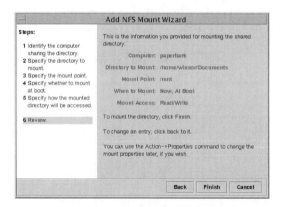

*Figure 188   Add NFS Mounts Window: Step 6*

7.  Review the information and click on Finish to create the NFS mount.

    You can change the information later from the Mount Properties window for this directory.

The Mounts tool uses the default options. If you want to change any of the options—for example, to mount NFS directories in the background—use the Properties window. See "Displaying or Modifying the Properties of Mounted File Systems" on page 197 for instructions and illustrations of the default NFS mount options.

## Unmounting a Mounted File System

When you use the Mounts tool to unmount a file system, the tool makes the file system inaccessible once you click on the Unmount button, removes all connections to the mounted resource, and removes the mount from the list of mounted directories.

Use the following steps to unmount a mounted file system.

1. In the View pane, highlight the file system you want to unmount.
2. From the Action menu, choose Unmount.

   The Unmount Resource warning is displayed, as shown in Figure 189.

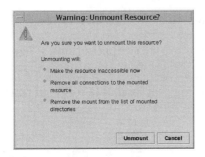

*Figure 189   Add NFS Mounts Window: Step 6*

3. Click on Cancel to leave the file system mounted. Click on Unmount to unmount the file system.

# Shares

Use the Shares tool to perform the following share tasks.

- Display a list of shared directories.
- Display or modify the properties of shared directories.
- Add shared directory.
- Unshare a directory.

## Sharing Files from a Server

NFS is a distributed file system that can be used to share files or directories from one system to other systems across a network. Computers that are running different operating systems can also share files. For example, systems running DOS can share files with systems running UNIX.

NFS makes the actual physical location of the file system irrelevant to the user. You can use NFS to enable users to see all the relevant files, regardless of location. Instead of placing copies of commonly used files on every system, with NFS you place one copy on one system's disk and let all other systems access it across the network. Under NFS, remote file systems are virtually indistinguishable from local ones.

A system becomes an NFS server if it has file systems to share or export over the network. A server keeps a list of currently exported file systems and their access restrictions (such as read/write or read-only).

You may want to share resources, such as files, directories, or devices from one system on the network (typically, a server) with other systems. For example, you might want to share third-party applications or source files with users on other systems.

When you share a resource, you make it available for mounting by remote systems. You can share a resource in the following ways.

- By using the `share` or `shareall` command.
- By adding an entry to the `/etc/dfs/dfstab` (distributed file system table) file.
- With the SMC Console Shares tool.

The default `/etc/dfs/dfstab` file shows the syntax and an example of entries.

```
paperbark% more /etc/dfs/dfstab

#       Place share(1M) commands here for automatic execution
#       on entering init state 3.
#
#       Issue the command '/etc/init.d/nfs.server start' to run the NFS
#       daemon processes and the share commands, after adding the very
#       first entry to this file.
#
#       share [-F fstype] [ -o options] [-d "<text>"] <pathname> [resource]
#       .e.g,
#       share  -F nfs  -o rw=engineering  -d "home dirs"  /export/home2

paperbark%
```

## Displaying a List of Shared Directories

To display a list of shared directories, double-click on the Shares icon in the View pane. Alternatively, you can highlight the Shares icon and, from the Action menu, choose Open. The list of shared directories on the server is displayed. If no directories are shared, the columns in the view are blank, as shown in Figure 190.

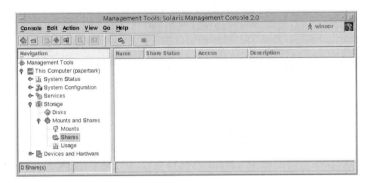

*Figure 190  Shares Window*

The default columns are described in Table 19.

*Table 19    Default Shares Columns*

| Column | Description |
| --- | --- |
| Name | Name of the shared directory. |
| Share Status | Whether the directory is shared now or both now and at boot time. |
| Access | Whether the directory has Read-only or Read/Write access. |
| Description | Description of the shared directory. You define the description in the Share Properties window. |

You can suppress display of any number of columns from the View > Columns menu. You can rearrange the width of the columns by dragging the right end of the label box. Existing columns are rearranged within the existing View pane.

You can also choose View > Refresh to refresh the view.

When the view is refreshed, the default column widths are used, any selected items are deselected, and the list is redisplayed from the top.

## Adding a Shared Directory

Use the following steps to add a shared directory.

1.  From the Action menu, choose Add Shared Directory.

The Add Shared Directory window is displayed, as shown in Figure 191.

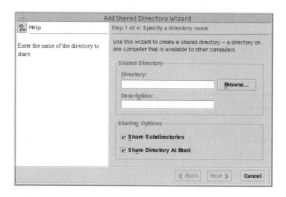

Figure 191   *Add Shared Directory Window: Step 1*

2.  Enter the name of the directory or browse through the file system and choose a directory.

3.  Enter a description of the shared directory for display in the View pane of the Shares tool.

4.  Specify the sharing options and click on Next.

    The next step is to assign access rights and authentication methods, as shown in Figure 192.

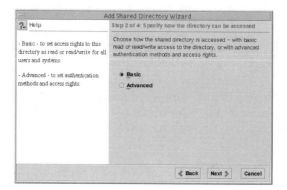

Figure 192   *Add Shared Directory Window: Step 2*

5.  Choose Basic to assign access permissions only.

    a.  Choose Basic and click on Next.

        The access step is displayed, as shown in Figure 193.

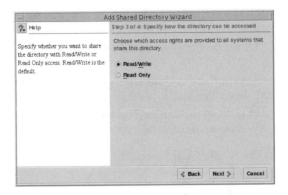

*Figure 193  Add Shared Directory Window: Step 3 (Basic)*

    b.   Choose Read/Write or Read Only access and click on Next.
          The summary screen is displayed.

    c.   Review the summary information and click on Finish.
          The directory is shared and added to the SMC shares list.

  6.  Choose Advanced to assign access permissions and authentication
     methods.

    a.   Choose Advanced and click on Next.
          The authentication method step is displayed, as shown in
          Figure 194.

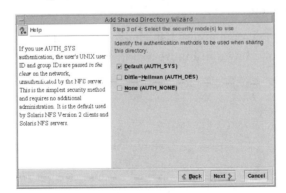

*Figure 194  Add Shared Directory Window: Step 3, Part 1*
*              (Authentication)*

    b.   Choose the authentication method and click on Next.
          AUTH_SYS passes unauthenticated UIDs and GIDs over the
          network.

AUTH_DES uses Diffie-Hellman public and secret keys for authentication.

AUTH_NONE maps the user identity to the `nobody` anonymous user.

When you click on the check box for an authentication method, the help text describes the authentication method checked.

The next part of Step 3 enables you to specify the default access and to build a custom access list, as shown in Figure 195.

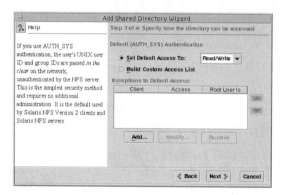

*Figure 195   Add Shared Directory Window: Step 3, Part 2 (Authentication)*

a.  Choose a default access from the drop-down menu.

b.  To build a custom access list, click on the Build Custom Access List radio button.

c.  To add to a custom access list, click on the Add button.
    The window shown in Figure 196 is displayed.

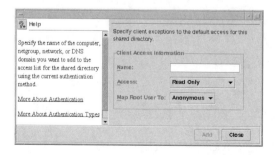

*Figure 196   Add Shared Directory Window: Step 3, Part 3 (Authentication)*

d.  Specify the name of a system, a netgroup, or a DNS domain to add to the access list for the shared directory and click on Add.

The name you specify is added and uses the current
authentication method.

e.  When you have completed adding custom access, click on Close.
    The client access you specified is added to the custom access list.

f.  Click on Next.
    The summary screen is displayed, as shown in Figure 197.

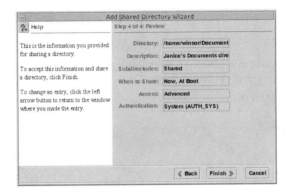

*Figure 197   Add Shared Directory Window: Step 4 (Authentication)*

g.  Review the summary information. To make corrections, click on
    the Back button and make the corrections required.

h.  Click on Finish to add the share.
    The appropriate files are updated and the share is added to the
    list in the Shares tool, as shown in Figure 198.

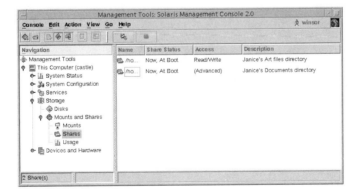

*Figure 198   List of Added Shares*

## Displaying or Modifying the Properties of Shared Directories

Use the following steps to display or modify the properties of a shared directory.

*NOTE. When you modify properties and click on the OK button, the properties are applied only to the current tab and the Properties window is dismissed. If you want to modify properties in more than one of the Share Directory Properties tabs, redisplay the Properties window for each relevant tab.*

1. In the View pane, double-click on the shared directory for which you want to view or modify properties.

   The Share Properties window is displayed, as shown in Figure 199.

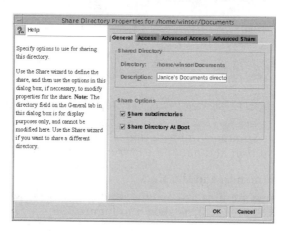

*Figure 199 Share Properties: General Tab*

2. Review general properties. Make any desired modifications and click on OK.

3. Click on the Access tab to display access properties. Figure 200 shows the Access tab.

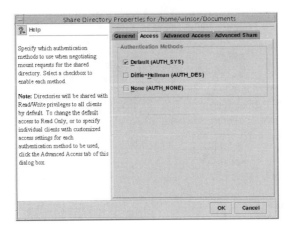

Figure 200 Share Properties: Access Tab

4. Review Access properties. Make any desired modifications and click on OK.

5. Click on the Advanced Access tab to display advanced access properties. Figure 201 shows the Advanced Access tab.

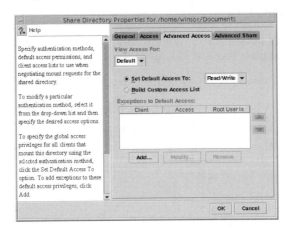

Figure 201 Share Properties: Advanced Access Tab

6. Review Advanced Access properties. Make any desired modifications and click on OK.

7. Click on the Advanced Share tab to display advanced share properties. Figure 202 shows the Advanced Share tab.

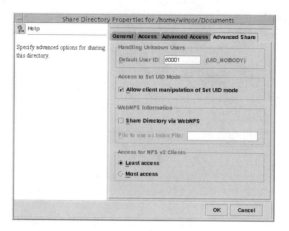

*Figure 202   Share Properties: Advanced Share Tab*

8.  Review Advanced Access properties. Click on Cancel to dismiss the Share Directory properties window or make any desired modifications and click on OK.

## Unsharing a Directory

Unsharing a directory makes all mounts of that directory inoperable and removes the directory from the list of shared directories.

Use the following steps to unshare a directory.

1.  In the Shares View pane, highlight the directory you want to unshare.
2.  From the Action menu, choose Unshare.

    The Unshare Resource warning is displayed, as shown in Figure 203.

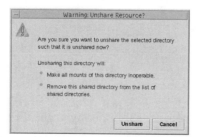

*Figure 203   Unshare Resource Warning*

3.  Click on Cancel to retain the shared directory. Click on Unshare to remove the directory from the list of available shares and make all mounts of the directory inoperable.

# Usage

You can use the Usage tool to view the following system usage information about currently mounted file systems.

- Mount points.
- Disks space usage.
- Disk space availability.

Double-click on the Usage icon to display usage information. The Usage is displayed, as shown in Figure 204.

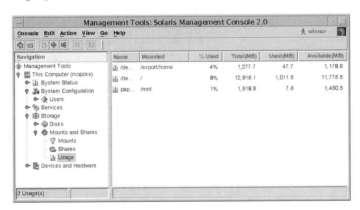

*Figure 204   Usage Window*

The default columns are described in Table 20.

*Table 20   Default Usage Columns*

| Column | Description |
|---|---|
| Name | Name of the shared directory. |
| Mounted | The mount point. |
| % Used | Percentage of the file system that is used. |
| Total (MB) | Total megabytes of the partition. |
| Used (MB) | Number of megabytes of the partition that are in use. |
| Available (MB) | Number of available megabytes of the partition. |

You can suppress display of any number of columns from the View > Columns menu. You can rearrange the width of the columns by dragging the right end of the label box. Existing columns are rearranged within the existing View pane.

You can also choose View > Refresh to refresh the view.

When the view is refreshed, the default column widths are used, any selected items are deselected, and the list is redisplayed from the top.

The Usage window has no editable fields.

# Part Six

# Devices and Hardware

The Storage folder contains the following chapter describing the Serial Ports tool.

# 16

# SERIAL PORTS

This chapter describes how to use the SMC Serial Ports tool. This tool provides a graphical user interface that you can use to manage terminals and modems in the current management scope.

Table 21 describes three tasks that are not supported in the SMC Serial Port tools. You must use SAF (Service Access Facility) commands to perform these tasks.

*Table 21    Tasks Not Supported by the Serial Port Tools*

| Task | SAF Command | Description |
| --- | --- | --- |
| Inform users that a port is disabled. | `ttyadm -i` | This command specifies the inactive (disabled) response message. The message is sent to a terminal or modem when a user logs in when the port is disabled. This functionality is not provided when you disable a port with the Serial Ports tools. |

*Table 21     Tasks Not Supported by the Serial Port Tools (Continued)*

| Task | SAF Command | Description |
|------|-------------|-------------|
| Keep the modem connected when a user logs out of a host. | ttyadm -h | This command specifies that the system does not hang up on a modem before setting or resetting to the default or specified value. If ttyadm -h is not used, the host hangs up the modem when the user logs out of that host. |
| Require the user to type a character before the system displays a prompt. | ttyadm -r | This command specifies that ttymon requires the user to type a character or press Return a specified number of times before the login prompt is displayed. When -r is not specified, pressing Return one or more times prints the prompt anyway. This option prevents a terminal server from issuing a welcome message that the Solaris host might misinterpret to be a user trying to log in. Without the -r option, the host and terminal server might begin looping and printing prompts to each other. |

# Starting the Serial Ports Tool

Use the following steps to start the Serial Ports tool.

1. Start SMC (if necessary) from the Tools menu by choosing Solaris Management Console.
2. If you want to open a different toolbox, from the Console menu, choose Open Toolbox.

   See "Opening a Toolbox" on page 25 for instructions on how to open server and local toolboxes.
3. In the Navigation pane, click on the Devices and Hardware turner.
4. Click on the Serial Ports icon.

5. If necessary, log in with your user name or role name and appropriate passwords.

The available serial ports are displayed in the View pane, as shown in Figure 205.

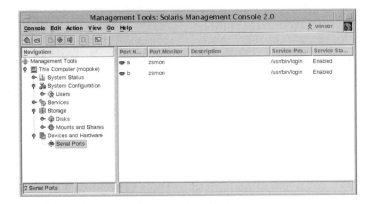

*Figure 205  Serial Ports Window*

The default columns are described in Table 22.

*Table 22  Default Shares Columns*

| Column | Description |
| --- | --- |
| Port Name | Name of the port: a, b, or another identifier. |
| Port Monitor | The type of port monitor. Default is `zsmon`. |
| Description | Description of the service provided. |
| Service Program | Program run by the port monitor. Default is `/usr/bin/login`. |
| Service Status | Status of the service. Default is enabled. The other possible status value is Disabled. |

You can suppress display of any number of columns from the View > Columns menu. You can rearrange the width of the columns by dragging the right end of the label box. Existing columns are rearranged within the existing View pane.

You can also choose View > Refresh to refresh the view.

When the view is refreshed, the default column widths are used, any selected items are deselected, and the list is redisplayed from the top.

## Files Used by the Serial Ports Tool

The Serial Ports tool uses the files listed in Table 23 to display information. The tool updates these files when you use the SMC Serial Ports windows to modify information for existing ports.

*Table 23      Files Used by the Serial Ports Tool*

| File | Description |
|------|-------------|
| /etc/saf/_sactab | |
| | Version, port monitor name (zsmon), service program (ttymon), and program path (/usr/lib/saf/ttymon). |
| /etc/saf/zsmon/_pmtab | |
| | Configuration information for all active ports monitored by the zsmon port monitor. If you configure another port monitor, for example zsmon2, configuration information for that port monitor is stored in a separate /etc/saf/zsmon2/_pmtab directory. |

# Viewing Serial Port Properties

Use the following steps to view or modify the properties of a serial port.

*NOTE. When you modify properties and click on the OK button, the properties are applied only to the current tab and the Properties window is dismissed. If you want to modify properties in more than one of the Properties tabs, redisplay the Properties window for each relevant tab.*

1. In the View pane, double-click on the port you want to view. Alternatively, you can highlight the port and, from the Action menu, choose Properties.

   The properties for the port are displayed, as shown in Figure 206.

*Figure 206  Serial Ports Properties Window: Basic Tab*

2.  From the Basic tab you can view or change the port name, description, service status, baud rate, terminal type, and login prompt. Click on the OK button to register any changes.

3.  Click on the Advanced tab to view or modify advanced properties. The default Advanced properties are shown in Figure 207.

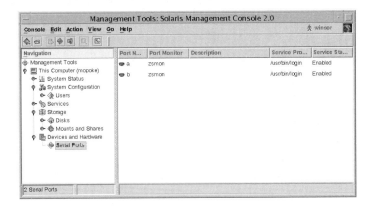

*Figure 207  Serial Ports Properties Window: Advanced Tab*

4.  From the Advanced tab, you can view or change carrier detection, connection method, timeout, port monitor, and service properties.

5.  Click on the Cancel button to dismiss the window. Click on OK to record any changes you have made in the Advanced tab.

# Setting Up Modems

You can set up a modem in three ways.

- Dial-out service—You can access other systems, but nobody outside can dial in and gain access to this system.
- Dial-in service—People can access this system from remote sites, but this system does not permit dial-out calls.
- Bidirectional service—This service provides both dial-in and dial-out capabilities.

## Modem Connection and Switch Settings

Connect the modem to a serial port with an RS-232-C cable that has pins 2 through 8 and pin 20 wired straight through. You can also use a full 25-pin cable to connect the modem to the system. Ensure that all of the connections are secure.

### Qualified Modems

The Solaris Operating Environment supports many popular modems. The following modems have been tested and qualified for use with Solstice PPP.

- AT&T DataPort Express.
- BocaModem V.34 DataFax.
- Cardinal V.34/V.FC 28.8 data/fax.
- Cardinal MVP288I 28.8 Kbps V.34 Fax Modem.
- Hayes Accura 144B and 288V.FC.
- Megahertz XJ2288 PCMCIA.
- Motorola Codex 326X V.34.
- MultiModem MT2834BLF.
- MultiModem MT1432BF.
- Olitec 288.
- Practical 14400 V32bis.
- SupraFaxModem 288.
- USRobotics Courier V.34.
- USRobotics Sporter 14400.
- USRobotics Sporter 288.
- Zoom V34.

*NOTE. This information does not imply a support contract or warranty from Sun Microsystems, Inc., for any of the listed devices.*

## Hayes-Compatible Modem Settings

Hayes-compatible modems that use the Hayes AT command set may work with cu and UUCP software. Use the following configurations.

- Use hardware data terminal ready (DTR). When the system drops DTR (for example, when someone logs out), the modem should hang up.
- Use hardware carrier detect (CD). The modem raises the CD line only when there is an active carrier signal on the phone connection. When the carrier drops, either because the other end of the connection is terminated or the phone connection is broken, the system is notified and acts appropriately. The CD signal is also used for coordinating dial-in *and* dial-out use on a single serial port and modem.
- Respond with numeric result codes.
- Send result codes.
- Do not echo commands.

## Modem Default Values

Table 24 shows the default values the Serial Ports tool uses for a dial-in modem.

*Table 24     Modem—Dial-In Only Default Values*

| Item | Default Value |
|---|---|
| Port | a \| b \| other port identifier |
| Service | enabled |
| Baud rate | 9600 |
| Terminal type | tvi925 |
| Option: Initialize only | no |
| Option: Bidirectional | no |
| Option: Software carrier | no |
| Login prompt | ttyn login: |
| Comment | Modem—Dial-In Only |
| Service tag | ttyn |
| Port monitor tag | zsmon |

*Table 24    Modem—Dial-In Only Default Values (Continued)*

| Item | Default Value |
|---|---|
| Create `utmpx` entry | `yes` |
| Connect on carrier | `no` |
| Service | `/usr/bin/login` |
| Streams modules | `ldterm,ttcompat` |
| Timeout (secs) | `never` |

Table 25 shows the default values the Serial Ports tool uses for a dial-out modem.

*Table 25    Modem—Dial-Out Only Default Values*

| Item | Default Value |
|---|---|
| Port | `a` &#124; `b` &#124; other port identifier |
| Service | `enabled` |
| Baud rate | `9600` |
| Terminal type | `tvi925` |
| Option: Initialize only | `yes` |
| Option: Bidirectional | `no` |
| Option: Software carrier | `no` |
| Login prompt | `ttyn login:` |
| Comment | `Modem—Dial-Out Only` |
| Service tag | `ttyn` |
| Port monitor tag | `zsmon` |
| Create `utmpx` entry | `yes` |
| Connect on carrier | `no` |
| Service | `/usr/bin/login` |
| Streams modules | `ldterm,ttcompat` |
| Timeout (secs) | `never` |

Table 26 shows the default values used by the Serial Ports tool for bidirectional modem service.

*Table 26    Modem—Bidirectional Default Values*

| Item | Default Value |
|---|---|
| Port | a \| b \| other port identifier |
| Service | enabled |
| Baud rate | 9600 |
| Terminal type | tvi925 |
| Option: Initialize only | no |
| Option: Bidirectional | yes |
| Option: Software carrier | no |
| Login prompt | ttyn login: |
| Comment | Modem—Bidirectional |
| Service tag | ttyn |
| Port monitor tag | zsmon |
| Create utmpx entry | yes |
| Connect on carrier | no |
| Service | /usr/bin/login |
| Streams modules | ldterm,ttcompat |
| Timeout (secs) | never |

## Configuring Modems

You can use the Serial Ports tool to configure modems within the current SMC management scope.

Refer to "Modem Default Values" on page 227 for a list of the default values the Serial Ports tool uses to configure modems.

1. Click on the port to which the modem is connected and, from the Action menu, choose the configuration you want for your modem.

   You can choose Modem (Dial In), Modem (Dial Out), or Modem (Dial In/Out).

   The Serial Port Basic properties are displayed, as shown in Figure 208.

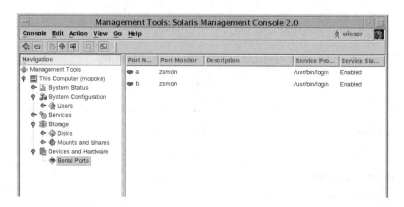

*Figure 208   SMC Serial Port Properties*

*NOTE. If you click on a port and choose a configuration option from
the Action menu, only the Basic options tab is displayed. You can
display the Advanced options only by double-clicking on a port, by
highlighting a port, or by highlighting a port and clicking on the
properties icon to the right of the View menu. First, configure the
modem with the default settings. If they don't work, display the
properties for the serial port and modify the Advanced settings.*

2.  Change the values of template entries if desired. If you change the
    values, make sure that you change the comment field so that other
    users know that you have changed the default values.

3.  Click OK to configure the port.

    The port is configured and the configuration information is displayed
    in the Serial Ports window, as shown in Figure 209.

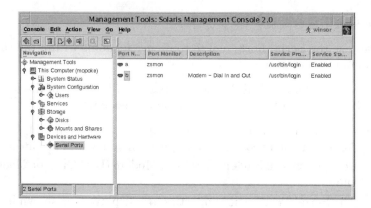

*Figure 209   Serial Ports Window*

## Troubleshooting Modem Connections

When troubleshooting problems with modem connections, first check the following list with the user.

- Was the correct login ID or password used?
- Is the serial cable loose or unplugged?
- Is the serial cable verified to work properly?

Sometimes the SAF settings don't work. In that case, you have to remove the port monitor completely and reinstall it. Even then, the hardware can get into a state that requires you to reboot the system for the port monitor to start properly.

Continue troubleshooting by checking the configuration of the modem.

- Was the proper `ttylabel` used?
- Does the `ttylabel` setting of the modem match the `ttylabel` of the SAF?
- If you have changed any modem switches, turn off the power to the modem, wait a few seconds, and turn it on again.

If the problem persists, check the system software.

- Was the port monitor configured to service the modem?
- Does the `type` definition match a setting in the `/etc/ttydefs` file?
- Is the port monitor enabled? (Use the `sacadm -l -p` *pmtag* command.)
- Is the service enabled? (Use the `pmadm -l -p` *pmtag* command.)

If the Service Access Controller is starting the `ttymon` port monitor, the service is enabled, and the configuration matches the port monitor configuration, continue to search for the problem by checking the physical serial connection. A serial connection consists of serial ports, cables, modems, and terminals. Test each of these parts by using it with two other parts that are known to be reliable.

To check for cable problems, you can use a breakout box. It plugs into the RS-232-C cable. A patch panel lets you connect any pin to any other pins. A breakout box often contains light-emitting diodes that show whether a signal is present on each pin.

Continue troubleshooting by checking each of the following:

- If you cannot access a port and the `ps` command shows that a process is running on it, make sure that pin 8 in the cable is connected. If the pin is connected, check that the device driver is configured properly to set the correct flag for the line to Off.

- If the error message `can't synchronize with hayes` is displayed when a Hayes-compatible modem is used, check the `/etc/remote` file and make sure that you have changed `at=ventel` to `at=hayes`.

- If the message `all ports busy` is displayed, the port may actually be busy running a dial-in user. Use the `ps` command to see what is running. You should also check to ensure that the carrier detect is set up properly. Type **pmadm -l** and press Return. If the last character on the line, at the end of the PMSPECIFIC field is y, delete the entry and reconfigure it, making sure that you use `-S n` (not `-S y`) as the last argument for *ttymon*.

- If the message `all ports busy` still displays after you have followed the above steps, the message may be bogus. Check the `/var/spool` and `/var/spool/locks` directories for leftover lock files. A lock file would have a name like `LCK.cua0`. If you find a lock file, remove it.

# Setting Up Character Terminals

The Solaris Operating Environment is automatically configured to work properly with Sun graphics display monitors. You do not need to do any additional SAF configuration to use them. The word *terminal* is used in this chapter to describe a *character terminal*—a serial port device that displays only letters, numbers, and other characters, such as those produced by a typewriter. The VT100 model, for example, is a popular type of character terminal that many other terminals emulate.

Not all systems require character terminals. You may want to attach a character terminal to a server as an inexpensive control console or to a malfunctioning system's serial port to use for diagnostics.

If you do attach a character terminal to a system, you need to configure it with the Serial Ports tool.

## Connecting the Terminal Cable

Use a null modem cable to connect a character terminal to serial ports on Sun systems. A null modem cable swaps lines 2 and 3 so that the proper transmit and receive signals are communicated between two DTE devices. Line 7 goes straight through, connecting pin 7 of the devices at each end of the null modem cable.

## Configuring Character Terminals

You can use the Serial Ports tool to add a character terminal. Table 27 shows the default settings for adding a character terminal.

*Table 27    Terminal—Hardwired Default Values*

| Item | Default Value |
|---|---|
| Port | a \| b \| other port identifier |
| Service | enabled |
| Baud rate | 9600 |
| Terminal type | tvi925 |
| Option: Initialize only | no |
| Option: Bidirectional | no |
| Option: Software carrier | yes |
| Login prompt | login: |
| Comment | Terminal—Hardwired |
| Service tag | ttyn |
| Port monitor tag | zsmon |
| Create utmpx entry | yes |
| Connect on carrier | no |
| Service | /usr/bin/login |
| Streams modules | ldterm,ttcompat |
| Timeout (secs) | never |

Use the following steps to configure a character terminal with the SMC Serial Ports tool.

1. Click on the port to which the character terminal is connected and then from the Action menu, choose Configure > Terminal.

    The Serial Port properties are displayed.

    *NOTE. If you click on a port and choose Configure from the Action menu, only the basic options tab is displayed. You can display the Advanced options only by double-clicking on a port or by highlighting a port and clicking on the properties icon to the right of the View menu.*

2. Terminal—Hardwired is the default choice from the Template menu. If it is not displayed, choose it.

3.   Change the values of template entries if desired.

If you change the values, make sure that you change the comment field so that other users know that you have changed the default values.

4.   Click on the OK button to configure the port.

## Troubleshooting the Terminal Connection

When troubleshooting problems with terminal connections, first check the following list with the user.

- Was the correct login ID or password used?
- Is the terminal waiting for the xon flow control key?
- Is the serial cable loose or unplugged?
- Is the serial cable verified to work properly?
- Is the terminal configuration correct?
- Is the terminal turned off?

Continue troubleshooting by checking the configuration of the terminal.

- Was the proper `ttylabel` used?
- Does the `ttylabel` setting of the modem match the `ttylabel` of the SAF?
- Do baud rates, parity, and stop bits match?

If the problem persists, check the system software.

- Was the port monitor configured to enable logins?
- Does it have the correct `ttylabel` associated with it?
- Is the port monitor enabled? (Use the `sacadm -l -p` *pmtag* command.)
- Is the service enabled? (Use the `pmadm -l -p` *pmtag* command.)

If the Service Access Controller is starting the `ttymon` port monitor, the service is enabled and if the configuration matches the port monitor configuration, continue to search for the problem by checking the physical serial connection. A serial connection consists of serial ports, cables, and terminals. Test each of these parts by using it with two other parts that are known to be reliable.

For checking cable problems, a breakout box is helpful. It plugs into the RS-232-C cable. A patch panel lets you connect any pin to any other pins. A breakout box often contains light-emitting diodes that show whether a signal is present on each pin.

If you cannot access a port and the `ps` command shows that a process is running on it, make sure that pin 8 in the cable is connected.

# Initializing Ports Without Configuring

The Serial Ports tool enables you to initialize a port without configuring it. Table 28 shows the Serial Ports tool default values for initializing a port without configuring it.

*Table 28    Initialize Only—No Connection Default Values*

| Item | Default Value |
|---|---|
| Port | a \| b \| other port identifier |
| Service | `enabled` |
| Baud rate | `9600` |
| Terminal type | `tvi925` |
| Option: Initialize only | `yes` |
| Option: Bidirectional | `no` |
| Option: Software carrier | `no` |
| Login prompt | `ttyn login:` |
| Comment | `Initialize Only—No Connection` |
| Service tag | `ttyn` |
| Port monitor tag | `zsmon` |
| Create `utmpx` entry | `yes` |
| Connect on carrier | `no` |
| Service | `/usr/bin/login` |
| Streams modules | `ldterm,ttcompat` |
| Timeout (secs) | `never` |

Use the following steps to initialize ports without configuring for a specific device.

1.  Click on the port you want to initialize.
2.  From the Action menu, choose Initialize Only—No Connection.

    The Configure Serial Port window is displayed.
3.  Change values of template entries if desired.

4.  Click OK to initialize the port.

# Removing Port Services

Use the following steps to delete services on configured ports with the Serial Ports tool.

1.  Click on the port service that you want to delete.
2.  From the Edit menu, choose Delete.

    A confirmation window is displayed, asking if you really want to delete the service for the specified port, as shown in Figure 210.

*Figure 210   Remove Serial Port Warning*

3.  Click on Cancel to stop the operation or Delete to delete the port service.

# *A*

# *SMC* COMMANDS

This appendix describes the set of commands listed in Table 29 that you can use as a supplement to SMC graphical user interface.

*Table 29    SMC Commands*

| Command | Description | Page |
|---------|-------------|------|
| smattrpop(1M) | Populate security-attribute databases in a nameservice. | page 238 |
| smc(1M) | Start SMC. | page 242 |
| smcconf(1M) | Configure SMC. | page 246 |
| smcron(1M) | Manage jobs in the crontab database. | page 260 |
| smdiskless(1M) | Manage diskless clients. Available only through the command line. | page 253 |
| smexec(1M) | Manage entries in the exec_attr database. | page 267 |
| smgroup(1M) | Manage group entries. | page 271 |
| smmaillist(1M) | Manage e-mail alias entries. | page 275 |
| smmultiuser(1M) | Batch user operations. | page 280 |

*Table 29   SMC Commands (Continued)*

| Command | Description | Page |
|---------|-------------|------|
| smosservice(1M) | List and manage OS services for diskless clients and manage patches on all existing diskless clients. | page 285 |
| smprofile(1M) | Manage profiles (rights) in the prof_attr and exec_attr databases. | page 290 |
| smrole(1M) | Manage roles and users in role accounts. | page 295 |
| smuser(1M) | Manage user entries. | page 301 |

# smattrpop

## Synopsis

    smattrpop [-c][-f][-m][-p policy][-r] -s scope -t scope [-v] database

## Description

Use the smattrpop command to populate security attribute databases in a nameservice. For example, you must run the smattrpop command before you can create a nameservice toolbox with the SMC toolbox editor. See "Creating a Nameservice Domain Toolbox" on page 52 for more information. The smattrpop command uses corresponding databases from a source nameservice—or corresponding /etc files—to update the role-based access control (RBAC) auth_attr(4), exec_attr(4), prof_attr(4), and user_attr(4) databases in a target NIS, NIS+, LDAP, or local /etc files nameservice.

This command processes the table entries from the source database and merges each source entry field into the same field in the corresponding table entry in the target database. If a source entry does not exist in the target database, it is created. If the source entry exists in the target database, the fields are merged or replaced according to the command options you specify.

Any errors encountered while the target entry is updated are reported to standard output, and the command processes the next source database entry.

## Options

-c              Perform cross-table checking. When a check error occurs, write a message identifying the check error to standard output.

The target entry values are checked against entries in related databases.

*auths* values  Each value must exist as the name of an authorization in the auth_attr(4) database.

*profiles* values

> Each value must exist as a name of a profile in the prof_attr(4) database.

*roles* values      Each value must exist as the name of a role identity in the user_attr(4) database.

For each exec_attr(4) entry in the source database, the name must exist as the name of a profile in the prof_attr(4) database.

-f      When the source entry field contains a value, replace the value in each field in target entry with the corresponding field in the source entry.

-m      For the *auths*, *profiles*, and *roles* attributes, merge the values in each field in the source entry with the values in the corresponding target entry field. If a source value does not exist in the target field, append the value to the set of target values. If the target field is empty, add the source value for the target field. The attribute values that merge depend on the database being updated.

> prof_attr(4)      Merge the *auths* and *profiles* attribute values.
>
> user_attr(4)      Merge the *auths*, *profiles*, and *roles* attribute values.
>
> exec_attr(4)      Merge the *uid*, *gid*, *euid*, and *egid* values.

-p *policy*      Specify the value of the policy field in the exec_attr(4) database. Valid values are suser (standard Solaris superuser) and tsol (Trusted Solaris). Process only the entries in the source exec_attr database with the specified policy. If you omit this option, process all entries in the source exec_attr database.

-r      Process role identities in the user_attr(4) database in the source nameservice. If you omit this option, process only the normal user entries in the user_attr source database.

-s *scope*      Specify the source nameservice or local file directory for database updates with the syntax *type:/server/domain* where *type* is the type of nameservice. Valid values for type are listed below.

> file      Local files.
>
> nis      NIS nameservice.
>
> nisplus      NIS+ nameservice.
>
> ldap      LDAP nameservice server indicates the local host name of the Solaris system on which the smattrpop command is executed and on which both the source and target databases exist.

*domain* specifies the management domain name for the nameservice.

You can use two special cases of *scope* values, as described below.

- To load from the databases in the /etc/security local system directory, use the scope file:/*server*, where *server* is the name of the local system.

- To load from databases in an arbitrary directory on the Solaris server, use the scope `file:/server/pathname`, where *server* is the name of the local system and *pathname* is the fully qualified directory path name to the database files.

-t *scope*     Specify the target nameservice or local file directory for database updates with the following syntax.

*type:/server/domain*

where *type* indicates the type of nameservice. Valid values for *type* are listed below.

file            Local files.

nis             NIS nameservice.

nisplus         NIS+ nameservice.

ldap            LDAP nameservice server indicates the local host name of the Solaris system on which the smattrpop command is executed, and on which both the source and target databases exist.

*domain* specifies the management domain name for the nameservice. You can use two special cases of scope values, as described below.

- To update to the databases in the /etc/security local system directory, use the scope *type:/server*, where *server* is the name of the local system.

- To update to databases in an arbitrary directory on the Solaris server, use the scope *type:/server/pathname*, where *server* is the name of the local system and *pathname* is the fully qualified directory path name to the database files.

-v             Write verbose messages. Write a message to standard output for each entry processed.

## Operands

*database*     Populate one or all databases. You can specify either the name of the database you want to process (for example, auth_attr), or all to process all databases.

If you specify all, the databases are processed in the following order.

1. auth_attr(4)

2. prof_attr(4)

3. exec_attr(4)

4. user_attr(4)

## Examples

The following example uses the RBAC databases from `file` on the server `mopoke` to populate the `nisplus` tables on the server `mopoke` in the `wellard.com.` domain for `all` of the databases.

```
mopoke# /usr/sadm/bin/smattrpop -s file:/mopoke -t nisplus:/mopoke/wellard.com. all

Populating the auth_attr table...

Read 67 source entries; updated 67 target entries.

Populating the prof_attr table...

Read 28 source entries; updated 28 target entries.

Populating the exec_attr table...

Read 204 source entries; updated 204 target entries.

Populating the user_attr table...

Read 1 source entries; updated 0 target entries.
mopoke#
```

## Environment Variables

See `environ`(5) for a description of the `JAVA_HOME` environment variable, which affects the execution of the `smattrpop` command. If you do not specify this environment variable, the `/usr/java` location is used. See `smc`(1M).

## Exit Status

Any errors encountered while updating the target entry are reported to standard output.

| | |
|---|---|
| 0 | The specified tables were updated. Individual entries may have encountered checking errors. |
| 1 | A syntax error occurred in the command line. |
| 2 | A fatal error occurred and the tables were not completely processed. Some entries may have been updated before the failure. |

## Files

`/etc/security/auth_attr`

Authorization description database. See `auth_attr`(4).

`/etc/security/exec_attr`

Execution profiles database. See `exec_attr`(4).

`/etc/security/prof_attr`

Profile description database. See `prof_attr`(4).

/etc/user_attr

>Extended user attribute database. See user_attr(4).

## Attributes

See attributes(5) for descriptions of the following attributes.

| Attribute Type | Attribute Value |
|---|---|
| Availability | SUNWmga |

## See Also

smc(1M), smexec(1M), smprofile(1M), auth_attr(4), exec_attr(4), prof_attr(4), user_attr(4), attributes(5), environ(5)

# smc

## Synopsis

```
smc [subcommand][args]
smc [subcommand][args] -T tool_name [-- tool_args]
```

## Description

The smc command starts the Solaris Management Console (SMC). SMC is a graphical user interface that provides access to a set of Solaris system administration tools. SMC relies on SMC servers running on one or more computers to perform modifications and report data. Each of these servers is a repository for code that the SMC console can retrieve after the user of the console has authenticated himself or herself to the server.

The console can also retrieve toolboxes from the server. These toolboxes are descriptions of organized collections of tools available on that and possibly other servers. Once one of these toolboxes is loaded, the console displays it and the tools referenced in it.

The /etc/init.d/init.wbem script runs the smc command when a system is booted. See Chapter 3, "SMC Server," for more information. You can also run the command manually to launch the SMC Editor to edit toolboxes and create custom toolboxes. See Chapter 4, "SMC Toolbox Editor," for more information about using SMC toolbox editor.

The console can also run in a terminal (nongraphically) for use over remote connections or noninteractively from a script.

### subcommands

open
: The default subcommand for SMC is open. This subcommand launches the console and enables you to run tools from the toolboxes you load. You do not need to specify this suboption on the command line.

edit
: Launch SMC toolbox editor. Use the SMC toolbox editor to create or edit an SMC toolbox. See Chapter 4, "SMC Toolbox Editor," for instructions on using the SMC toolbox editor.

## Options

You can also specify the following options with their equivalent option words preceded by a double dash. For example, for the domain argument, you can specify either -D or --domain. Precede any *tool_args* with the -- option separated by spaces.

--auth-data *file*

> Specify a file that the console can read to collect authentication data. When running SMC noninteractively, the console still needs to authenticate itself with the server to retrieve tools. You can either pass this data, insecurely, on the command line with the -u, -p, -r, and -1 options or put it in a file for the console to read. For security reasons, ensure the file is readable only by the user running the console; the console does not enforce this restriction.
>
> Contents of *file* have the following formats.
>
> hostname=*host_name*
>
> username=*user_name*
>
> password=*password_for_user_name*
>
> rolename=*role_name*
>
> rolepassword=*password_for_role_name*
>
> You can specify only one set of hostname-username-password-rolename-rolepassword in any one file. If you do not specify *role name*, assume no role.

-B | --toolbox *toolbox*

> Load the specified toolbox. *toolbox* can be either a fully qualified URL or a file name. If you specify an HTTP URL, for example,
>
> http://*host_name*:*port*/. . .
>
> the URL must point to a *host_name* and *port* on which an SMC server is running. If you omit *port*, the default port, 898, is used. This option overrides the -H option.

-D | --domain *domain*

> Specify the default domain that you want to manage. The syntax of domain is *type*:/*host_name*/*domain_name*, where *type* is nis, nisplus, dns, ldap, or file; *host_name* is the name of the system that serves the domain; and *domain_name* is the name of the domain you want to manage. (Note: Do not use nis+ for nisplus.) This option applies only to a single tool run in the terminal console.
>
> If you do not specify this option, SMC assumes the file default domain on whatever server you choose to manage, which means that changes are local to the server. Toolboxes can change the domain on a tool-by-tool basis; this option specifies the domain for all other tools.

-h | --help    Print a usage statement about the smc command and its subcommands to the terminal window. To print a usage statement for one of the subcommands, enter -h after the subcommand. For example, to print a usage statement for the edit subcommand, type smc edit -h and press Return.

-H | --hostname *host_name:port*

Specify the *host_name* and *port* to which you want to connect. If you do not specify a port, the system connects to the default port, 898. If you do not specify *host_name:port*, SMC connects to the local host on port 898. You may still need to choose a toolbox to load into the console. To override this behavior, use the -B option or set your console preferences to load a home toolbox by default. See "Specifying SMC Console Preferences" on page 20 for information about setting console preferences.

-J*java_option*

Specify an option that can be passed directly to the Java runtime (see java(1)). Do not enter a space between -J and the argument. This option is most useful for developers.

-l | --rolepassword *role_password*

Specify the password for the *role_name* (see the -r option) If you specify a *role_name* but do not specify a *role_password*, the system prompts you to supply a *role_password*. Because passwords specified on the command line can be seen by any user on the system who runs the ps command, this option is considered insecure.

-p | --password *password*

Specify the password for the *user_name* (see the -u option). If you do not specify a password, the system prompts you for one. Because passwords specified on the command line can be seen by any user on the system who runs the ps command, this option is considered insecure.

-r | --rolename *role_name*

Specify a role name for authentication. If you are running smc in a terminal and you do not specify this option, assume no role. The GUI console may prompt you for a role name, although you may not need to assume a role.

-s | --silent

Disable informational messages printed to the terminal.

-t    Run SMC in terminal mode. If you do not specify this option, SMC automatically runs in terminal mode if it cannot find a graphical display.

--trust    Trust all downloaded code implicitly. Use this option when you are running the terminal console noninteractively and you cannot wait for user input.

-T | --tool *tool_name*

> Run the tool with the Java class name that corresponds to
> *tool_name*. If you do not specify this option and SMC is running in
> terminal mode, the system prompts you. If SMC is running in
> graphical mode, the system either loads a toolbox or prompts you for
> one (see options -H and -B).

-u | --username *user_name*

> Specify the user name for authentication. If you do not specify this
> option, assume the user identity running the console process.

-v | --version

> Print the version of SMC to the terminal. In the graphical console,
> this information can be found in the About box, available from the
> Help menu.

-y | --yes    Answer yes to all yes/no questions. Use this option when you are
> running the terminal console noninteractively and you cannot wait
> for user input.

## Examples

The following example prints a usage statement about SMC command to the terminal
window.

```
mopoke% smc -h
Solaris Management Console
Usage: smc [flags] command [flags]

Common flags:
       -h, -?, --help, --usage              : Print out this usage
     statement. (optional)
         -v, --version, --about             : Print version information.
     (optional)

Commands:
       edit    Edit a toolbox.
       open    Open a tool or toolbox.
mopoke%
```

The following example passes an option through to the Java virtual machine, which
sets the com.example.boolean system property to true. This system property is only
an example; SMC does not actually use it.

```
mopoke% smc -J-Dcom.example.boolean=true
```

## Environment Variables

See environ(5) for a description of the following environment variable that affects the
execution of the smc command.

JAVA_HOME     If you do not specify this environment variable, the /usr/java1.2
> location is used.

## Exit Status

Other error codes may be returned if you specify a tool (with the $-T$ $tool\_name$ option) that has its own error codes. See the documentation for the appropriate tool.

| | |
|---|---|
| 0 | Successful completion. |
| 1 | An error occurred. |

## Attributes

See attributes(5) for descriptions of the following attributes.

| Attribute Type | Attribute Value |
|---|---|
| Availability | SUNWmcc |

## See Also

auths(1), java(1), profiles(1), roles(1), smcconf(1M), attributes(5), environ(5), X(7)

# smcconf

## Synopsis

/usr/sadm/bin/smcconf [-h][-v] toolbox [*action*][*target*][*parameters*]
    [*options*]
/usr/sadm/bin/smcconf [-h][-v] repository [*action*][*target*][*parameters*]
    [*options*]

## Description

Use smcconf command to configure the Solaris Management Console (SMC). See smc(1M). This command enables you to add to, remove from, and list the contents of the toolboxes and bean repository.

Using smcconf to edit toolboxes is not as feature-rich as using the SMC console graphical editor. Use the command-line interface for packaging scripts that do not require user interaction. To edit all the properties of a toolbox or to modify the hierarchy of folders in a toolbox, you must use the specialized graphical editor, smc edit. See Chapter 4, "SMC Toolbox Editor," and smc(1M) for more information.

---

**Note —** All standard shell quoting rules apply.

---

## Options

| | |
|---|---|
| -h | Print a usage summary for the command. |
| -v | Display the debugging output at any time. |

### Toolbox Configuration

| | |
|---|---|
| *action* | Legal values are listed below. |

| | | |
|---|---|---|
| add | | Add a target to the toolbox. Specify the path to the toolbox with the -B *toolboxpath* option and, optionally, provide locale information with the -L *locale* option. |
| remove | | Remove a target from the toolbox. Specify the path to the toolbox with the -B *toolboxpath* option and, optionally, provide locale information with the -L *locale* option. |
| create | | Create a new toolbox with no tools in it. The only target recognized is toolbox. |
| list | | List the contents of the toolbox. No target is recognized. If you specify a parameter, it is taken as the path to a toolbox and the contents of that toolbox are listed. If you do not specify a parameter, the contents of the default toolbox are listed. |

*target*   Legal values are listed below.

| | |
|---|---|
| tool | If you specify the add action, add a native SMC tool from the toolbox. The required parameter is the full Java classname of the tool you are adding. If you specify a folder name with the -F option, the tool is placed inside that folder (the folder is not created if it does not already exist). Otherwise, the tool is appended to the end of the toolbox and not placed inside any folder. If you specify the remove action, remove a native SMC tool from the toolbox. The required parameter is the full Java classname of the tool you want to remove. If you specify a folder name with the -F option, any tool with the given name in that folder is removed. If you specify no folder name, remove all tools with the given name in the toolbox. |

For the tool to show up in the console, you must also register the tool in the repository. See "Repository Configuration" on page 250 for more information. If a tool is referenced in a toolbox but is not registered, it does not appear in the console when the toolbox is loaded.

Removing a tool from a toolbox does not remove the tool from the server repository

| | |
|---|---|
| tbxURL | If you specify the add or remove action, add a link from this target to another toolbox or remove a link from this target to another toolbox. The required parameter is the URL to the other toolbox. The properties of addition and removal are the same as for the tool target. |

toolbox  If you specify the create action, create a skeleton toolbox with no tools. Four parameters are required: the toolbox name, description, and small and large icon paths. You must follow these parameters with the -B `toolbox-path` and -D `scope` options.

legacy  If you specify the add or remove action, add or remove legacy applications (applications based on the command-line, X-Windows, and the Web) to or from the toolbox. The -N, -T, -E, and -B options are required, and the -A option is optional.

Placement in the toolbox with the -F option follows the same rules as for the tool and tbxURL targets.

Legacy applications (applications based on the command-line, X-Windows, and the Web) are handled differently from native SMC tools. Legacy tools are handled by an instantiation of a native SMC tool, LegacyAppLauncher, which, through the toolbox, is given the necessary information to run the legacy application: path, options, and so forth. You do not register a legacy application into the repository as you would a native SMC tool. Instead, legacy applications appear only in toolboxes.

folder  If you specify the add action, add a folder to the toolbox. Four parameters are required: the folder name, description, and small and large icon paths.

If you specify the remove action, remove a folder from the toolbox. If the folder to be removed is itself inside a folder, you must specify the containing folder with the -F option.

parameters  Specify values that may be required depending on the combination of action and target.

options  Supported options for various action and target combinations for the toolbox configuration are listed below.

-A parameters

Specify the parameters to pass to the legacy application. This option is available only for the legacy target.

-B toolboxpath

Specify the path of the toolbox that is being modified. If you do not specify this option, the modifications are be performed on the default toolbox, This Computer.

-D *scope*        Specify the scope (domain) in which the tool should
                  be run. The legal values for scope are file, nis,
                  nisplus, dns, and ldap. You can also specify scope
                  for a folder or a toolbox. For a folder, all tools in that
                  folder and its subfolders are run in that scope; for a
                  toolbox, all tools in the toolbox are to be run in that
                  scope.

-E *appPath*      Specify the absolute executable path of the legacy
                  application. This option is available only for the
                  legacy target.

-F *folder*       Specify the full path of the container folder. If you do
                  not specify this option, the default folder is the root
                  folder of the toolbox.

-H [*host_name*][:*port*]

                  Specify the host and port from which a tool should be
                  loaded. If you do not specify *host_name*, use the
                  default host (localhost, if the toolbox is loaded from
                  the local file system, or the host from which the
                  toolbox is loaded if loaded from a remote SMC
                  server). If you do not specify :*port*, use the default
                  port. If you do not specify this option, both the default
                  host and the default port are used.

-L *locale*       Specify the locale of the toolbox being modified. The
                  default is the C locale.

-N *appName*      Specify the name of the legacy application being
                  registered. This name is used in the console. This
                  option is available only for the legacy target.

-P *key*:*value*

                  Specify the key:value pairs that define parameters to
                  a tool. You can specify multiple key:value pairs at a
                  time.

-T *appType*      Specify the legacy application type. Legal values are
                  CLI, XAPP, or HTML. This option is available only for
                  the legacy target.

## Repository Configuration

SMC repository stores information about the registered tools and services, as well as libraries (for instance, resource jars) and properties attached to tools or services.

*action*      Legal values are listed below.

add            Add information to the repository. If you specify the -f option to add, the information overwrites any information of the same name already in the repository. If you do not specify the -f option, an error may be returned if the information is already in the repository.

remove       Remove information from the repository.

list             List the contents of the repository.

- All registered tools.

- All registered services.

- All libraries attached to all tools.

- All libraries attached to all services.

- All libraries attached to all tools and services.

*target*      Legal values are listed below.

bean          If you specify the add action, add a tool or service bean (which kind is determined by the contents of the bean) to the repository. The required parameter is the path to the jar file that contains the bean to be added.

                   If you specify the remove action, remove a tool or service bean from the repository. The required parameter is the full Java classname of the desired bean.

library        If you specify the add action, add a library jar file to a tool or service bean. The two required parameters are the full Java classname of the desired bean and the path to the jar file to be attached. The bean name can also be one of the pseudo-beans, ALL, ALLTOOL, or ALLSERVICE, in which case the library is attached to all beans, all tools, or all services in the repository.

                   If you specify the remove action, detach a library jar file from a tool or service bean. The two required parameters are the full Java classname of the desired bean and the name of the jar file that is attached. As with the add action, you can use the three pseudo-beans ALL, ALLTOOL, or ALLSERVICE.

property      If you specify the add action, define a property on a tool or service. You must specify one or more key:value pairs in the form -P *key=value*.

Following this property list is a pseudo-bean name, pseudoBeanName, as defined for the library target, on which the properties are defined. Optionally, you can follow the pseudo-bean name with a library name, in which case the properties are defined on the library that is attached to the named bean.

If you specify the remove action, undefine a property on a tool or service. The key:value pairs, pseudo-bean name, and optional library are specified as for the add action.

## Examples

The following example adds the Command Line Interface (CLI) application, /usr/bin/ls with arguments -al -R to the default toolbox and gives it the name Directory Listing.

```
# /usr/sadm/bin/smcconf toolbox add legacy -N "Directory Listing" -T CLI -E
    /usr/bin/ls -A "-al -R"
```

The following example adds a folder with the name New Folder to the standard Management Tools toolbox, with the description This is a new folder, and the small and large icons, folder_s.gif and folder_l.gif.

```
# /usr/sadm/bin/smcconf toolbox add folder "New Folder" "This is a new folder"
    folder_s.gif folder _l.gif -B /var/sadm/smc/toolboxes/smc/smc.tbx
```

The following example adds a native SMC tool to the default toolbox. The Java classname of the tool is HelloWorld.client.HelloTool. The name, description, and icons visible in the console are provided by the tool itself. When loaded, it is run in the NIS domain, syrinx, which is hosted by the machine, temple, and is retrieved from port 2112 on the machine from which the toolbox was loaded.

```
# /usr/sadm/bin/smcconf toolbox add tool HelloWorld.client.HelloTool -D
    nis:/temple/syrinx -H :2112
```

The following example adds the bean found in HelloWorld.jar to the repository. The jar file contains information that the bean is a tool.

```
# /usr/sadm/bin/smcconf repository add bean HelloWorld.jar
```

The following example removes a bean from the repository. Although the name of the bean implies that it is a service, that is merely convention; the repository knows whether a particular registered bean is a tool or a service.

```
# /usr/sadm/bin/smcconf repository remove bean HelloWorld.server.HelloService
```

The following example adds the library jar file, HelloWorld_fr.jar (a French localized version of the HelloTool's resources) to the bean, HelloWorld.client.HelloTool.

```
# /usr/sadm/bin/smcconf repository add library HelloWorld.client.HelloTool
    HelloWorld_fr.jar
```

The following example adds the library jar file, widgets.jar, to all tools in the repository. The library contains a widget set that might be useful to any registered tools.

```
# /usr/sadm/bin/smcconf repository add library ALLTOOL widgets.jar
```

## Environment Variables

See environ(5) for descriptions of the following environment variables that affect the execution of smcconf command.

| | |
|---|---|
| JAVA_HOME | If you do not specify this environment variable, the /usr/java1.2 location is used. |
| DISPLAY | If you do not set this environment variable, set it to null, or set it to an X(7) display to which you are not authorized to connect, SMC starts in terminal mode instead of graphical mode. |

## Exit Status

| | |
|---|---|
| 0 | Successful completion. |
| 1 | An error occurred. |

## Attributes

See attributes(5) for descriptions of the following attributes.

| Attribute Type | Attribute Value |
|---|---|
| Availability | SUNWmc |

## See Also

jar(1), java(1), javac(1), smc(1M), attributes(5), environ(5)

# smdiskless

## Synopsis

/usr/sadm/bin/smdiskless *subcommand* [*auth_args*] -- [*subcommand_args*]

## Description

Use the smdiskless command in combination with the smosservice command to manage diskless clients from the command line. The SMC Console does not provide GUI support for diskless clients. The smdiskless subcommands are listed below.

add
: Add a new diskless client support to a server. You can specify two usages for this command. You can specify either all the optional arguments directly on the command line or provide a sysidcfg(4) formatted file as input. A future enhancement will enable you to specify both a sysidcfg(4) formatted file and optional arguments that override the values in the sysidcfg(4) file.

delete
: Delete an existing diskless client from the system databases and remove any server support associated with the host, depending on the host type.

list
: List existing diskless clients served by *hostname*.

modify
: Modify the specified attributes of the diskless client host.

## Options

The smdiskless authentication arguments, *auth_args*, are derived from the smc(1M) argument set and are the same regardless of the subcommand you use.

The subcommand-specific options, *subcommand_args*, must come after *auth_args* separated by the -- option.

### auth_args

The valid, optional *auth_args* are -D, -H, -l, -p, -r, and -u. If you specify no *auth_args*, certain defaults are assumed and you may be prompted for additional information, such as a password for authentication purposes. You can also specify these letter options by their equivalent option words preceded by a double dash. For example, for the domain option, you can use either -D or --domain.

-D | --domain *domain*

Specify the default domain that you want to manage. The syntax of domain is *type*:/*host_name*/*domain_name*, where *type* is nis, nisplus, dns, ldap, or file; *host_name* is the name of the system that serves the domain; and *domain_name* is the name of the domain you want to manage. (Note: Do not use nis+ for nisplus.)

If you do not specify this option, SMC assumes the file default domain on whatever server you choose to manage, which means that changes are local to the server. Toolboxes can change the domain on a tool-by-tool basis; this option specifies the domain for all other tools.

`-H | --hostname` *host_name:port*

> Specify the *host_name* and *port* to which you want to connect. If you do not specify a port, the system connects to the default port, 898. If you do not specify *host_name:port*, SMC connects to the local host on port 898. You may still need to choose a toolbox to load into the console. To override this behavior, use the smc(1M) `-B` option or set your console preferences to load a home toolbox by default. See "Console Preferences" on page 20 for information on specifying console preferences.

`-l | --rolepassword` *role_password*

> Specify the password for the *role_name*. If you specify a *role_name* but do not specify a *role_password*, the system prompts you to supply a *role_password*. Because passwords specified on the command line can be seen by any user on the system, this option is considered insecure.

`-p | --password` *password*

> Specify the password for the *user_name*. If you do not specify a password, the system prompts you for one. Because passwords specified on the command line can be seen by any user on the system, this option is considered insecure.

`-r | --rolename` *role_name*

> Specify a role name for authentication. If you do not specify this option, assume no role.

`-u | --username` *user_name*

> Specify the user name for authentication. If you do not specify this option, assume the user identity running the console process.

`--`

> This required option must always follow the preceding options. If you do not specify any preceding options, you still must include the `--` option.

## subcommand_args

Enclose descriptions and other argument options with white spaces in double quotes. Options for the add subcommand are listed below.

`-h`

> (Optional) Display the usage statement for the command.

`-i` *IP_address*

> Specify the IP address for the host in the form of 129.9.200.1.

`-e` *ethernet_addr*

> Specify the Ethernet address.

`-n` *host=client_name*

> Specify the client name.

-o *host_os*          (Optional) Specify the name of the host where the OS service file systems reside. If you do not specify this option, the host is the same as that specified in the smc(1M) -D option. This option is useful when the nameservice server and the OS server are not the same.

-x platform=*platform*

Specify the operating system. The syntax for *platform* is

*instruction_set.implementation.Solaris_version*

where

*instruction_set* is one of sparc or i386.

*implementation* is the implementation architecture, for example, i86pc, sun4c (for Solaris 2.6 and 7 only), sun4d, sun4m, and sun4u.

*version* is the Solaris version number. The supported version numbers are 2.6, 2.7 (for Solaris 7), 8, and 9. Examples are sparc.sun4c.Solaris_2.7, sparc.sun4d.Solaris_8.

-x root=*directory*

(Optional) Specify the absolute or full path of the directory in which to create the root directory for diskless clients. The default is /export/root/*client_name*.

-x swap=*directory*

(Optional) Specify the absolute or full path of the directory in which to create the swap file for diskless clients. The default is /export/swap/*client_name*.

-x swapsize=*size*

(Optional) Specify the size, in megabytes, of the swap file for diskless clients. The default swap size is 24M.

-x dump=*directory*

(Optional) Specify the absolute or full path of the dump directory for diskless clients. The default is /export/dump/*client_name*.

-x dumpsize=*size*

(Optional) Specify the size, in megabytes, of the dump file for diskless clients. The default dump file size is 24M.

-x pw=Y                (Optional) Prompt for the system's root password. The default is not to prompt.

The following options are used to configure workstations on first boot by sysidtool(1M). You can specify the options either on the command line or in a sysidcfg(4) formatted file. Note: Use the sysidcfg(4) file to add a DNS client.

-x domain=*domain*

(Optional) Specify the client's domain. The default is the server's domain.

`-x locale=`*`locale`*

> (Optional) Specify the client's system locale. The default is the server's locale.

`-x nameserver=`*`hostname`*

> (Optional) Specify the nameserver's host name. The default is the server's nameserver.

`-x nameserver_ipaddress=`*`ip_address`*

> (Optional) Specify the nameserver's IP address.

`-x netmask=`*`ip_address`*

> (Optional) Specify the client's IP address netmask. The default is the server's netmask.

`-x ns=NIS | NIS+ | NONE | DNS`

> (Optional) Specify the client's nameservice. This is one of NIS, NIS+, NONE (for /etc files), or DNS. The default is the server's nameservice. The default is obtained by reading the server's `nsswitch.conf`(4) file.

`-x passwd=`*`root_password`*

> (Optional) Specify the system's root password. The default is no password.

`-x security_policy=kerberos | none`

> (Optional) Specify the security policy. If you specify kerberos, more information is required. The default is none.

`-x sysidcfg=`*`path_to_sysidcfg_file`*

> (Optional) Specify the file to be placed in the /etc directory of the diskless client. On first boot, /etc/.UNCONFIGURED exists and `sysidtool`(1M) is run. If a file called /etc/sysidcfg exists, `sysidtool`(1M) reads this file and uses the information in it for system configuration. The keywords and syntax of `sysidcfg`(4) are shown below.
>
> `install_locale=locale during install (optional)`
>
> `system_locale=runtime locale`
>
> `terminal=terminal`
>
> `timezone=timezone`
>
> `timeserver=IP address | domain name (optional)`
>
> `root_password=encrypted root password` (The encrypted password, usually taken from an /etc/shadow root password entry of a known password)
>
> `network_interface="none" (or)`
>
> `network_interface="primary" {`
>
> `hostname=client hostname |`
>
> `ip_address=client IP address |`

```
netmask=client net mask |
}
```
(can have one or more sets of attributes, hostname, IP
address, and so on, within the braces)

```
name_service="nisplus" | "nis" {
        domain_name=domain name |
        name_server=hostname ( IP address ) }
```
(can have one or more sets of attributes,
domain_name, name_server, and so on,
within the braces)

```
(or) name_service="dns" {
        domain_name=domain name |
        name_server=hostname ( IP address ) |
        search=domain name , . . . , }
```
(can have one or more sets of attributes,
domain_name, name_server, search, and so
on, within the braces)

```
(or) name_service="other" | "none"
security_policy="kerberos" {
        default_realm=ident
        admin_server= ident |
        kdc=ident, . . . }
```
(can have one or more sets of attributes,
default_realm, admin_server, kdc, and so on,
within the braces)

```
(or) security_policy="none"
```

For example:

```
install_locale=C
system_locale=C
terminal=xterms
timezone=US/Eastern
root_password=hJ9ai4b1x9VIw
network_interface=primary \
{ hostname=maerzen ip_address=129.148.4.4 \
        netmask=255.255.255.0 }
name_service=nis \
        { domain_name=Ecd.East.Sun.COM \
        name_server=teton (129.148.171.44)
```

```
                              }
                   security_policy=none
```

-x terminal=*term*

> (Optional) Specify the workstation's terminal type, typically, sun or xterms.

-x tz=*timezone*

> (Optional) Specify the path of a timezone file, relative to /usr/share/lib/zoneinfo. The default is the server's timezone.

The delete subcommand accepts the following options.

-h
> (Optional) Display the usage statement for the command.

-n *host*
> Specify the host name of the diskless client to delete. Delete this host from relevant tables and delete OS Services for this client.

-o *host_os*
> (Optional) Specify the name of the host where the OS service file systems reside. If you do not specify this option, the host is the same as that specified in the smc(1M) -D option. This option is useful when the nameservice server and the OS server are not the same.

The list subcommand accepts the following options.

-h
> (Optional) Display the usage statement for the command.

-o host_os
> (Optional) Specify the name of the host where the OS service file systems reside. If you do not specify this option, the host is the same as that specified in the smc(1M) -D option. This option is useful when the nameservice server and the OS server are not the same.

The modify subcommand accepts the following options.

-e *ethernet_addr*

> Change the specified diskless client's Ethernet address to *ethernet_addr*.

-h
> (Optional) Display the usage statement for the command.

-n *host*
> Specify the host name of the diskless client to modify.

-o *host_os*
> (Optional) Specify the name of the host where the OS service file systems reside. If you do not specify this option, the host is the same as that specified in the smc(1M) -D option. This option is useful when the nameservice server and the OS server are not the same.

-x tz=*timezone*

> (Optional) Change the time zone of the specified diskless client.

## Examples

The following example adds a new diskless client named client1 that runs Solaris 8 on a sun4u machine.

```
example% /usr/sadm/bin/smdiskless add -- -i 129.9.200.1 -e 8:0:11:12:13:14 -n
    client1 -x os=sparc.sun4u.Solaris_8 -x root=/export/root/client1 -x
    swap=/export/swap/client1  -x swapsize=32 -x tz=US/Eastern -x
    locale=en_US
```

The following example deletes the diskless client named client1 from the OS server named osserver, where the OS server is using NIS+ and the NIS+ server is nisplusserve.

```
example% /usr/sadm/bin/smdiskless delete -D
    nisplus:/nisplusserver/my.domain.com -- -o osserver -n client1
```

The following example lists the diskless clients running on the OS server, osserver.

```
example% /usr/sadm/bin/smdiskless list -D file:/osserver/osserver --
    -o osserver
```

The following example modifies the Ethernet address for the client named client1 on the OS server, osserver, to 8:0:11:12:13:15.

```
example% /usr/sadm/bin/smdiskless modify -D file:/osserver/osserver -- -o
    osserver -n client1 -e 8:0:11:12:13:15
```

## Environment Variables

See environ(5) for a description of the JAVA_HOME environment variable, which affects the execution of the smdiskless command. If you do not specify this environment variable, the /usr/java location is used. See smc(1M).

## Exit Status

| | |
|---|---|
| 0 | Successful completion. |
| 1 | Invalid command syntax. A usage message is displayed. |
| 2 | An error occurred while the command was executing. An error message is displayed. |

## Attributes

See attributes(5) for descriptions of the following attributes.

| Attribute Type | Attribute Value |
|---|---|
| Availability | SUNWdclnt |

## See Also

smc(1M), smosservice(1M), sysidtool(1M), nsswitch.conf(4), sysidcfg(4),
attributes(5), environ(5)

# smcron

## Synopsis

/usr/sadm/bin/smcron subcommand [*auth_args*] -- [*subcommand_args*]

## Description

Use smcron command to manage jobs in the crontab(1) database.
smcron subcommands are listed below.

| | |
|---|---|
| add | Add a job to the crontab(1) database. |
| delete | Delete a job from the crontab(1) database. |
| list | List one or more jobs in the crontab(1) database. |
| modify | Modify a job in the crontab(1) database. |

## Options

The smcron authentication arguments, *auth_args*, are derived from the smc(1M)
argument set and are the same regardless of which subcommand you use.

You must place the subcommand-specific options, *subcommand_args*, after
*auth_args* separated by the -- option.

### auth_args

The valid, optional *auth_args* are -D, -H, -l, -p, -r, and -u. If you specify no *auth_arg*,
certain defaults are assumed and you may be prompted for additional information, such
as a password for authentication purposes. You can also specify these letter options as
their equivalent option words preceded by a double dash. For example, you can use
either -D or --domain with the *domain* argument.

-D | --domain *domain*

Specify the default domain that you want to manage. The syntax of
domain is *type*:/*host_name*/*domain_name*, where type is nis,
nisplus, dns, ldap, or file; *host_name* is the name of the system
that serves the domain; and *domain_name* is the name of the domain
you want to manage. (Note: Do not use nis+ for nisplus.)

If you do not specify this option, SMC assumes the file default
domain on whatever server you choose to manage, which means that
changes are local to the server. Toolboxes can change the domain on a
tool-by-tool basis; this option specifies the domain for all other tools.

-H | --hostname *host_name*:*port*

Specify the *host_name* and *port* to which you want to connect. If you do not specify a port, the system connects to the default port, 898. If you do not specify *host_name:port*, SMC connects to the local host on

port 898. You may still need to choose a toolbox to load into the console. To override this behavior, use the smc(1M) -B option or set your console preferences to load a home toolbox by default. See "Specifying SMC Console Preferences" on page 20 for information on specifying console preferences.

-l | --rolepassword *role_password*

Specify the password for the *role_name*. If you specify a *role_name* but do not specify a *role_password*, the system prompts you to supply a *role_password*. Because passwords specified on the command line can be seen by any user on the system running the ps command, this option is considered insecure.

-p | --password *password*

Specify the password for the *user_name*. If you do not specify a password, the system prompts you for one. Because passwords specified on the command line can be seen by any user on the system running the ps command, this option is considered insecure.

-r | --rolename *role_name*

Specify a role name for authentication. If you do not specify this option, assume no role.

-u | --username *user_name*

Specify the user name for authentication. If you do not specify this option, assume the user identity running the console process.

--

This required option must always follow the preceding options. If you do not enter the preceding options, you must still enter the -- option.

## subcommand_args

Enclose descriptions and other argument options with white spaces in double quotes. The following list describes the add subcommand.

-c *command*     Specify the command that you want to run.

-h               (Optional) Display the usage statement for the command.

-m *day of month*

(Optional) Specify the day of the month you want to run the job. Valid values are 1-31. If you specify both -t and -m options, execute the job one day a month at the time specified by -t.

-M *month*       (Optional) Specify the month that you want to run the job. Valid values are 1-12. If you specify both -t and -M options, execute the job during the specified month at the time specified by -t.

-n *name*        Specify the unique name of the job.

-o *owner*     (Optional) Specify the user name that is the owner of the job. If you do not specify this option, assume the user name specified by the -U option.

-t *time_of_day*

Specify the time (in *hh*:*mm*) that you want to execute the command. Note that you specify *hh* with a 24-hour clock. For example, you specify 1:00 p.m. as 13:00. If you specify no other time-related options (-m, -M, or -w), execute the job every day at the time specified by -t. If you specify both -t and -w options, execute the job one day a week at the time specified by -t. If you specify both -t and -m options, execute the job one day a month at the time specified by -t. If you specify both -t and -M options, execute the job each day during the specified month at the time specified by -t.

-w *day_of_week*

(Optional) Specify the day of the week you want to execute the command. Valid values are shown below

0 = Sunday

1 = Monday

2 = Tuesday

3 = Wednesday

4 = Thursday

5 = Friday

6 = Saturday

If you specify both -t and -w options, execute the job one day a week at the time specified by -t.

The following list describes the options for the delete subcommand.

-h     (Optional) Display the usage statement for the command.

-n *name*     Specify the unique name of the job.

-o *owner*     (Optional) Specify the name of the user who owns the job. If you do not specify this option, assume the user name specified by the -U option.

The following list describes the options for the list subcommand.

-f n|s|v     (Optional) Specify the format of the output. See "Examples" on page 265 for examples of each output type.

n     Display the data in native format, as it appears in the crontab(1) database.

s     Default format. Display the data in summary format.

v     Display the data in verbose format.

-h     (Optional) Display the usage statement for the command.

-o *owner*    (Optional) List all jobs for the specified owner (user name). If you do not specify this option, all jobs in the crontab(1) database are listed.

---

The following list describes the modify subcommand.

-c *command*    (Optional) Specify the command that you want to run.

-h    (Optional) Display the usage statement for the command.

-m *day_of_month*

(Optional) Specify the day of the month you want to run the job. Valid values are 1-31. If you specify both -t and -m options, execute the job one day a month at the time specified by -t.

-M *month*    (Optional) Specify the month that you want to run the job. Valid values are 1-12. If you specify both -t and -M options, execute the job during the specified month at the time specified by -t.

-n *name*    Specify the current unique name of the job.

-N *new_name*    (Optional) Specify the new unique name of the job.

-o *owner*    (Optional) Specify the name of the user who owns the job. If you do not specify this option, assume the user name specified by the -U option.

-O *new_owner*

(Optional) Specify the new owner of the job.

-t *time_of_day*

(Optional) Specify the time (in *hh*:*mm*) that you want to execute the command. If you specify no other time-related options (-m, -M, or -w), then execute the job every day at the time specified by -t. If you specify both -t and -w options, execute the job one day a week at the time specified by -t. If you specify both -t and -m options, execute the job one day a month at the time specified by -t. If you specify both -t and -M, then execute the job each day during the specified month at the time specified by -t.

-w *day_of_week*

(Optional) Specify the day of the week you want to execute the command. Valid values are shown below.

0 = Sunday

1 = Monday

2 = Tuesday

3 = Wednesday

4 = Thursday

5 = Friday

6 = Saturday

If you specify both -t and -w options, execute the job one day a week at the time specified by -t.

## Examples

The following example adds a new job, owned by root, that removes the old log files from /tmp daily at 1:30 AM.

```
mopoke# /usr/sadm/bin/smcron add -H mopoke -u root -p rootpasswd -- -n "Remove
    old logs" -t 1:30 -c "rm /tmp/*.log" -o root

Loading Tool: com.sun.admin.taskschedmgr.cli.TaskSchedMgrCli from mopoke
Login to mopoke as user root was successful.
Download of com.sun.admin.taskschedmgr.cli.TaskSchedMgrCli from mopoke was
    successful.
mopoke#
```

The following example deletes the job Remove old logs owned by root. However, the argument for the -n option does not match and an error message is returned.

```
mopoke# /usr/sadm/bin/smcron delete -H mopoke -u root -p rootpasswd -- -n
    "remove old logs" -o root
Loading Tool: com.sun.admin.taskschedmgr.cli.TaskSchedMgrCli from mopoke
Login to mopoke as user root was successful.
Download of com.sun.admin.taskschedmgr.cli.TaskSchedMgrCli from mopoke was
    successful.
The management server cannot perform the operation requested.  Verify that the
    CIMOM is running.

If this problem persists, please see the Log Viewer for additional
    information, or contact your Sun Microsystems support provider.

The actual error reported was: CIM_ERR_FAILED
mopoke#
```

The following example successfully deletes the Remove old logs job owned by root.

```
mopoke# /usr/sadm/bin/smcron delete -H mopoke -u root -p rootpasswd -- -n
    "Remove old logs" -o root
Loading Tool: com.sun.admin.taskschedmgr.cli.TaskSchedMgrCli from mopoke
Login to mopoke as user root was successful.
Download of com.sun.admin.taskschedmgr.cli.TaskSchedMgrCli from mopoke was
    successful.
mopoke#
```

The following example lists all jobs in native, or crontab(1), format.

```
mopoke# /usr/sadm/bin/smcron list -H mopoke -u root -p rootpasswd -- -f n
    MINUTE HOUR DATE MONTH DAY COMMAND
10 3 * * 0,4 /etc/cron.d/logchecker
10 3 * * o /usr/lib/newsyslog
15 3 * * 0 /usr/lib/fs/nfs/nfsfind
1 2 * * * [-x /usr/sbin/rtc] && /usr/sbin/rtc -c > /dev/null 2>&1
mopoke#
```

The following example lists all jobs owned by lp in standard format.

```
mopoke# /usr/sadm/bin/smcron list -H mopoke -u root -p rootpasswd -- -f s -o
    lp NAME::OWNER::SCHEDULE::COMMAND
```

```
NoName_1765663371::lp::Weekly on Sundays at 3:13 AM::cd /var/lp/logs; if [-f
    requests]; then if [-f requests.1]; then /bin/mv requests.1 requests.2;
    fi; /usr/bin/cp requests requests.1; > requests; fi
NoName_512822673::lp::Weekly on Sundays at 4:15 AM::cd /var/lp/logs; if [-f
    lpsched]; then if [-f lpsched.1]; then /bin/mv lpsched.1 lpsched.2; fi;
    /usr/bin/cp lpsched lpsched.1; >lpsched; fi
mopoke#
```

The following example lists all jobs in verbose format.

```
mopoke# /usr/sadm/bin/smcron list -H mopoke -u root -p rootpasswd -- -f v
    NAME::OWNER::SCHEDULE::NEXT_RUN::STATUS::COMMAND
NoName_1075488942::root::Advanced::::Finished on Feb 10 3:10 with code 1
    :::/etc/cron.d/logchecker
databackup::root::Weekly on Sundays at 3:10 AM::3/19/00 3:10 AM ::Finished on
    Sep 19 3:10::/usr/lib/newsyslog
runlog::root::Daily at 2:01 AM::3/14/00 2:01 AM::Finished on Feb 11 2:01
    AM::/usr/sbin/rtc
mopoke#
```

The following modifies the Remove old logs job owned by root to execute daily at
2:00 A.M.

```
mopoke# /usr/sadm/bin/smcron modify -H mopoke -u root -p rootpasswd -- -n
    "Remove old logs" -o root -t 2:00
Loading Tool: com.sun.admin.taskschedmgr.cli.TaskSchedMgrCli from mopoke
Login to mopoke as user root was successful.
Download of com.sun.admin.taskschedmgr.cli.TaskSchedMgrCli from mopoke was
    successful.
mopoke#
```

## Environment Variables

See environ(5) for a description of the JAVA_HOME environment variable, which affects
the execution of smcron command. If you do not specify this environment variable, the
/usr/java location is used. See smc(1M).

## Exit Status

| | |
|---|---|
| 0 | Successful completion. |
| 1 | Invalid command syntax. A usage message is displayed. |
| 2 | An error occurred while the command was executing. An error message is displayed. |

## Attributes

See attributes(5) for descriptions of the following attributes.

| Attribute Type | Attribute Value |
|---|---|
| Availability | SUNWmga |

### See Also

crontab(1), cron(1M), smc(1M), attributes(5), environ(5)

# smexec

### Synopsis

/usr/sadm/bin/smexec *subcommand* [*auth_args*] -- [*subcommand_args*]

### Description

Use the smexec command to manage an entry in the exec_attr(4) database in the local /etc files nameservice or in an NIS or NIS+ nameservice.

The smexec subcommands are listed below.

| | |
|---|---|
| add | Add a new entry to the exec_attr(4) database. |
| delete | Delete an entry from the exec_attr(4) database. |
| modify | Modify an entry in the exec_attr(4) database. |

### Options

The smexec authentication arguments, *auth_args*, are derived from the smc(1M) argument set and are the same regardless of which subcommand you use.

Put the subcommand-specific options, *subcommand_args*, after *auth_args*, separated by the -- option.

#### auth_args

The valid, optional *auth_args* are -D, -H, -l, -p, -r, and -u. If you specify no *auth_args*, certain defaults are assumed and you may be prompted for additional information, such as a password for authentication purposes. You can also specify these letter options by their equivalent option words preceded by a double dash. For example, you can use either -D or --domain with the *domain* argument.

-D | --domain *domain*

> Specify the default domain that you want to manage. The syntax of domain is *type*:/*host_name*/*domain_name*, where *type* is nis, nisplus, dns, ldap, or file; *host_name* is the name of the system that serves the domain; and *domain_name* is the name of the domain you want to manage. (Note: Do not use nis+ for nisplus.)

> If you do not specify this option, SMC assumes the file default domain on whatever server you choose to manage, which means that changes are local to the server. Toolboxes can change the domain on a tool-by-tool basis; this option specifies the domain for all other tools.

-H | --hostname *host_name:port*

> Specify the *host_name* and *port* to which you want to connect. If you do not specify a port, the system connects to the default port, 898. If you do not specify *host_name:port*, SMC connects to the local host on port 898. You may need to choose a toolbox to load into the console. To

override this behavior, use the smc(1M) -B option or set your console preferences to load a home toolbox by default. See "Specifying SMC Console Preferences" on page 20 for information on specifying console preferences.

-l | --rolepassword *role_password*

> Specify the password for the *role_name*. If you specify a *role_name* but do not specify a *role_password*, the system prompts you to supply a *role_password*. Because passwords specified on the command line can be seen by any user on the system who runs the ps command, this option is considered insecure.

-p | --password *password*

> Specify the password for the *user_name*. If you do not specify a password, the system prompts you for one. Because passwords specified on the command line can be seen by any user on the system, this option is considered insecure.

-r | --rolename *role_name*

> Specify a role name for authentication. If you do not specify this option, assume no role.

-u | --username *user_name*

> Specify the user name for authentication. If you do not specify this option, assume the user identity running the console process.

--

> This required option must always follow the preceding options. If you do not enter the preceding options, you must still enter the -- option.

## subcommand_args

Enclose descriptions and other argument options with white spaces in double quotes. The options for the add subcommand are listed below.

-c *command_path*

> Specify the full path to the command associated with the new exec_attr entry.

-g *egid*        (Optional) Specify the effective group ID that executes with the command.

-G *gid*        (Optional) Specify the real group ID that executes with the command.

-h              (Optional) Display the usage statement for the subcommand.

-n *profile_name*

> Specify the name of the profile associated with the new exec_attr entry.

-t *type*        Specify the type cmd for command.

-u *euid*        (Optional) Specify the effective user ID that executes with the command.

-U *uid*         (Optional) Specify the real user ID that executes with the command.

The options for the delete subcommand are listed below.

-c *command_path*

    Specify the full path to the command associated with the exec_attr entry.

-h     (Optional) Display the usage statement for the subcommand.

-n *profile_name*

    Specify the name of the profile associated with the exec_attr entry.

-t *type*     Specify the type cmd for command.

The options for the modify subcommand are listed below.

-c *command_path*

    Specify the full path to the command associated with the exec_attr entry that you want to modify.

-g *egid*     (Optional) Specify the new effective group ID that executes with the subcommand.

-G *gid*     (Optional) Specify the new real group ID that executes with the subcommand.

-h     (Optional) Display the usage statement for the subcommand.

-n *profile_name*

    Specify the name of the profile associated with the exec_attr entry.

-t *type*     Specify the type cmd for command.

-u *euid*     (Optional) Specify the new effective user ID that executes with the subcommand.

-U *uid*     (Optional) Specify the new real user ID that executes with the subcommand.

## Examples

The following example creates a new exec_attr entry for the User Manager profile on the local file system. The entry type is cmd for the command /usr/bin/cp. The command has an effective user ID of 0 and an effective group ID of 0.

```
mopoke# /usr/sadm/bin/smexec add -H mopoke -p rootpasswd -u root -- -n "User
    Manager" -t cmd -c /usr/bin/cp -u 0 -g 0
Loading Tool: com.sun.admin.usermgr.cli.execs.UserMgrExecCli from mopoke
Login to mopoke as user root was successful.
Download of com.sun.admin.usermgr.cli.execs.UserMgrExecCli from mopoke was
    successful.
mopoke#
```

The following example deletes an exec_attr database entry for the User Manager profile from the local file system. The entry designated for the command /usr/bin/cp is deleted.

```
mopoke# /usr/sadm/bin/smexec delete -H mopoke -p rootpasswd -u root -- -n
     "User Manager" -t cmd -c /usr/bin/cp
Loading Tool: com.sun.admin.usermgr.cli.execs.UserMgrExecCli from mopoke
Login to mopoke as user root was successful.
Download of com.sun.admin.usermgr.cli.execs.UserMgrExecCli from mopoke was
     successful.
mopoke#
```

The following example modifies the attributes of the exec_attr database entry for the User Manager profile on the local file system. The /usr/bin/cp entry is modified to execute with the real user ID of 0 and the real group ID of 0.

```
mopoke# /usr/sadm/bin/smexec modify -H mopoke -p rootpasswd -u root -- -n
     "User Manager" -t cmd -c /usr/bin/cp -U 0 -G 0
Loading Tool: com.sun.admin.usermgr.cli.execs.UserMgrExecCli from mopoke
Login to mopoke as user root was successful.
Download of com.sun.admin.usermgr.cli.execs.UserMgrExecCli from mopoke was
     successful.
mopoke#
```

## Environment Variables

See environ(5) for a description of the JAVA_HOME environment variable, which affects the execution of the smexec command. If you do not specify this environment variable, the /usr/java location is used. See smc(1M).

## Exit Status

| 0 | Successful completion. |
|---|---|
| 1 | Invalid command syntax. A usage message is displayed. |
| 2 | An error occurred while the command was executing. An error message is displayed. |

## Files

/etc/security/exec_attr

Execution profiles database. See exec_attr(4).

## Attributes

See attributes(5) for descriptions of the following attributes.

| Attribute Type | Attribute Value |
|---|---|
| Availability | SUNWmga |

## See Also

smc(1M), exec_attr(4), attributes(5), environ(5)

# smgroup

## Synopsis

/usr/sadm/bin/smgroup *subcommand* [*auth_args*] -- [*subcommand_args*]

## Description

Use the smgroup command to manage one or more group definitions in the group database for the appropriate files in the local /etc files nameservice or in an NIS or NIS+ nameservice.

### subcommands

The smgroup subcommands are listed below.

| | |
|---|---|
| add | Add a new group entry. |
| delete | Delete a group entry. You can delete only one entry at a time. Note: You cannot delete the system accounts with IDs less than 100, or the accounts 60001, 60002, or 65534. |
| list | List one or more group entries in the form of a three-column list containing the group name, group ID, and group members, separated by colons (:). |
| modify | Modify a group entry. |

## Options

The smgroup authentication arguments, *auth_args*, are derived from the smc(1M) argument set and are the same regardless of which subcommand you use.

Put the subcommand-specific options, *subcommand_args*, after the *auth_args* separated by the -- option.

### auth_args

The valid, optional *auth_args* are -D, -H, -l, -p, -r, and -u. If you specify no *auth_args*, certain defaults are assumed and you may be prompted for additional information, such as a password for authentication purposes. You can also specify these letter options by their equivalent option words preceded by a double dash. For example, you can use either -D or --domain with the *domain* argument.

-D | --domain *domain*

Specify the default domain that you want to manage. The syntax of *domain* is *type*:/*host_name*/*domain_name*, where *type* is nis, nisplus, dns, ldap, or file; *host_name* is the name of the system that serves the domain; and *domain_name* is the name of the domain you want to manage. (Note: Do not use nis+ for nisplus.)

If you do not specify this option, SMC assumes the `file` default domain on whatever server you choose to manage, which means that changes are local to the server. Toolboxes can change the domain on a tool-by-tool basis; this option specifies the domain for all other tools.

`-H | --hostname host_name:port`

Specify the `host_name` and `port` to which you want to connect. If you do not specify a port, the system connects to the default port, `898`. If you do not specify `host_name:port`, SMC connects to the local host on port 898. You may still need to choose a toolbox to load into the console. To override this behavior, use the smc(1M) `-B` option or set your console preferences to load a home toolbox by default. See "Specifying SMC Console Preferences" on page 20 for information on specifying console preferences.

`-l | --rolepassword role_password`

Specify the password for the `role_name`. If you specify a `role_name` but do not specify a `role_password`, the system prompts you to supply a `role_password`. Because passwords specified on the command line can be seen by any user on the system who runs the ps command, this option is considered insecure.

`-p | --password password`

Specify the password for the `user_name`. If you do not specify a password, the system prompts you for one. Because passwords specified on the command line can be seen by any user on the system, this option is considered insecure.

`-r | --rolename role_name`

Specify a role name for authentication. If you do not specify this option, assume no role.

`-u | --username user_name`

Specify the user name for authentication. If you do not specify this option, assume the user identity running the console process.

`--`

This required option must always follow the preceding options. If you do not enter the preceding options, you must still enter the `--` option.

## subcommand_args

Enclose descriptions and other argument options with white spaces in double quotes. Options for the add subcommand are listed below.

`-g gid`

(Optional) Specify the group ID for the new group. The group ID must be a non-negative decimal integer with a maximum value of 2 Mbytes (2,147,483,647). Group IDs 0–99 are reserved for the system and should be used with care. If you do not specify a `gid`, the system automatically assigns the next available `gid`. To maximize interoperability and compatibility, administrators are advised to assign groups using the range of GIDs below 60000 when possible.

-h            (Optional) Display the usage statement for the subcommand.

-m *group_member1* -m *group_member2* . . .

         (Optional) Specify the new members to add to the group.

-n *group_name*

         Specify the name of the new group. The group name must be unique within a domain, contain 2–32 alphanumeric characters, begin with a letter, and contain at least one lowercase letter.

Options for the `delete` subcommand are listed below.

-h            (Optional) Display the usage statement for the subcommand.

-n *group_name*

         Specify the name of the group you want to delete.

Options for the `list` subcommand are listed below.

-h            (Optional) Display the usage statement for the subcommand.

-n *group_name*

         (Optional) Specify the name of the group you want to list. If you do not specify a group name, list all groups.

Options for the `modify` subcommand are listed below.

-h            (Optional) Display the usage statement for the subcommand.

-m *group_member1* -m *group_member2* . . .

         (Optional) Specify the new members to add to the group.

-n *group_name*

         Specify the name of the group you want to modify.

-N *new_group*

         (Optional) Specify the new group name. The group name must be unique within a domain, contain 2–32 alphanumeric characters, begin with a letter, and contain at least one lowercase letter.

## Examples

The following example creates a `test_group` entry with a group ID of 123 and adds two members to the group.

```
mopoke# /usr/sadm/bin/smgroup add -H mopoke -p rootpasswd -u root -- -n
    test_group -m winsor -m ray -g 123
Loading Tool: com.sun.admin.usermgr.cli.group.UserMgrGroupCli from mopoke
Login to mopoke as user root was successful.
Download of com.sun.admin.usermgr.cli.group.UserMgrGroupCli from mopoke was
    successful.
mopoke#
```

The following example lists all of the groups in a three-column format with group name, group ID, and a comma-separated list of group members.

```
mopoke# /usr/sadm/bin/smgroup list -H mopoke -p rootpasswd -u root --
Loading Tool: com.sun.admin.usermgr.cli.group.UserMgrGroupCli from mopoke
Login to mopoke as user root was successful.
Download of com.sun.admin.usermgr.cli.group.UserMgrGroupCli from mopoke was
     successful.
root : 0 : root
other : 1 :
bin : 2 : root, bin, daemon
sys : 3 : root, bin, sys, adm
adm : 4 : root, adm, daemon
uucp : 5 : root, uucp
mail : 6 : root
tty : 7 : root, tty, adm
lp : 8 : root, lp, adm
nuucp : 9 : root, nuucp
staff : 10 : winsor
daemon : 12 : root, daemon
sysadmin : 14 :
nobody : 60001 :
noaccess : 60002 :
nogroup : 65534 :
test_group : 123 : winsor, ray
mopoke#
```

The following example deletes the test_group group.

```
mopoke# /usr/sadm/bin/smgroup delete -H mopoke -p rootpasswd -u root -- -n
     test_group
Loading Tool: com.sun.admin.usermgr.cli.group.UserMgrGroupCli from mopoke
Login to mopoke as user root was successful.
Download of com.sun.admin.usermgr.cli.group.UserMgrGroupCli from mopoke was
     successful.
mopoke#
```

The following example lists the contents of the staff group in a three-column format.

```
mopoke# /usr/sadm/bin/smgroup list -H mopoke -p rootpasswd -u root -- -n staff
Loading Tool: com.sun.admin.usermgr.cli.group.UserMgrGroupCli from mopoke
Login to mopoke as user root was successful.
Download of com.sun.admin.usermgr.cli.group.UserMgrGroupCli from mopoke was
     successful.
staff : 10 : winsor, ray, des, rob
mopoke#
```

The following example changes the name of the finance group to accounting.

```
mopoke# /usr/sadm/bin/smgroup modify -H mopoke -p rootpasswd -u root -- -n
     finance -N accounting
Loading Tool: com.sun.admin.usermgr.cli.group.UserMgrGroupCli from mopoke
Login to mopoke as user root was successful.
Download of com.sun.admin.usermgr.cli.group.UserMgrGroupCli from mopoke was
     successful.
mopoke#
```

## Environment Variables

See environ(5) for a description of the JAVA_HOME environment variable, which affects the execution of the smgroup command. If you do not specify this environment variable, the /usr/java location is used. See smc(1M).

## Exit Status

| | |
|---|---|
| 0 | Successful completion. |
| 1 | Invalid command syntax. A usage message is displayed. |
| 2 | An error occurred while the command was executing. An error message is displayed. |

## Files

/etc/group　　　Group file. See group(4).

## Attributes

See attributes(5) for descriptions of the following attributes.

| Attribute Type | Attribute Value |
|---|---|
| Availability | SUNWmga |

## See Also

smc(1M), group(4), attributes(5), environ(5)

# smmaillist

## Synopsis

/usr/sadm/bin/smmaillist *subcommand* [*auth_args*] -- [*subcommand_args*]

## Description

Use the smmaillist command to manage one or more e-mail alias entries for the appropriate files in the local /etc files or in an NIS or NIS+ nameservice.

### subcommands

The subcommands for smmaillist are listed below.

| | |
|---|---|
| add | Create a new e-mail alias definition and add it to the appropriate files. |
| delete | Delete an e-mail alias entry. You can delete only one entry at a time. Note: You cannot delete Postmaster or Mailer-Daemon aliases. |
| list | List one or more e-mail alias entries. |
| modify | Modify an e-mail alias entry. |

## Options

The smmaillist authentication arguments, *auth_args*, are derived from the smc(1M) argument set and are the same regardless of which subcommand you use.

Put the subcommand-specific options, *subcommand_args*, after the *auth_args* and separated by the -- option.

### auth_args

The valid, optional *auth_args* are -D, -H, -l, -p, -r, and -u. If you specify no *auth_args*, certain defaults are assumed and you may be prompted for additional information, such as a password for authentication purposes. You can also specify these letter options by their equivalent option words preceded by a double dash. For example, you can use either -D or --domain with the *domain* argument.

-D | --domain *domain*

> Specify the default domain that you want to manage. The syntax of domain is *type*:/*host_name*/*domain_name*, where *type* is nis, nisplus, dns, ldap, or file; *host_name* is the name of the system that serves the domain; and *domain_name* is the name of the domain you want to manage. (Note: Do not use nis+ for nisplus.)
>
> If you do not specify this option, SMC assumes the file default domain on whatever server you choose to manage, which means that changes are local to the server. Toolboxes can change the domain on a tool-by-tool basis; this option specifies the domain for all other tools.

-H | --hostname *host_name*:*port*

> Specify the *host_name* and *port* to which you want to connect. If you do not specify a port, the system connects to the default port, 898. If you do not specify *host_name*:*port*, SMC connects to the local host on port 898. You may still need to choose a toolbox to load into the console. To override this behavior, use the smc(1M) -B option or set your console preferences to load a home toolbox by default. See "Specifying SMC Console Preferences" on page 20 for information on specifying console preferences.

-l | --rolepassword *role_password*

> Specify the password for the *role_name*. If you specify a *role_name* but do not specify a *role_password*, the system prompts you to supply a *role_password*. Because passwords specified on the command line can be seen by any user on the system, this option is considered insecure.

-p | --password *password*

> Specify the password for the *user_name*. If you do not specify a password, the system prompts you for one. Because passwords specified on the command line can be seen by any user on the system, this option is considered insecure.

-r | --rolename *role_name*

> Specify a role name for authentication. If you do not specify this option, assume no role.

```
-u | --username user_name
```
        Specify the user name for authentication. If you do not specify this option, assume the user identity running the console process.

```
--
```
        This required option must always follow the preceding options. If you do not enter the preceding options, you must still enter the -- option.

### subcommand_args

Enclose descriptions and other argument options with white spaces in double quotes. Options for the add subcommand are listed below.

```
-a address1 -a address2 . . .
```
        (Optional) Specify the new e-mail address. See sendmail(1M).

```
-h
```
        (Optional) Display the usage statement for the subcommand.

```
-n alias_name
```
        Specify the name of the alias you want to add. See sendmail(1M).

Options for the delete subcommand are listed below.

```
-h
```
        (Optional) Display the usage statement for the subcommand.

```
-n alias_name
```
        Specify the alias you want to delete.

Options for the list subcommand are listed below.

```
-h
```
        (Optional) Display the usage statement for the subcommand.

```
-n alias_name
```
        (Optional) Specify the name of the alias you want to display. If you do not specify an alias, list all aliases.

Options for the modify subcommand are listed below.

```
-a address1 -a address2 . . .
```
        (Optional) Specify new e-mail address(es) to replace the existing one(s). See sendmail(1M).

```
-h
```
        (Optional) Display the usage statement for the subcommand.

```
-n alias_name
```
        (Optional) Specify the name of the alias you want to modify.

```
-N new_alias_name
```
        Specify the new alias name. Use only when renaming an alias. See sendmail(1M).

## Examples

The following example creates the coworkers alias and adds rob@castle, ray@paperbark, and maris@mr1

```
mopoke# /usr/sadm/bin/smmaillist add -H mopoke -p rootpasswd -u root -- -n
     coworkers -a rob@castle -a ray@paperbark -a maris@mr1
Loading Tool: com.sun.admin.usermgr.cli.mail.UserMgrMailCli from mopoke
Login to mopoke as user root was successful.
Download of com.sun.admin.usermgr.cli.mail.UserMgrMailCli from mopoke was
     successful.
mopoke#
```

The following example displays the list of members belonging to the coworkers alias.

```
mopoke# /usr/sadm/bin/smmaillist list -H mopoke -p rootpasswd -u root -- -n
     coworkers
Loading Tool: com.sun.admin.usermgr.cli.mail.UserMgrMailCli from mopoke
Login to mopoke as user root was successful.
Download of com.sun.admin.usermgr.cli.mail.UserMgrMailCli from mopoke was
     successful.
coworkers : rob@castle, ray@paperbark, maris@mr1

mopoke#
```

The following example displays members of all aliases.

```
mopoke# /usr/sadm/bin/smmaillist list -H mopoke -p rootpasswd -u root --
Loading Tool: com.sun.admin.usermgr.cli.mail.UserMgrMailCli from mopoke
Login to mopoke as user root was successful.
Download of com.sun.admin.usermgr.cli.mail.UserMgrMailCli from mopoke was
     successful.
Postmaster :  root

MAILER-DAEMON :  postmaster

nobody :  /dev/null

winsor : winsor@mopoke

project : winsor, ray, des, rob

coworkers : rob@castle, ray@paperbark, maris@mr1

mopoke#
```

The following example deletes the coworkers alias.

```
mopoke# /usr/sadm/bin/smmaillist delete -H mopoke -p rootpasswd -u root
     -- -n coworkers
Loading Tool: com.sun.admin.usermgr.cli.mail.UserMgrMailCli from mopoke
Login to mopoke as user root was successful.
Download of com.sun.admin.usermgr.cli.mail.UserMgrMailCli from mopoke was
     successful.
mopoke#
```

The following example changes the name of the project alias to coworkers.

```
mopoke# /usr/sadm/bin/smmaillist modify -H mopoke -p rootpasswd -u root -- -n
    project -N coworkers
Loading Tool: com.sun.admin.usermgr.cli.mail.UserMgrMailCli from mopoke
Login to mopoke as user root was successful.
Download of com.sun.admin.usermgr.cli.mail.UserMgrMailCli from mopoke was
    successful.
mopoke#
```

The following example changes the recipients of the coworkers alias to
winsor@mopoke. Any previous recipients are deleted from the alias.

```
mopoke# /usr/sadm/bin/smmaillist modify -H mopoke -p rootpasswd -u root -- -n
    coworkers -a winsor@mopoke
Loading Tool: com.sun.admin.usermgr.cli.mail.UserMgrMailCli from mopoke
Login to mopoke as user root was successful.
Download of com.sun.admin.usermgr.cli.mail.UserMgrMailCli from mopoke was
    successful.
mopoke#
```

## Environment Variables

See environ(5) for a description of the JAVA_HOME environment variable, which affects
the execution of the smmaillist command. If this environment variable is not specified,
the /usr/java location is used. See smc(1M).

## Exit Status

| | |
|---|---|
| 0 | Successful completion. |
| 1 | Invalid command syntax. A usage message is displayed. |
| 2 | An error occurred while the command was executing. An error message is displayed. |

## Files

/var/mail/aliases

Aliases for sendmail(1M). See aliases(4).

## Attributes

See attributes(5) for descriptions of the following attributes.

| Attribute Type | Attribute Value |
|---|---|
| Availability | SUNWmga |

## See Also

sendmail(1M), smc(1M), aliases(4), attributes(5), environ(5)

# smmultiuser

## Synopsis

/usr/sadm/bin/smmultiuser *subcommand* [*auth_args*] -- [*subcommand_args*]

## Description

Use the smmultiuser command to perform bulk operations on user entries in the local /etc file system or in an NIS or NIS+ nameservice with either an input file or piped input.

---

**Note** — Both input files and piped input contain a cleartext (nonencrypted) password for each new user entry. Be aware that information provided in this way is potentially insecure.

---

### subcommands

The smmultiuser subcommands are listed below.

add             Add multiple user entries to the appropriate files.

delete          Delete one or more user entries from the appropriate files.

modify          Modify existing user entries in the user account database. You can modify the following things with the modify subcommand.

      *UserName*      The modifications done based on lookups of the user name in the user tables. If a user name can not be found in this lookup, SMC performs a secondary check to see if the *uid* and *FullName* can be found in the user tables. If both are found, assume that a user rename has occurred. If neither is found, assume that the user account does not exist and cannot be modified.

      *Password*      If no password is supplied, assume that there is no change to the password information. If a password is being changed, it should be supplied in cleartext as piped input, although this is not required. The password can be supplied in the input file also. Once read in, the password is changed accordingly.

      *Description*

      *Primary Group ID*

      *Shell type*

      *FullName*

The /etc/passwd file format is used by both the add and modify subcommands. In addition, you can use a mutated version of this file format with an extra field at the end of each line to be used for the Full Name. If you append the extra field to the end of each line, it is used for the Full Name value; if you omit the extra field, it is assumed that no Full Name modification is being done. The extra field is separated with a colon (:), just as are all the other fields, as shown in the following examples.

The following example shows the regulation /etc/passwd entry.

```
ray:x:1002:10:description1:/home/ray:/bin/sh
```

The following example shows the variant /etc/passwd entry with an extra field at the end of the line.

```
ray:x:1002:10:description1:/home/rick2:/bin/sh:Ray Gun
```

## Options

The smmultiuser authentication arguments, *auth_args*, are derived from the smc(1M) argument set and are the same regardless of which subcommand you use.

Put the subcommand-specific options, *subcommand_args*, after the *auth_args* separated by the -- option.

### auth_args

The valid, optional *auth_args* are -D, -H, -l, -p, -r, --trust, and -u. If you specify no *auth_args*, certain defaults are assumed and you may be prompted for additional information, such as a password for authentication purposes. You can also specify letter options by their equivalent option words preceded by a double dash. For example, you can use either -D or --domain with the *domain* argument.

-D | --domain *domain*

Specify the default domain that you want to manage. The syntax of *domain* is *type:/host_name/domain_name*, where *type* is nis, nisplus, dns, ldap, or file; *host_name* is the name of the machine that serves the domain; and *domain_name* is the name of the domain you want to manage. (Note: Do not use nis+ for nisplus.)

If you do not specify this option, SMC assumes the file default domain on whatever server you choose to manage, which means that changes are local to the server. Toolboxes can change the domain on a tool-by-tool basis; this option specifies the domain for all other tools.

-H | --hostname *host_name:port*

Specify the *host_name* and *port* to which you want to connect. If you do not specify a port, the system connects to the default port, 898. If you do not specify *host_name:port*, SMC connects to the local host on port 898. You may still need to choose a toolbox to load into the console. To override this behavior, use the smc(1M) -B option or set your console preferences to load a home toolbox by default. See "Specifying SMC Console Preferences" on page 20 for information on specifying console preferences.

-l | --rolepassword *role_password*

Specify the password for the *role_name*. If you specify a *role_name* but do not specify a *role_password*, the system prompts you to supply a *role_password*. Because passwords specified on the command line can be seen by any user on the system who runs the ps command, this option is considered insecure.

-p | --password *password*

Specify the password for the *user_name*. If you do not specify a password, the system prompts you for one. Because passwords specified on the command line can be seen by any user on the system who runs the ps command, this option is considered insecure.

-r | --rolename *role_name*

Specify a role name for authentication. If you do not specify this option, assume no role.

--trust

Trust all downloaded code implicitly. Use this option when you are running the terminal console noninteractively and cannot let the console wait for user input.

When piping input into any of the smmultiuser subcommands, you now should use the --trust option with the -L *logfile* option.

-u | --username *user_name*

Specify the user name for authentication. If you do not specify this option, assume the user identity running the console process.

--

This required option must always follow the preceding options. If you do not enter the preceding options, you must still enter the -- option.

## subcommand_args

Enclose descriptions and other argument options with white spaces in double quotes. Options for the add subcommand are listed below.

-h

(Optional) Display the usage statement for the subcommand.

-i *input_file*

Specify the input file that contains the user account information. After the command is executed, SMC removes the input file. The input file must follow the /etc/passwd file format. If you do not specify the -i *input_file* option, you must include a *piped_input* operand immediately before the command.

-L *logfile*

(Optional) Specify the full path name to the text file that stores the success/failure data for the command. This text file is an ASCII-formatted log file; it is different from and unrelated to the output of the normal logging mechanism that also occurs within the Log Viewer tool. Use the -L *logfile* option to dump additional logging information into a text file.

Options for the `delete` subcommand are listed below.

-h                      (Optional) Display the usage statement for the subcommand.

-i *input_file*

Specify the input file that contains the user account information. After the command is executed, the `smmultiuser` command removes the input file. The input file must follow the `/etc/passwd` file format. If you do not specify the `-i` *input_file* option, you must include a *piped_input* operand immediately before the command.

-L *logfile*            (Optional) Specify the full path name to the text file that stores the success/failure data for the command.

Options for the `modify` subcommand are listed below.

-h                      (Optional) Display the usage statement for the subcommand.

-i *input_file*

Specify the input file that contains the user account information. After the command is executed, the `smmultiuser` command removes the input file. The input file must follow the `/etc/passwd` file format. If you do not specify the `-i` *input_file* option, you must include a *piped_input* operand immediately before the command. When modifying passwords, use the piped input because it is more secure than keeping passwords in a file.

-L *logfile*            (Optional) Specify the full path name to the text file that stores the success/failure data for the subcommand.

## Operands

piped_input    If you do not specify an *input_file*, you must include *piped_input*. Include the piped input immediately before the command. The piped input must follow the `/etc/passwd` file format. Note that you should use the `--trust` option for piped input with the `-L` *logfile* option to avoid the user prompt from the Security Alert Manager, which normally asks the user whether to create the log file. Without the `--trust` option, the piped input is improperly taken as the answer to the prompt before the user can answer `Y` or `N` and the logging operation probably fails.

## Examples

The following examples read user account data from a file named `/tmp/newusers` that contains the following data formatted in `/etc/password` format.

```
mopoke% more /tmp/newusers
ray:x:1002:10:Ray Gun:/home/ray:/bin/csh
des:x:1003:10:Desmond Tornado:/home/des:/bin/csh
rob:x:1004:10:Rob Roy:/home/rob:/bin/csh
mopoke%
```

> **Note** — If you want to maintain a record of the contents of the input file, make a copy with a different name, say, newusers1. The smmultiuser command automatically removes the input file after it has read the file contents.

The following example reads in user account data from the /tmp/newusers file and creates new user accounts on the local file system.

```
mopoke# /usr/sadm/bin/smmultiuser add -H mopoke -p rootpasswd -u root -- -i
    /tmp/newusers
Loading Tool: com.sun.admin.usermgr.cli.user.UserMgrCli from mopoke
Login to mopoke as user root was successful.
Download of com.sun.admin.usermgr.cli.user.UserMgrCli from mopoke was
    successful.

[ Security Manager Alert ]
A Tool loaded from mopoke:898 wishes to read from the file located at
    /tmp/newusers.
Do you wish to allow this action? [Y | n] : y

Do you wish to trust all actions by tools from this location? [Y | n] : y
mopoke#
```

If you want to eliminate the Security Manager prompts, use the --trust option as shown in the following example.

```
mopoke# /usr/sadm/bin/smmultiuser add --trust -H mopoke -p rootpasswd -u root
    -- -i /tmp/newusers
Loading Tool: com.sun.admin.usermgr.cli.user.UserMgrCli from mopoke
Login to mopoke as user root was successful.
Download of com.sun.admin.usermgr.cli.user.UserMgrCli from mopoke was
    successful.
mopoke#
```

The following example deletes from the local file system the user accounts it reads in from the /tmp/newusers input file.

```
mopoke# /usr/sadm/bin/smmultiuser delete -H mopoke -p rootpasswd -u root -- -i
    /tmp/newusers
Loading Tool: com.sun.admin.usermgr.cli.user.UserMgrCli from mopoke
Login to mopoke as user root was successful.
Download of com.sun.admin.usermgr.cli.user.UserMgrCli from mopoke was
    successful.

[ Security Manager Alert ]
A Tool loaded from mopoke:898 wishes to read from the file located at
    /tmp/newusers.
Do you wish to allow this action? [Y | n] : y

Do you wish to trust all actions by tools from this location? [Y | n] : y
mopoke#
```

The following example creates a log file, using the required --trust option.

```
mopoke# cat /tmp/users.txt | /usr/sadm/bin/smmultiuser add --trust -H mopoke
    -p rootpasswd -u root -- -L /tmp/mylog.txt
Loading Tool: com.sun.admin.usermgr.cli.user.UserMgrCli from mopoke
Login to mopoke as user root was successful.
```

## Environment Variables

See environ(5) for a description of the JAVA_HOME environment variable, which affects the execution of the smmultiuser command. If you do not specify this environment variable, the /usr/java location is used. See smc(1M).

## Exit Status

| | |
|---|---|
| 0 | Successful completion. |
| 1 | Invalid command syntax. A usage message is displayed. |
| 2 | An error occurred while the command was executing. An error message is displayed. |

## Files

| | |
|---|---|
| /etc/passwd | Contains the file format to use for the *input_file* and *piped_input*. See passwd(4). |

## Attributes

See attributes(5) for descriptions of the following attributes.

| Attribute Type | Attribute Value |
|---|---|
| Availability | SUNWmga |

## See Also

smc(1M), passwd(4), attributes(5), environ(5)

# smosservice

## Synopsis

/usr/sadm/bin/smosservice *subcommand* [*auth_args*] -- [*subcommand_args*]

## Description

Use the smosservice command together with the smdiskless command to manage diskless clients from the command line.

The smosservice subcommands are listed below.

| | |
|---|---|
| add | Add the specified OS services. |
| delete | Delete the specified OS services. |

list
: Either list all the installed OS services for the server if you do not specify a host name, or list the OS services for the specified diskless client if you do specify a host name.

patch
: Manage patches on all existing diskless clients. For example, you can use this subcommand to initially establish a patch spool directory on an OS server. Then, you can apply the patch to the spool area, verifying the patch as needed. Once the patch exists in the spool area, you can apply the patch to the clone area. In addition, you can migrate the patched clone area to clients.

## Options

The smosservice authentication arguments, *auth_args*, are derived from the smc(1M) argument set and are the same regardless of which subcommand you use.

Put the subcommand-specific options, *subcommand_args*, after the *auth_args* separated by the -- option.

### auth_args

The valid, optional *auth_args* are -D, -H, -l, -p, -r, and -u. If you specify no *auth_args*, certain defaults are assumed and you may be prompted for additional information, such as a password for authentication purposes. You can also specify these letter options by their equivalent option words preceded by a double dash. For example, you can use either -D or --domain with the *domain* argument.

-D | --domain *domain*

Specify the default domain that you want to manage. The syntax of *domain* is *type:/host_name/domain_name*, where type is nis, nisplus, dns, ldap, or file; *host_name* is the name of the machine that serves the domain; and *domain_name* is the name of the domain you want to manage. (Note: Do not use nis+ for nisplus.)

If you do not specify this option, SMC assumes the file default domain on whatever server you choose to manage, which means that changes are local to the server. Toolboxes can change the domain on a tool-by-tool basis; this option specifies the domain for all other tools.

-H | --hostname *host_name:port*

Specify the *host_name* and *port* to which you want to connect. If you do not specify a port, the system connects to the default port, 898. If you do not specify *host_name:port*, SMC connects to the local host on port 898. You may still need to choose a toolbox to load into the console. To override this behavior, use the smc(1M) -B option or set your console preferences to load a home toolbox by default. See "Specifying SMC Console Preferences" on page 20 for information on specifying console preferences.

-l | --rolepassword *role_password*

Specify the password for the *role_name*. If you specify a *role_name* but do not specify a *role_password*, the system prompts you to supply a *role_password*. Because passwords specified on the command line can be seen by any user on the system who runs the ps command, this option is considered insecure.

-p | --password *password*

Specify the password for the *user_name*. If you do not specify a password, the system prompts you for one. Because passwords specified on the command line can be seen by any user on the system who runs the ps command, this option is considered insecure.

-r | --rolename *role_name*

Specify a role name for authentication. If you do not specify this option, assume no role.

-u | --username *user_name*

Specify the user name for authentication. If you do not specify this option, assume the user identity running the console process.

--

This required option must always follow the preceding options. If you do not enter the preceding options, you must still enter the -- option.

## subcommand_args

Enclose descriptions and other argument options with white spaces in double quotes. Options for the add subcommand are listed below.

-h

(Optional) Display the usage statement for the subcommand.

-o *host_os*

(Optional) Specify the name of the host where the OS service file systems reside. If you do not specify this option, the host is the same as that specified in the smc(1M) -D option. This option is useful when the nameservice server and the OS server are not the same.

-x cluster=*cluster*

Specify the Solaris cluster to install. For example, SUNWCall.

-x locale=*locale*[*locale*, . . .]

(Optional) Specify the locales to install from the specified cluster. You can specify a comma-delimited list of locales.

-x mediapath=*path*

Specify the full path to the Solaris CD image.

-x platform=*platform*

Specify the OS service to add. The instruction architecture, machine class, OS, and version are given in the following form.

*instruction_set.machine_class.Solaris_os_version*, for example, sparc.sun4m.Solaris_8.

Options for the `delete` subcommand are listed below.

| | |
|---|---|
| -h | (Optional) Display the usage statement for the subcommand. |
| -o *host_os* | (Optional) Specify the name of the host where the OS service file systems reside. If you do not specify this option, the host is the same as that specified in the smc(1M) -D option. This option is useful when the nameservice server and the OS server are not the same. |

-x *rmplatform=platform*

> Specify the OS service to remove. The instruction architecture, machine class, OS, and version are given in the following form.
>
> *instruction_set.machine_class.Solaris_os_version*
>
> For example, sparc.all.Solaris_8.
> Note: Only a machine class of all is supported.

Options for the `list` subcommand are listed below.

| | |
|---|---|
| -h | (Optional) Display the usage statement for the subcommand. |
| -o *host_os* | (Optional) Specify the name of the host where the OS service file systems reside. If you do not specify this option, the host is the same as that specified in the smc(1M) -D option. This option is useful when the nameservice server and the OS server are not the same. |

Options for the `patch` subcommand are listed below.

-a *patch_directory/patch_ID*

> Add the specified patch, *patch_ID*, to the spool directory. *patch_directory* specifies the source path of the patch to be spooled; the source path includes the patch ID directory name. Patches are spooled to /export/diskless/Patches/. If the patch being added obsoletes an existing patch in the spool, smosservice moves the obsolete patch to the archive area, /export/diskless/Patches/Archive (to be restored if this new patch is ever removed).

| | |
|---|---|
| -h | (Optional) Display the usage statement for the subcommand. |
| -m | (Optional) Synchronize spooled patches with offline copies of each diskless client OS service on the server. Compare spooled patches and applied patches so that newly spooled patches can be installed and patches recently removed from the spool can be backed out. This option does not apply patches directly to diskless client OS services or diskless clients; you must use the -u option to update the services and clients with the changes. Clients are not required to be down at this time, because all patching is done offline. Note: The server is fully available during this operation. |
| -P | List all currently spooled patches with an associated synopsis. The list is split up into sections detailing the patches for each OS and architecture in the following format. |

```
Solaris os_rel1 architecture1:
patchid Synopsis
patchid Synopsis
...
Solaris os_rel1 architecture2:
patchid Synopsis
...
patchid Synopsis
...
```

-r *patchid*

Remove the specified *patchid* from the spool if it is not a requirement for any of the other patches in the spool. Restore to the spool all archived patches that were obsoleted by the removed patch.

-U

(Optional) Update all diskless client OS services and diskless clients with any changes after synchronizing patches with the –m option. You must bring down clients during this operation. Once execution has completed, boot each client again.

## Examples

The following command adds an OS service for Solaris 8 for the sun4u machine class where the OS server is not using a nameservice.

```
example% /usr/sadm/bin/smosservice add -- -x
     mediapath=/net/imageserver/5.8/sparc -x platform=sparc.sun4u.Solaris_8
     -x cluster=SUNWCXall -x locale=en_US
```

The following command adds an OS service for Solaris 8 for the sun4u machine class where the OS server is using NIS and the NIS server is nisserver.

```
example% /usr/sadm/bin/smosservice add -D nis:/nisserver/my.domain.com -- -x
     mediapath=/net/imageserver/5.8/sparc -x platform=sparc.sun4u.Solaris_8
     -x cluster=SUNWCXall -x locale=en_US
```

The following command deletes the OS service for Solaris 8 for the sun4u machine class where the OS server is using NIS and the NIS server is nisserver.

```
example% /usr/sadm/bin/smosservice delete -D nis:/nisserver/my.domain.com --
     -x rmplatform=sparc.all.Solaris_8
```

The following command lists the OS services installed on the machine, osserver.

```
example% /usr/sadm/bin/smosservice list -D file:/osserver/osserver -- -o
     osserver
```

## Environment Variables

See environ(5) for a description of the JAVA_HOME environment variable, which affects the execution of the smosservice command. If you do not set this environment variable, the /usr/java location is used. See smc(1M).

## Exit Status

| | |
|---|---|
| 0 | Successful completion. |
| 1 | Invalid command syntax. A usage message is displayed. |
| 2 | An error occurred while the command was executing. An error message is displayed. |

## Attributes

See attributes(5) for descriptions of the following attributes.

| Attribute Type | Attribute Value |
|---|---|
| Availability | SUNWdclnt |

## See Also

smc(1M), smdiskless(1M), attributes(5), environ(5)

# smprofile

## Synopsis

/usr/sadm/bin/smprofile subcommand [auth_args] -- [subcommand_args]

## Description

Use the smprofile command to manage one or more profiles in the prof_attr(4) or exec_attr(4) databases in the local /etc files nameservice or in an NIS or NIS+ nameservice.

### subcommands

The smprofile subcommands are listed below.

| | |
|---|---|
| add | Add a new profile (right) to the prof_attr(4) database. |
| delete | Delete a profile from the prof_attr(4) database, delete all associated entries from the exec_attr(4) database, and delete the assigned profile from the user_attr(4) database. |
| list | List one or more profiles from the prof_attr(4) or exec_attr(4) databases. |
| modify | Modify a profile in the prof_attr(4) database. |

## Options

The smprofile authentication arguments, *auth_args*, are derived from the smc(1M) argument set and are the same regardless of which subcommand you use.

Put the subcommand-specific options, *subcommand_args*, after the *auth_args* separated by the -- option.

### auth_args

The valid, optional *auth_args* are -D, -H, -1, -p, -r, and -u. If you specify no *auth_args*, certain defaults are assumed and you may be prompted for additional information, such as a password for authentication purposes. You can also specify these letter options by their equivalent option words preceded by a double dash. For example, you can use either -D or --domain with the *domain* argument.

-D | --domain *domain*

Specify the default domain that you want to manage. The syntax of domain is *type:/host_name/domain_name*, where type is nis, nisplus, dns, ldap, or file; *host_name* is the name of the machine that serves the domain; and *domain_name* is the name of the domain you want to manage. (Note: Do not use nis+ for nisplus.)

If you do not specify this option, SMC assumes the file default domain on whatever server you choose to manage, which means that changes are local to the server. Toolboxes can change the domain on a tool-by-tool basis; this option specifies the domain for all other tools.

-H | --hostname *host_name:port*

Specify the *host_name* and port to which you want to connect. If you do not specify a port, the system connects to the default port, 898. If you do not specify *host_name:port*, SMC connects to the local host on port 898. You may still need to choose a toolbox to load into the console. To override this behavior, use the smc(1M) -B option or set your console preferences to load a home toolbox by default. See "Specifying SMC Console Preferences" on page 20 for information on specifying console preferences.

-1 | --rolepassword *role_password*

Specify the password for the *role_name*. If you specify a *role_name* but do not specify a *role_password*, the system prompts you to supply a *role_password*. Because passwords specified on the command line can be seen by any user on the system, this option is considered insecure.

-p | --password *password*

Specify the password for the *user_name*. If you do not specify a password, the system prompts you for one. Because passwords specified on the command line can be seen by any user on the system, this option is considered insecure.

-r | --rolename *role_name*

Specify a role name for authentication. If you do not specify this option, assume no role.

-u | --username *user_name*

> Specify the user name for authentication. If you do not specify this option, assume the user identity running the console process.

--

> This option is required and must always follow the preceding options. If you do not enter the preceding options, you must still enter the -- option.

## subcommand_args

Enclose descriptions and other argument options with white spaces in double quotes. Options for the add subcommand are listed below.

-a *addauth1* -a *addauth2* . . .

> (Optional) Specify the authorization name(s) to add to the new profile.

-d *description*

> Specify the description of the new profile.

-h

> (Optional) Display the usage statement for the subcommand.

-m *html_help*

> Specify the HTML help file name for the new profile. The help file name must be put in the /usr/lib/help/profiles/locale/C directory.

-n *name*   Specify the name of the new profile.

-p *addprof1* -p *addprof2* . . .

> (Optional) Specify the supplementary profile name(s) to add to the new profile.

Options for the delete subcommand are listed below.

-h

> (Optional) Display the usage statement for the subcommand.

-n *name*   Specify the name of the profile you want to delete.

Options for the list subcommand are listed below.

-h

> (Optional) Display the usage statement for the command.

-l

> (Optional) Display the detailed output for each profile in a block of key:value pairs, followed by a blank line that delimits each profile block. Each key:value pair is displayed on a separate line. All the attributes associated with a profile from the prof_attr and exec_attr databases are displayed. If you do not specify this option, display only the specified profile name(s) and associated profile description(s).

-n *name1* -n *name2* . . .

> (Optional) Specify the profile(s) that you want to display. If you do not specify a profile name, display all profiles.

Options for the `modify` subcommand are listed below.

-a *addauth1* -a *addauth2* . . .
　　　　　　(Optional) Specify the authorization name(s) to add to the profile.

-d *description*
　　　　　　(Optional) Specify the new description of the profile.

-h　　　　　(Optional) Display the usage statement for the subcommand.

-m *html_help*　(Optional) Specify the new HTML help file name of the profile. If you change this name, you must accordingly rename the help file name entered in the `/usr/lib/help/profiles/locale/C` directory.

-n *name*　　Specify the name of the profile you want to modify.

-p *addprof1* -p *addprof2* . . .
　　　　　　(Optional) Specify the supplementary profile name(s) to add to the profile.

-q *delprof1* -q *delprof2* . . .
　　　　　　(Optional) Specify the supplementary profile name(s) to delete from the profile.

-r *delauth1* -r *delauth2* . . .
　　　　　　(Optional) Specify the authorization name(s) to delete from the profile.

## Examples

The following example creates a new `User Manager` profile on the local file system. The new profile description is `Manage users and groups`, and the authorizations assigned are `solaris.admin.usermgr.write` and `solaris.admin.usermgr.read`. The supplementary profile assigned is `Operator`. The help file name is `RtUserMgmt.html`.

```
mopoke# /usr/sadm/bin/smprofile add -H mopoke -p rootpasswd -u root -- -n
    "User Manager" -d "Manage users and groups" -a
    solaris.admin.usermgr.write -a solaris.admin.usermgr.read -p Operator -m
    RtUserMgmt.html
Loading Tool: com.sun.admin.usermgr.cli.profile.UserMgrProfCli from mopoke
Login to mopoke as user root was successful.
Download of com.sun.admin.usermgr.cli.profile.UserMgrProfCli from mopoke was
    successful.
mopoke#
```

The following example lists all profiles on the local file system and their associated profile descriptions.

```
mopoke# /usr/sadm/bin/smprofile list -H mopoke -p rootpasswd -u root --
Loading Tool: com.sun.admin.usermgr.cli.profile.UserMgrProfCli from mopoke
Login to mopoke as user root was successful.
Download of com.sun.admin.usermgr.cli.profile.UserMgrProfCli from mopoke was
    successful.
Profile name: Primary Administrator   Description: Can perform all
    administrative tasks
Profile name: System Administrator   Description: Can perform most
    non-security administrative tasks
```

```
Profile name: Operator    Description: Can perform simple administrative tasks
Profile name: Audit Control    Description: Configure BSM auditing
Profile name: Basic Solaris User    Description: Automatically assigned rights
Profile name: Device Management    Description: Control Access to Removable
    Media
Profile name: Device Security    Description: Manage devices and Volume Manager
Profile name: File System Management    Description: Manage, mount, share file
    systems
Profile name: File System Security    Description: Manage file system security
    attributes
Profile name: Maintenance and Repair    Description: Maintain and repair a
    system
Profile name: Process Management    Description: Manage current processes and
    processors
Profile name: User Management    Description: Manage users, groups, home
    directory
Profile name: User Security    Description: Manage passwords, clearances
Profile name: Printer Management    Description: Manage printers, daemons,
    spooling
Profile name: Software Installation    Description: Add application software to
    the system
Profile name: Network Management    Description: Manage the host and network
    configuration
Profile name: Media Restore    Description: Restore files and file systems from
    backups
Profile name: Name Service Security    Description: Security related name
    service scripts/commands
Profile name: Media Backup    Description: Backup files and file systems
Profile name: Mail Management    Description: Manage sendmail & queues
Profile name: Audit Review    Description: Review BSM auditing logs
Profile name: Network Security    Description: Manage network and host security
Profile name: Cron Management    Description: Manage at and cron jobs
Profile name: Name Service Management    Description: Non-security name service
    scripts/commands
Profile name: Object Access Management    Description: Change ownership and
    permission on files
Profile name: DHCP Management    Description: Manage the DHCP service
Profile name: Rights Delegation    Description: Delegate ability to assign
    rights to users and roles
Profile name: All    Description: Execute any command as the user or role
Profile name: User Manager    Description: Manage users and groups
mopoke#
```

The following example modifies the description of the User Manager profile on the local system. It also assigns the new authorization assignment solaris.admin.usermgr.* and the new supplementary profile assignment All. You must enclose the argument to the -a option in double quotes because the wildcard character (*) is used.

```
mopoke# /usr/sadm/bin/smprofile modify -H mopoke -p rootpasswd -u root -- -n
    "User Manager" -d "Manage world" -a "solaris.admin.usermgr.*" -p All
Loading Tool: com.sun.admin.usermgr.cli.profile.UserMgrProfCli from mopoke
Login to mopoke as user root was successful.
Download of com.sun.admin.usermgr.cli.profile.UserMgrProfCli from mopoke was
    successful.
mopoke#
```

The following example deletes the User Manager profile from the local system.

```
# /usr/sadm/bin/smprofile delete -H mopoke -p rootpasswd -u root -- -n "User
    Manager"
Loading Tool: com.sun.admin.usermgr.cli.profile.UserMgrProfCli from mopoke
Login to mopoke as user root was successful.
Download of com.sun.admin.usermgr.cli.profile.UserMgrProfCli from mopoke was
    successful.
#
```

## Environment Variables

See environ(5) for a description of the JAVA_HOME environment variable, which affects the execution of the smprofile command. If you do not specify this environment variable, the /usr/java location is used. See smc(1M).

## Exit Status

| | |
|---|---|
| 0 | Successful completion. |
| 1 | Invalid command syntax. A usage message is displayed. |
| 2 | An error occurred while the command was executing. An error message is displayed. |

## Files

/etc/security/exec_attr

Execution profiles database. See exec_attr(4).

/etc/security/prof_attr

Profile description database. See prof_attr(4).

/etc/user_attr

Extended user attribute database. See user_attr(4).

## Attributes

See attributes(5) for descriptions of the following attributes.

| Attribute Type | Attribute Value |
|---|---|
| Availability | SUNWmga |

## See Also

smc(1M), exec_attr(4), prof_attr(4), user_attr(4), attributes(5), environ(5)

# smrole

## Synopsis

/usr/sadm/bin/smrole *subcommand* [*auth_args*] -- [*subcommand_args*]

## Description

Use the smrole command to manage roles and add or delete users in role accounts.

### subcommands

The smrole subcommands are listed below.

add         Add a new role entry.

| | |
|---|---|
| delete | Delete one or more roles. |
| list | List one or more roles. If you do not specify a role name, list all roles. |
| modify | Add or delete users from a role account. |

## Options

The smrole authentication arguments, *auth_args*, are derived from the smc(1M) argument set and are the same regardless of which subcommand you use.

Put the subcommand-specific options, *subcommand_args*, after the *auth_args* separated by the -- option.

### auth_args

The valid, optional *auth_args* are -D, -H, -l, -p, -r, and -u. If you specify no *auth_args*, certain defaults are assumed and you may be prompted for additional information, such as a password for authentication purposes. You can also specify these letter options by their equivalent option words preceded by a double dash. For example, you can use either -D or --domain with the *domain* argument.

-D | --domain *domain*

> Specify the default domain that you want to manage. The syntax of domain is *type*:/*host_name*/*domain_name*, where type is nis, nisplus, dns, ldap, or file; *host_name* is the name of the machine that serves the domain; and *domain_name* is the name of the domain you want to manage. (Note: Do not use nis+ for nisplus.)
>
> If you do not specify this option, SMC assumes the file default domain on whatever server you choose to manage, which means that changes are local to the server. Toolboxes can change the domain on a tool-by-tool basis; this option specifies the domain for all other tools.

-H | --hostname *host_name:port*

> Specify the *host_name* and *port* to which you want to connect. If you do not specify a port, the system connects to the default port, 898. If you do not specify *host_name:port*, SMC connects to the local host on port 898. You may still need to choose a toolbox to load into the console. To override this behavior, use the smc(1M) -B option or set your console preferences to load a home toolbox by default. See "Specifying SMC Console Preferences" on page 20 for information on specifying console preferences.

-l | --rolepassword *role_password*

> Specify the password for the *role_name*. If you specify a *role_name* but do not specify a *role_password*, the system prompts you to supply a *role_password*. Because passwords specified on the command line can be seen by any user on the system who runs the ps command, this option is considered insecure.

-p | --password *password*

> Specify the password for the *user_name*. If you do not specify a
> password, the system prompts you for one. Because passwords
> specified on the command line can be seen by any user on the system
> who runs the ps command, this option is considered insecure.

-r | --rolename *role_name*

> Specify a role name for authentication. If you do not specify this
> option, assume no role.

-u | --username *user_name*

> Specify the user name for authentication. If you do not specify this
> option, assume the user identity running the console process.

--

> This required option must always follow the preceding options. If you
> do not enter the preceding options, you must still enter the -- option.

## subcommand_args

Enclose descriptions and other argument options with white spaces in double quotes.
Options for the add subcommand are listed below.

-a *adduser1* -a *adduser2* . . .

> (Optional) Specify the user name(s) to add to the new role.

-c *comment*     (Optional) Include a short description of the role. The comment
> consists of a string of up to 256 printable characters, excluding the
> colon ( : ).

-d *dir*     (Optional) Specify the home directory of the new role, limited to 1024
> characters.

-F *full_name* (Optional) Specify the full, descriptive name of the role. The
> *full_name* must be unique within a domain and can contain
> alphanumeric characters and spaces. If you use spaces, you must
> enclose the *full_name* in double quotes.

-G *group1* -G *group2* . . .

> (Optional) Specify the supplementary group membership for the new
> role in the system group database with the character string names of
> one or more existing groups. Note: You cannot assign a primary group
> to a role. A role's primary group is always sysadmin (group 14).

-h     (Optional) Display the usage statement for the subcommand.

-n *rolename*     Specify the name of the role you want to create.

-p *addprof1* -p *addprof2* . . .

> (Optional) Specify the profile(s) to add to the role.

-P *password*   (Optional) Specify the role password. The password can contain up to eight characters. If you do not specify a password, the system prompts you for one. Note: When you specify a password with the -P option, you type the password in plain text. Specifying a password with this method introduces a security gap while the command is running. However, if you do not specify a password (and the system prompts you for one), echo is turned off when you type in the password.

-s *shell*      (Optional) Specify the full path name of the program used as the role shell on login. Valid entries are /bin/pfcsh (C shell), /bin/pfksh (Korn shell), and /bin/pfsh (Bourne shell), the default.

-u *uid*        (Optional) Specify the ID of the role you want to add. If you do not specify this option, the system assigns the next available unique ID of 100 or greater.

-x autohome=Y|N

                (Optional) Set the role home directory. The home directory path in the password entry is set to /home/*login_name*.

-x perm=*home_perm*

                (Optional) Set the permissions on the role home directory. perm is interpreted as an octal number, and the default is 0775.

-x serv=*homedir_server*

                (Optional) If -D is nis, nisplus, or ldap, use this option to specify the name of the server where the user's home directory resides. Users created in a local scope must have their home directory server created on their local machines.

Options for the delete subcommand are listed below.

-h              (Optional) Display the usage statement for the subcommand.

-n *rolename1* -n *rolename2* . . .

                Specify the name of the role(s) you want to delete.

Options for the list subcommand are listed below.

-h              (Optional) Display the usage statement for the subcommand.

-l              (Optional) Display the output for each user in a block of key:value pairs (for example, user name:root), followed by a blank line that delimits each user block. Each key:value pair is displayed on a separate line. The keys are autohome setup, comment, home directory, login shell, primary group, secondary groups, server, user ID (UID), and user name.

-n *role1* -n *role2* . . .

                (Optional) Specify the role(s) that you want to list. If you do not specify a role name, list all roles.

Options for the `modify` subcommand are listed below.

`-a` *adduser1* `-a` *adduser2* . . .
> (Optional) Specify the user name(s) to add to the role.

`-c` *comment*   (Optional) Include a short description of the role. The comment can be a string of up to 256 printable characters, excluding the colon ( : ).

`-d` *dir*   (Optional) Specify the home directory of the new role, limited to 1024 characters.

`-F` *full_name*
> (Optional) Specify the full, descriptive name of the role. The *full_name* must be unique within a domain and can contain alphanumeric characters and spaces. If you use spaces, enclose the *full_name* in double quotes.

`-G` *group1* `-G` *group2* . . .
> (Optional) Specify the new role's secondary group membership in the system group database with the character string names of one or more existing groups. Note: You cannot assign a primary group to a role. A role's primary group is always `sysadmin` (group 14).

`-h`   (Optional) Display the usage statement for the subcommand.

`-n` *rolename*   Specify the name of the role you want to modify.

`-N` *new_rolename*
> (Optional) Specify the new name of the role.

`-p` *addprof1* `-p` *addprof2* . . .
> (Optional) Specify the profile(s) to add to the role.

`-P` *password*   (Optional) Specify the role password. The password can contain up to eight characters. Note: When you specify a password, you type the password in plain text. Specifying a password with this method introduces a security gap while the command is running.

`-q` *delprof1* `-q` *delprof2* . . .
> (Optional) Specify the profile(s) to delete from the role.

`-r` *deluser1* `-r` *deluser2* . . .
> (Optional) Specify the user name(s) to delete from the role.

`-s` *shell*   (Optional) Specify the full path name of the program used as the role shell on login. Valid entries are `/bin/pfcsh` (C shell), `/bin/pfksh` (Korn shell), and `/bin/pfsh` (Bourne shell), the default.

`-x` autohome=Y|N
> (Optional) Set the role home directory. The home directory path in the password entry is set to `/home/`*login_name*.

`-x` perm=*home_perm*
> (Optional) Set the permissions on the role home directory. `perm` is interpreted as an octal number, and the default is 0775.

## Examples

The following example creates the `security` role with a full name of `Security and Audit` and a `password` of `abc123` on the local file system and assigns user accounts `winsor` and `ray` to the role. This role has `Name Service Security` and `Audit Review` rights. The system assigns the next available unique UID of 100 or greater.

```
mopoke# /usr/sadm/bin/smrole add -H mopoke -p rootpasswd -u root -- -n
       security -F "Security and Audit" -P abc123 -a winsor -a ray -p "Name
       Service Security" -p "Audit Review"
Loading Tool: com.sun.admin.usermgr.cli.role.UserMgrRoleCli from mopoke
Login to mopoke as user root was successful.
Download of com.sun.admin.usermgr.cli.role.UserMgrRoleCli from mopoke was
       successful.
mopoke#
```

The following example lists all roles on the local system in summary form, which shows the role name and the role UID.

```
mopoke# /usr/sadm/bin/smrole list -H mopoke -p rootpasswd -u root --
Loading Tool: com.sun.admin.usermgr.cli.role.UserMgrRoleCli from mopoke
Login to mopoke as user root was successful.
Download of com.sun.admin.usermgr.cli.role.UserMgrRoleCli from mopoke was
       successful.
security                100
mopoke#
```

The following example modifies the `security` role account to use the Korn shell, add the `des` user account, and remove the `ray` user account.

```
mopoke# /usr/sadm/bin/smrole modify -H mopoke -p rootpasswd -u root -- -n
       security -s /bin/pfksh -a des -r ray
Loading Tool: com.sun.admin.usermgr.cli.role.UserMgrRoleCli from mopoke
Login to mopoke as user root was successful.
Download of com.sun.admin.usermgr.cli.role.UserMgrRoleCli from mopoke was
       successful.
mopoke#
```

The following example deletes the security role account from the local system.

```
mopoke# /usr/sadm/bin/smrole delete -H mopoke -p rootpasswd -u root -- -n
       security
Loading Tool: com.sun.admin.usermgr.cli.role.UserMgrRoleCli from mopoke
Login to mopoke as user root was successful.
Download of com.sun.admin.usermgr.cli.role.UserMgrRoleCli from mopoke was
       successful.
mopoke#
```

## Environment Variables

See environ(5) for a description of the JAVA_HOME environment variable, which affects the execution of the smrole command. If you do not specify this environment variable, the /usr/java location is used. See smc(1M).

## Exit Status

| | |
|---|---|
| 0 | Successful completion. |
| 1 | Invalid command syntax. A usage message is displayed. |
| 2 | An error occurred while the command was executing. An error message is displayed. |

## Files

`/etc/aliases`    Mail aliases. See `aliases`(4).

`/etc/auto_home`

Automatic mount points. See `automount`(1M).

`/etc/group`    Group file. See `group`(4).

`/etc/passwd`    Password file. See `passwd`(4).

`/etc/security/policy.conf`

Configuration file for security policy. See `policy.conf`(4).

`/etc/shadow`    Shadow password file. See `shadow`(4).

`/etc/user_attr`

Extended user attribute database. See `user_attr`(4).

## Attributes

See `attributes`(5) for descriptions of the following attributes.

| **Attribute Type** | **Attribute Value** |
|---|---|
| Availability | SUNWmga |

## See Also

`automount(1M)`, `smc(1M)`, `aliases(4)`, `group(4)`, `passwd(4)`, `policy.conf(4)`, `shadow(4)`, `user_attr(4)`, `attributes(5)`, `environ(5)`

# smuser

## Synopsis

`/usr/sadm/bin/smuser` *subcommand* [*auth_args*] `--` [*subcommand_args*]

## Description

Use the `smuser` command to manage one or more user entries in the local `/etc` file system or in an NIS or NIS+ target nameservice.

### subcommands

The smuser subcommands are listed below.

add            Add a new user entry to the appropriate files. You can use a template and input file instead of supplying the additional command-line options. If you use a template and command-line options, the command-line options take precedence and override any conflicting template values. To add an entry, the administrator must have the solaris.admin.usermgr.write authorization.

delete       Delete one or more user entries from the appropriate files. To delete an entry, the administrator must have the solaris.admin.usermgr.write authorization. Note: You cannot delete the system accounts 60001, 60002, 65534, or accounts with IDs lower than 100.

list           List one or more user entries from the appropriate files. To list entries, the administrator must have the solaris.admin.usermgr.read authorization.

modify      Modify a user entry in the appropriate files. To modify an entry, the administrator must have the solaris.admin.usermgr.write authorization.

## Options

The smuser authentication arguments, *auth_args*, are derived from the smc(1M) argument set and are the same regardless of which subcommand you use.

Put the subcommand-specific options, *subcommand_args*, after the *auth_args* separated by the -- option.

### auth_args

The valid, optional *auth_args* are -D, -H, -l, -p, -r, and -u. If you specify no *auth_args*, certain defaults are assumed and you may be prompted for additional information, such as a password for authentication purposes. You can also specify these letter options by their equivalent option words preceded by a double dash. For example, you can use either -D or --domain with the *domain* argument.

-D | --domain *domain*

Specify the default domain that you want to manage. The syntax of *domain* is *type*:/*host_name*/*domain_name*, where *type* is nis, nisplus, dns, ldap, or file; *host_name* is the name of the machine that serves the domain; and *domain_name* is the name of the domain you want to manage. (Note: Do not use nis+ for nisplus.)

If you do not specify this option, SMC assumes the file default domain on whatever server you choose to manage, which means that changes are local to the server. Toolboxes can change the domain on a tool-by-tool basis; this option specifies the domain for all other tools.

-H | --hostname *host_name*:*port*

Specify the *host_name* and *port* to which you want to connect. If you do not specify a port, the system connects to the default port, 898. If you do not specify `host_name:port`, SMC connects to the local host on port 898. You may still need to choose a toolbox to load into the console. To override this behavior, use the smc(1M) -B option or set your console preferences to load a home toolbox by default. See "Specifying SMC Console Preferences" on page 20 for information on specifying console preferences.

-l | --rolepassword `role_password`

Specify the password for the `role_name`. If you specify a `role_name` but do not specify a `role_password`, the system prompts you to supply a `role_password`. Because passwords specified on the command line can be seen by any user on the system who runs the ps command, this option is considered insecure.

-p | --password `password`

Specify the password for the `user_name`. If you do not specify a password, the system prompts you for one. Because passwords specified on the command line can be seen by any user on the system who runs the ps command, this option is considered insecure.

-r | --rolename `role_name`

Specify a role name for authentication. If you do not specify this option, assume no role.

-u | --username `user_name`

Specify the user name for authentication. If you do not specify this option, assume the user identity running the console process.

--

This required option must always follow the preceding options. If you do not enter the preceding options, you must still enter the -- option.

## subcommand_args

Enclose descriptions and other argument options with white spaces in double quotes. Options for the add subcommand are listed below.

-c `comment`

(Optional) Include a short description of the login, which is typically the user's name. `comment` is a string of up to 256 printable characters, excluding the colon (:).

-d `dir`

(Optional) Specify the home directory of the new user, limited to 1024 characters.

-e `ddmmyyyy`

(Optional) Specify the expiration date for a login. After this date, no user can access this login. This option is useful for creating temporary logins. Specify a null value (" ") to indicate that the login is always valid. The administrator must have the solaris.admin.usermgr.pswd authorization.

-f `inactive`

(Optional) Specify the maximum number of days allowed between uses of a login ID before that ID is declared invalid. Normal values are positive integers. Enter 0 to indicate that the login account is always active.

| | |
|---|---|
| -F *full_name* | (Optional) Specify the full, descriptive name of the user. The *full_name* must be unique within a domain and can contain alphanumeric characters and spaces. If you use spaces, enclose *full_name* in double quotes. |
| -g *group* | (Optional) Specify the new user's primary group membership in the system group database with an existing group's integer ID. |
| -G *group1* -G *group2* . . . | |
| | (Optional) Specify the new user's supplementary group membership in the system group database with the character string names of one or more existing groups. Duplicates of groups specified with the -g and -G options are ignored. |
| -h | (Optional) Display the usage statement for the subcommand. |
| -n *login* | Specify the new user's login name. The login name must be unique within a domain, contain 2–32 alphanumeric characters, begin with a letter, and contain at least one lowercase letter. |
| -P *password* | (Optional) Specify up to an eight-character password assigned to the user account. Note: When you specify a password, you type the password in plain text. Specifying a password with this method introduces a security gap while the command is running. To set the password, the administrator must have the solaris.admin.usermgr.pswd authorization. |
| -s *shell* | (Optional) Specify the full path name (limited to 1024 characters) of the program used as the user's shell on login. Valid entries are a user-defined shell, /bin/csh (C shell), /bin/ksh (Korn shell), and the default, /bin/sh (Bourne shell). |
| -t *template* | (Optional) Specify a template, created with the User Manager tool, that contains a set of predefined user attributes. You may have entered a nameservice server in the template. However, when a user is actually added with this template, if a nameservice is unavailable, the user's local server is used for both the Home Directory Server and Mail Server. |
| -u *uid* | (Optional) Specify the user ID of the user you want to add. If you do not specify this option, the system assigns the next available unique user ID of 100 or greater. |
| -x autohome=Y\|N | |
| | (Optional) Set the home directory to automount if set to Y. The user's home directory path in the password entry is set to /home/*login_name*. |
| -x mail=*mail_server* | |
| | (Optional) Specify the host name of the user's mail server and create a mail file on the server. Users created in a local scope must have a mail server created on their local machines. |

-x perm=*home_perm*

> (Optional) Set the permissions on the user's home directory. perm is interpreted as an octal number, and the default is 0775.

-x

    pwmax=*da*
     *ys*

> (Optional) Specify the maximum number of days that the user's password is valid. The administrator must have the solaris.admin.usermgr.pswd authorization.

-x pwmin=*days*

> (Optional) Specify the minimum number of days between user password changes. The administrator must have the solaris.admin.usermgr.pswd authorization.

-x pwwarn=*days*

> (Optional) Specify the number of days relative to pwmax that the user is warned about password expiration before the password expires. The administrator must have the solaris.admin.usermgr.pswd authorization.

-x serv=*homedir_server*

> (Optional) Specify the name of the server where the user's home directory resides. Users created in a local scope must have their home directory server created on their local machines.

Options for the delete subcommand are listed below.

-h            (Optional) Display the usage statement for the subcommand.

-n *login1*    Specify the login name of the user you want to delete.

-n *login2*...

> (Optional) Specify the additional login name(s) of the user(s) you want to delete.

Options for the list subcommand are listed below.

-h            (Optional) Display the usage statement for the subcommand.

-l

> Display the output for each user in a block of key:value pairs (for example, user name:root,) followed by a blank line to delimit each user block. Each key:value pair is displayed on a separate line. The keys are autohome setup, comment, days to warn, full name, home directory, home directory permissions, login shell, mail server, max days change, max days inactive, min days change, password expires, password type, primary group, rights, roles, secondary groups, server, user ID (UID), and user name.

-n *login1*    Specify the login name of the user you want to list.

-n *login2* . . .

(Optional) Specify the additional login name(s) of the user(s) you want to list.

Options for the `modify` subcommand are listed below.

`-a addrole1 -a addrole2 . . .`

>(Optional) Specify the role(s) to add to the user account. To assign a role to a user, the administrator must have the `solaris.role.assign` authorization or must have the `solaris.role.delegate` authorization and be a member of each of the roles specified.

`-c comment`   (Optional) Describe the changes you made to the user account. `comment` is a string of up to 256 printable characters, excluding the colon (`:`).

`-d description`

>(Optional) Specify the description of the user's home directory, limited to 1024 characters.

`-e ddmmyyyy`   (Optional) Specify the expiration date for a login in a format appropriate to the locale. After this date, no user can access this login. This option is useful for creating temporary logins. Specify a null value (`" "`) to indicate that the login is always valid.

`-f inactive`   (Optional) Specify the maximum number of days allowed between uses of a login ID before the ID is declared invalid. Normal values are positive integers. Specify 0 to indicate that the login account is always active.

`-F full_name`

>(Optional) Specify the full, descriptive name of the user. The `full_name` must be unique within a domain and can contain alphanumeric characters and spaces. If you use spaces, enclose the `full_name` in double quotes.

`-g group`   (Optional) Specify the new user's primary group membership in the system group database with an existing group's integer ID.

`-G group1 -G group2 . . .`

>(Optional) Specify the new user's supplementary group membership in the system group database with the character string names of one or more existing groups. Duplicates of groups specified with the `-g` and `-G` options are ignored.

`-h`   (Optional) Display the usage statement for the subcommand.

`-n name`   Specify the user's current login name.

`-N new_name`   (Optional) Specify the user's new login name. The login name must be unique within a domain, contain 2–32 alphanumeric characters, begin with a letter, and contain at least one lowercase letter.

`-p addprof1 -p addprof2 . . .`

|  | (Optional) Specify the profile(s) to add to the user account. To assign a profile to a user, the administrator must have the `solaris.profmgr.assign` or `solaris.profmgr.delegate` authorization. |
|---|---|
| `-P password` | (Optional) Specify up to an eight-character password assigned to the user account. |
|  | When you specify a password, you type the password in plain text. Specifying a password with this method introduces a security gap while the command is running. |
| `-q delprof1 -q delprof2 . . .` | |
|  | (Optional) Specify the profile(s) to delete from the user account. |
| `-r delrole1 -r delrole2 . . .` | |
|  | (Optional) Specify the role(s) to delete from the user account. |
| `-s shell` | (Optional) Specify the full path name (limited to 1024 characters) of the program used as the user's shell on login. Valid entries are a user-defined shell, `/bin/csh` (C shell), `/bin/ksh` (Korn shell), and the default, `/bin/sh` (Bourne shell). |
| `-x autohome=Y|N` | |
|  | (Optional) Set up the home directory to automount if set to `Y`. The user's home directory path in the password entry are set to `/home/login_name`. |
| `-x pwmax=days` | |
|  | (Optional) Specify the maximum number of days that the user's password is valid. |
| `-x pwmin=days` | |
|  | (Optional) Specify the minimum number of days between password changes. |
| `-x pwwarn=days` | |
|  | (Optional) Specify the number of days relative to `pwmax` that the user is warned about password expiration before the password expires. |

## Examples

The following example creates a new user account on the local file system. The account name is `ignatz`, and the full name is `Iggy Ignatz`. The comment field verifies that the account is for Iggy. The system assigns the next available user ID of 100 or greater to this account. No password is set for this account, so when Iggy logs in for the first time, he is prompted to enter a password.

```
mopoke# /usr/sadm/bin/smuser add -H mopoke -p rootpasswd -u root -- -F "Iggy
    Ignatz" -n ignatz -c "Iggy's account"
Loading Tool: com.sun.admin.usermgr.cli.user.UserMgrCli from mopoke
Login to mopoke as user root was successful.
Download of com.sun.admin.usermgr.cli.user.UserMgrCli from mopoke was
    successful.
```

```
mopoke#
```

The following example lists all of the user accounts on the local system.

```
mopoke# /usr/sadm/bin/smuser list -H mopoke -p rootpasswd -u root --
Loading Tool: com.sun.admin.usermgr.cli.user.UserMgrCli from mopoke
Login to mopoke as user root was successful.
Download of com.sun.admin.usermgr.cli.user.UserMgrCli from mopoke was
     successful.
root            0                  Super-User
daemon          1
bin             2
sys             3
adm             4                  Admin
lp              71                 Line Printer Admin
uucp            5                  uucp Admin
nuucp           9                  uucp Admin
listen          37                 Network Admin
nobody          60001              Nobody
noaccess        60002              No Access User
nobody4         65534              SunOS 4.x Nobody
ray             1002               Ray Gun
des             1003               Desmond Tornado
rob             1004               Rob Roy
winsor          1001
ignatz          101                Iggy's account
mopoke#
```

The following example modifies the ignatz user account to use the C shell and assigns the account to the sysadmin secondary group.

```
mopoke# /usr/sadm/bin/smuser modify -H mopoke -p rootpasswd -u root -- -n
     ignatz -s /bin/csh -G sysadmin
Loading Tool: com.sun.admin.usermgr.cli.user.UserMgrCli from mopoke
Login to mopoke as user root was successful.
Download of com.sun.admin.usermgr.cli.user.UserMgrCli from mopoke was
     successful.
mopoke#
```

The following example deletes the des user account from the local system.

```
mopoke# /usr/sadm/bin/smuser delete -H mopoke -p rootpasswd -u root -- -n des
Loading Tool: com.sun.admin.usermgr.cli.user.UserMgrCli from mopoke
Login to mopoke as user root was successful.
Download of com.sun.admin.usermgr.cli.user.UserMgrCli from mopoke was
     successful.
mopoke#
```

## Environment Variables

See environ(5) for a description of the JAVA_HOME environment variable, which affects the execution of the smuser command. If you do not specify this environment variable, the /usr/java location is used. See smc(1M).

## Exit Status

0                    Successful completion.

| | |
|---|---|
| 1 | Invalid command syntax. A usage message is displayed. |
| 2 | An error occurred while the command was executing. An error message is displayed. |

## Files

`/etc/aliases`   Mail aliases. See `aliases`(4).

`/etc/auto_home`

Automatic mount points. See `automount`(1M).

`/etc/group`   Group file. See `group`(4).

`/etc/passwd`   Password file. See `passwd`(4).

`/etc/security/policy.conf`

Configuration file for security policy. See `policy.conf`(4).

`/etc/shadow`   Shadow password file. See `shadow`(4).

`/etc/user_attr`

Extended user attribute database. See `user_attr`(4).

## Attributes

See `attributes`(5) for descriptions of the following attributes.

| Attribute Type | Attribute Value |
|---|---|
| Availability | SUNWmga |

## See Also

`automount`(1M), `smc`(1M), `aliases`(4), `group`(4), `passwd`(4), `policy.conf`(4), `shadow`(4), `user_attr`(4), `attributes`(5), `environ`(5)

# GLOSSARY

**active fdisk partition**

The `fdisk` partition used to boot the computer.

**alias**

An alternative name or names assigned to a program or to an electronic mail address.

**Admintool**

A graphical user interface tool that you can use to manage local systems. SMC Console replaces Admintool and expands its capabilities for administering systems on the network from a central system.

**bean**

Short for a component written to the JavaBeans specification. A bean is a portable, platform independent reusable software component. Native SMC tools are written as a set of beans. SMC services are often written as combination of beans and platform-specific code.

**block**

See sector.

*Bourne shell*

One of the Solaris command interpreters. The Bourne shell is the default user shell, and it is the shell language in which most system administration shell scripts are written. See also C shell, Korn shell.

*character terminal*

A serial port device that displays only letters, numbers, and other characters, such as those produced by a typewriter.

*client*

A system or program that receives system resources from a remote system—called a server—over the network.

*C shell*

One of the Solaris command interpreters. See also Bourne shell, Korn shell.

*cylinder group*

One or more consecutive disk cylinders that include inode slots for files.

*cylinder group map*

A bitmap in a UFS file system that stores information about block use and availability within each cylinder. The cylinder group replaces the traditional free list.

*disc*

An optical disc, a CD-ROM, or a DVD-ROM.

*disk*

A hard-disk storage device.

*diskette*

A removable portable storage medium used to store and access data magnetically. Solaris Operating Environment supports 3.5-inch, double-sided, high-density (DS, HD) diskettes.

*domain*

A hierarchical directory structure for e-mail addressing and network address naming. Within the United States, top-level domains include com for commercial organizations; edu for educational organizations; gov for governments; mil for the military; net for networking organizations; and org for other organizations. Outside the United States, top-level domains designate the country. Subdomains designate the organization, department or group, and the individual system.

*domain addressing*

> Using an address to specify the destination of an e-mail message or the identity of a system.

*e-mail*

> Electronic mail. A set of programs that transmit mail messages from one system to another.

*fdisk partition*

> The portion of a disk on an IA computer that is used to hold a particular operating system, such as Solaris.

*file system*

> A hierarchical arrangement of directories and files organized on a portion of a magnetic or optical disk.

*floppy diskette*

> See diskette.

*folder*

> A container for grouping tools within a toolbox.

*free list*

> See cylinder group map.

*GID*

> The group identification number used by the system to control access to information owned by other users.

*group*

> A collection of user accounts that can access common data.

*Group database*

> The database that is used to create new group accounts or to modify existing group accounts.

*group ID*

> See GID.

*home directory*

> The part of the file system that is allocated to an individual user account for private files.

*IA computer*

> An Intel architecture computer.

*JavaBeans specification*

> See bean.

*kernel*

> The master program set of Solaris software that manages all of the physical resources of the computer, including file system management, virtual memory, reading and writing of files to disks and tapes, scheduling of processes, and communications over a network.

*Korn shell*

> One of the Solaris command interpreters. The Korn shell is upward-compatible with the Bourne shell and provides an expanded set of features. See also Bourne shell, C shell.

*launch*

> To start a computer application. For SMC, launch is the act of launching legacy (non-SMC-aware) applications.

*legacy application*

> An application that is not an SCM tool. A legacy application could be a script, an X application, or a URL.

*login name*

> The name assigned to an individual user account to control that user's access to a system.

*mailbox*

> A file on a mail hub where mail messages are stored for a user.

*metacharacter*

> A symbol used in file names and extensions to represent another character or string of characters. An asterisk (*) matches any number of characters. A question mark (?) matches a single character.

*MNTFS file system*

> A file system, introduced in the Solaris 8 release, that provides read-only information directly from the kernel about mounted file systems for the local system.

*modem*

A device that modulates a digital signal so that it can be transmitted across analog telephone lines and then demodulates the analog signal to a digital signal at the receiving end. The name is a contraction for modulate/demodulate. A modem is one way to connect a UNIX workstation or PC to a remote server or network.

*mount*

To extend a file system directory hierarchy by attaching a file system from somewhere else in the hierarchy. See also mount point.

*mount point*

A directory in the file system hierarchy where another file system is attached to the hierarchy.

*mount table*

The system file (/etc/mnttab) that keeps track of currently mounted file systems. Starting with the Solaris 8 release, the /etc/mnttab file is no longer a text-based file. Instead, it is an MNTFS file system. See also MNTFS file system.

*NFS*

The default Solaris distributed file system that provides file sharing among systems. NFS servers can also provide kernels and swap files to diskless clients.

*NIS*

The SunOS 4.x network information service.

*NIS+*

The Solaris network information service.

*null modem cable*

A cable that swaps RS-232 transmit and receive signals so that the proper transmit and receive signals are communicated between two data termination equipment (DTE) devices. The RS-232 ground signal is wired straight through.

*partition*

A discrete portion of a disk, configured with the format program or with the Disks tool. A partition is also known as a slice.

*path*

> A list of directories that is searched to find a file. PATH is a shell environment variable used to find user commands.

*path name*

> A list of directory names, separated with slashes (/), that specifies the location of a particular file or directory. For example, /var/adm/messages.

*port*

> A physical connection between a device such as a terminal, printer, or modem and the device controller. Also a logical access point on a system used to initiate and accept connections over a network.

*port monitor*

> A program that continuously watches for requests to log in or requests to access printers or files. The ttymon and listen port monitors are part of the Service Access Facility (SAF).

*Primary Administrator*

> An RBAC right that grants a user permission to perform all tasks that the root user can perform while logged in with the person's customary user name instead of as root.

*RBAC*

> Role-based access control is a new Solaris security feature that provides a flexible way to package certain superuser privileges for assignment to user accounts. You no longer need to give users all superuser privileges to enable them to perform a set of tasks that require superuser privileges. You can assign rights to a user to perform a specific set of tasks and you can create a role account with specific rights that are granted to a set of users.

*rights*

> A named collection that includes three components: commands; authorizations to use specific applications or to perform specific functions within an application; and other, previously created rights.

*role*

> An account with all the attributes of a user account, including a name, user ID (UID), password, and home directory. A role also has a specific set of administrative rights. Instead of a login shell, a role has a *role shell* (for example, Administrator's Bourne instead of Bourne shell). The root account is a role with all rights, whereas other roles have more limited rights.

**role shell**

> A shell designed specifically for use with RBAC roles. Role shells are Administrator's Bourne, Administrator's C, and Administrator's Korn.

**root**

> The highest level in a hierarchical system. As a login ID, the user name of the system administrator or superuser who has responsibility for an entire system. Root has permissions for all users files and processes on the system. In a file system, root is the topmost directory.

**SAC**

> See Service Access Controller.

**SAF**

> See Service Access Facility.

**sector**

> The smallest unit on a disk platter; usually contains 512 bytes. Also called a block.

**server**

> A system that provides network service, such as disk storage and file transfer or access to a database. Alternatively, a program that provides such a service. See also client.

**service**

> An application consisting of one or more processes that respond to a connection request.

**Service Access Controller (SAC)**

> The process that manages access to system services provided by the Service Access Facility.

**Service Access Facility (SAF)**

> The part of the system software that is used to register and monitor port activity for modems, terminals, and printers. SAF replaces /etc/getty as a way to control logins.

**share**

> To make a file system available (mountable) to other systems on the network. See also mount, NFS.

*slice*

An alternate name for a partition. See also partition.

*SMC client*

The GUI tool you can use for routine system administration tasks. Also called SMC or the Console.

*SMC Console*

The graphical user interface tool that provides a way to centralize basic system administration tasks.

*SMC SDK*

A software development kit with which developers can build an SMC tool.

*SMC server*

Started with the `/etc/inet.d/init.wbem` command, the SMC server is the back end to the SMC Console, `smc(1M)`. The SMC server provides tools that the console uses to download and perform common services for the console and its tools, for example authentication, authorization, logging, and persistence.

*SMC toolbox editor*

An SMC tool that enables you to customize the SMC Console. You can modify existing toolboxes or create additional toolboxes. You can manage multiple servers from one toolbox and group similar tools in a toolbox.

*superuser*

A user with special privileges granted if the correct password is supplied when the user is logging in as root or using the `su` command. For example, only the superuser can edit administrative files in the `/etc` directory. The superuser has the user name root.

*swap file*

A disk partition or file used for virtual memory storage.

*system*

Another name for a computer, PC, or workstation. A system can have either local or remote disks and may have additional peripheral devices, such as CD-ROM players, DVD-ROM drives, tape drives, diskette drives, modems, and printers.

*tool*

An SMC-compatible application or applet that integrates seamlessly into the Console. An SMC tool is built with the SMC software development kit (SDK).

*toolbox*

> A hierarchical collection that consists of folders, tools, legacy applications, and links to other toolboxes and that has been registered with smcconf(1m).

*toolbox URL or link*

> A pointer to another toolbox, which may be on the current SMC server on any other SMC server.

*track*

> One of several concentric rings on a hard-disk platter, made up of sectors.

*turner icon*

> The icon displayed in the SMC Console Navigation pane next to items that represent a group. Clicking on the turner icon expands or collapses the group.

*UDFS file system*

> Universal Disk Format file system, which is the industry-standard format for storing information on the optical media technology called DVD.

*UFS (UNIX file system)*

> The default disk-based file system for the Solaris operating system.

*UID number*

> The user identification number assigned to each login name. UID numbers are used by the system to identify, by number, the owners of files and directories. The UID of root is 0.

*UNIX Group*

> See group.

*unmount*

> To remove a file system from a mount point so that the files are no longer accessible. See also mount, NFS.

*unresolved mail*

> Mail with an address for which sendmail cannot find a recipient in the specified domain.

*user account*

> An account set up for an individual user. Account information is stored in the /etc/passwd file or the Passwd database and includes the user's login name, full name, password, UID, GID, login directory, and login shell.

*User Account Manager*

> The SMC Users tool you can use to administer users in a nameservice environment or on a local system.

*value*

> Data, either numeric or alphanumeric.

*variable*

> A name that refers to a temporary storage area in memory. A variable holds a value.

*virtual file system table*

> The file (`/etc/vfstab`) that specifies which file systems are mounted by default. Local UFS file systems and NFS file systems that are mounted automatically when a system boots are specified in this file.

*zombie*

> A process that has terminated but remains in the process table because its parent process has not sent the proper exit code. Zombie processes do not consume any system resources and are removed from the process table when a system is rebooted.

# INDEX

321

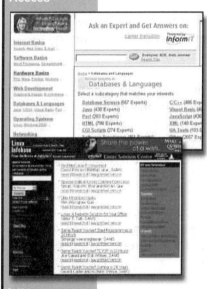